The
Greatest
Golf Stories
Ever Told

The
Greatest
Golf Stories
Ever Told

**EDITED AND WITH AN INTRODUCTION BY
JEFF SILVERMAN**

THE LYONS PRESS
Guilford, Connecticut
An imprint of The Globe Pequot Press

The Globe Pequot Press, P.O. Box 480, Guilford, CT 06437.

The Lyons Press is an imprint of The Globe Pequot Press.

Printed in the United States of America

10 9 8 7 6 5 4 3 2 1

ISBN 1-58574-367-4

Design by Compset, Inc.

The Library of Congress Cataloging-in-Publication Data is available on file.

To Abby, Mud, and Tuba

. . . for making the foursome complete

Acknowledgments

I'd like to thank Nick Lyons, Tony Lyons, and Bill Wolfsthal for their support; Mark Weinstein, for the heavy lifting; Dan Jenkins, Gary McCord, Ron Shelton, and Bud Shrake for the generosity of their contributions; and Abby Van Pelt, whose swing I covet, for her daily encouragement and graceful follow-through.

Contents

INTRODUCTION	ix	Jeff Silverman
WHAT GOLF IS	1	Grantland Rice
THE ONLY TWO ACCEPTABLE THEORIES	5	Ron Shelton and John Norville
THE GOLFOMANIAC	11	Stephen Leacock
THE CHARM OF GOLF	15	A. A. Milne
STARK	19	Michael Bamberger
THE WAY THE BALL BOUNCES	27	John P. Marquand
THE LONG HOLE	33	P. G. Wodehouse
WINTER DREAMS	49	F. Scott Fitzgerald
MR. FRISBIE	71	Ring Lardner
DRESSING THE PART FOR GOLF	83	Glenna Collett Vare
OVER THE WIRE IS OUT OF BOUNDS	93	Pat Ward-Thomas
SEPTEMBER 20, 1913	103	Al Laney
THE GREATEST OF GOLFERS	115	Robert T. Jones Jr.
BACK TO CHERRY HILLS	119	Herbert Warren Wind
DAY OF GLORY FOR A GOLDEN OLDIE	131	Rick Reilly
THE CARRY	139	George Plimpton
THEY MIGHT BE GIANTS	143	John Paul Newport
A GOOD WALK SPOILED	155	Mark Kram
THE RIVERCLIFF GOLF KILLINGS	167	Don Marquis
TITANIC THOMPSON	175	John Lardner
BIG DIVORCES AND SMALL DIVOTS	189	Gary McCord
CARE TO JOIN OUR LITTLE OLD GAME?	199	Edwin "Bud" Shrake
GOLF WITH THE BOSS	205	Dan Jenkins
GOLDFINGER	219	Ian Fleming

THE FINEST COURSE OF ALL **241** *Peter Dobereiner*

WORKERS, ARISE! SHOUT FORE **245** *Alistair Cooke*

LEFT-HANDED GOLF COURSES:

OUR GREATEST NEED **251** *Rube Goldberg*

THE HUMORS OF GOLF **255** *The Right Hon. A. Balfour, M.P.*

THE WOODEN PUTTER **269** *Bernard Darwin*

THE BLISS OF GOLF **281** *John Updike*

ABOUT THE EDITOR **285**

PERMISSIONS ACKNOWLEDGMENTS **286**

Introduction

S ome people grow up on the wrong side of the tracks. I grew up on the wrong side of the golf course.

The course was part of the local country club, which my parents never belonged to because they liked the beach better. Still, the three holes I could spy on from my second-floor bedroom window offered a marvelous laboratory for my young eyes to study the best and worst of the human race. Week after week, year after year, I'd peer beyond the chain-link fence that separated us and watch my friends' parents and my parents' friends—hostages to a small white ball that would rarely bend to their wills (or, more typically, bend too much)—as they'd go deliciously ballistic with every flub and foozle. And there were many.

I was mesmerized by this exercise that made the neighborhood authority figures seem so screamingly foolish. Did they have any idea how ridiculous they looked? Where was the appeal? What could they possibly be getting from this frustrating, humiliating, and self-flagellating ordeal? Existentially precocious, I made it my mission to find out.

My father had stashed an old set of hickory shafts he hadn't swung in decades behind some ratty furniture in the attic. The summer that I turned 11, I took the clubs, cut a hole in the fence big enough to slip myself and my weapons of destruction through, and, with the sun setting and the course clear, took off on an adventure I hope never ends.

After all these years, I readily admit that I haven't come close to solving the mysteries that my preteen mind tried to wrap itself around. But I'm pretty certain of this: the lure of golf lies in the beckoning essence of a game that hasn't changed much since a Scot first shanked a shot, broke his brassie, cursed the breezes blowing through his native heath, and *still* managed to scramble for his par. Golf beats you to a pulp with hope; latent perfection always lurks in the next swing. No matter how well you play or how badly, a day out on a golf course—be it Pebble Beach or the shaggy muni up the road—exhales hints of intoxication, and is rarely less than interesting.

Golf is unlike any other major sport. It has no age limits, no size limits, no sex limits, no class limits, no time limits, no domed stadiums, no artificial turf, no salary caps or contract renegotiations, no teams, no trades, no owners or free agents, no strikes, no arbitrations, and no waves. What it has is what it's always had: an individual—usually of natural human proportion—some clubs, a ball, some decorum and tradition, and a whole lot of natural beauty to complicate things. The human dilemma in a nutshell. Which makes it a writer's game, too, and, thus, a game that's par—or better—for the reader, as well.

With its long history, its considerable roster of heroes and hustlers, its myriad memorable moments, its psychological trials, and its fairways full of myth, golf has teed up a rich and lasting literature as funny, poignant, personal, surprising, exasperating, and fulfilling as the very endeavor it attempts to unlock, understand, excuse, and explain. Yet, after all the good words set down on the subject by smart and engaging minds, the brilliance of golf's continuing allure remains its essential elusiveness. On the course. And on the page.

No law says we golfers and golf lovers can't have a good time chipping away at it, though, and in compiling *The Greatest Golf Stories Ever Told,* I've tried to find the writers and stories that have done their chipping with a maximum of wit, grace, insight, and understanding whether they are writing about their own relationships to the game, or charting the ups and downs of others.

Let me say something here about the collection's title, because it sits like a Titleist on a tee daring a driver to make perfect, resonant, unarguable contact. Given the vicissitudes of golf and taste, I fully understand the hazards inherent in the boast. My drive could just as easily wind up whiffed, that Titleist guffawing at my overswing from five pathetic feet away, as it is likely to soar some 275 yards straight down the middle, and there are, of course, various horrors that lurk in between. Are these the *greatest* golf stories ever told? To me the stories that follow are surely among them. But to have brought together *every* story I would have liked to have sheltered under this umbrella would have meant felling too many of the stately elms and maples that line my favorite fairways, and where's the fun—or challenge—in that? Will you agree with my choices? With some, sure, with others, you'll doubtless have your druthers. I'd love to discuss them with you on a warm spring day, as we amble down a fairway, our approach shots stiff to the pin within gimme birdie range.

Until that opportunity presents itself, I hope you'll find some forgotten old friends here, make the acquaintance of a few new ones, share a laugh here and there, empathize with the disasters, revel in the triumphs, inhale a whiff or two of inspiration, and perhaps even pick up a stroke-saving tip. If that sounds something like a round of golf itself, terrific; when we're on the golf course, we're all on the same side of the fence at last.

Fore!
Jeff Silverman
March 2001

The
Greatest
Golf Stories
Ever Told

What Golf Is

BY GRANTLAND RICE

It's not unusual to find a writer obsessed by his subject, but to be privy to a writer's lifelong romance is a whole other ball game. For Grantland Rice (1880–1954), the acknowledged dean of American sportswriters for much of the first half of the 20th century, golf was no mere ball-game with a hole—it was his grand passion. A near-scratch player, he took the editorial helm of *The American Golfer* from founder Henry Travis in 1919, and for nearly 20 years steered the course of one of the most sophisticated sporting journals ever published.

Away from the golf course, his colorful—sometimes purple—prose dubbed Notre Dame's backfield "The Four Horsemen," Red Grange "The Galloping Ghost," and Jack Dempsey "The Manassa Mauler." In addition to his syndicated daily column, he offered radio commentaries, produced short films, picked the annual All-America football team, and wrote verse. Lots of it. Which brings us back to golf, at least tangentially. Among the treasures proudly displayed in his great friend Bobby Jones's office was a personalized print of Rice's most enduring inspirational rhyme: "For when the one great scorer comes to mark against your name / He writes—not that you won or lost—but how you played the game."

How Rice played the game of golf was as often as possible. For years, he formed the nucleus of a series of small social clubs primarily organized to tee it up in the South when the weather was cold in the North. Since, he believed, every club needs to hold meetings, and since he was in charge, he called those meetings to coincide with his own annual forays to Florida to cover spring training. His legion of friends found it hard to argue with the scheduling. In time, a single organization would evolve from its smaller forebears, and given its membership roll, is there a golf dreamer among us who wouldn't have lined up to caddie just for the privilege of eavesdropping on the conversations?

Called The Artists and Writers, the club was born in New York in 1925, and flourished into the early '40s. Long after its demise, it remains one of the most stellar—and exclusive—golf clubs ever to take a swing, though it never had a permanent clubhouse or grounds. Rice was its first and only president, and its reasons for existence couldn't have been more appealing: exceptional good fellowship; an annual, winter golf tournament held over several days in Palm Beach; Rice himself won the inaugural—communal card-playing and drinking into the wee hours; and the commemoration of the entire experience in a photo- and cartoon-filled yearbook put together by some of the cleverest minds of the time solely for their own amusement.

It would have been folly to expect less from them. Besides Rice, the club's founding members included his fellow knight of the pressbox Ring Lardner (see page 71); writers George Ade, Rex Beach, George Abbott, and "Barney Google" creator Billy deBeck; *Vanity Fair* editor Frank Crownin-shield; and artists Rube Goldberg (see page 271) and John Montgomery Flagg. Guests were encouraged—as long as they could keep up the 'round-the-clock pace; Babe Ruth, Bobby Jones (see page 115), Gene Tunney, and promoter Tex Rickard all left their divots.

In his memoirs, the sentimentalist in Rice let his prose drip with nostalgia as he resurrected the yearly outings and the strong friendships they cemented, calling them "the richest reward known to man." "In our various meetings," he went on unabashedly, "that wonderful bunch contributed a large share of whatever deep pleasure I've found along the endless, winding road."

So, of course, did golf itself. In 1926, he published a collection of droll instructional essays called *A Duffer's Handbook*. Most of it was pretty tongue-in-cheek—"How to Make a Nine," for instance, includes this unerring gem of advice: "The surest way is to miss a short putt on the preceding green and then advance to the next tee thinking about that missed short putt while applying to the game of golf in general every known epithet that one can remember." Still, he began the volume with this rhapsodic exercise that beautifully captures the game that captured his heart.

G olf is, in part, a game; but only in part. It is also in part a religion, a fever, a vice, a mirage, a frenzy, a fear, an abscess, a joy, a thrill, a pest, a disease, an uplift, a brooding melancholy, a dream of yester-day, a disappointing to-day and a hope for to-morrow.

"Hope deferred maketh the heart sick," and golf is hope deferred. Golf is light on the hills and a shadow in the valley. It is the first whisper of the trees in early spring. And late in the fall it is the gaunt spectre of leafless oaks that stand stark against a coming winter sky.

It is the song of streams and the lash of surf against the shore.

It is the strong wine that looseneth all tongues and starts a babble longer and louder than Babel ever knew.

It is philosophy making a losing fight, ambition shattered and the eternal ego held in bitter bounds.

It is also philosophy triumphant just often enough to show that miracles can happen.

Golf is everything that represents outdoors—trees, rivers, lakes, hills, valleys, ponds, sky, turf, surf, rain, sun, wind, sand and grass through mile after mile.

There may be few who can see any beauty around except that of a well-hit shot or a lucky bound, but it is at least there for them to see in case the grip of the ancient game can be broken only for the moment.

Golf is companionship and feud, friendliness and fury, ambition and despair. It is concentration, disintegration, inflammation, elation and desperation.

In short it is the Soul of the Race with the cover taken off.

The Only Two Acceptable Theories

BY RON SHELTON AND JOHN NORVILLE

I feel compelled to include this scene from what I believe is the ace golf movie of all time for two reasons, not the least of which is that if I didn't, Ron Shelton would never invite me out to play Riviera again. So, here goes. First, good writing is good writing whatever form it takes. Good screenwriting is deceptively difficult, and Shelton is a virtuoso in the field. As a member of the Writers Guild, the union representing screen and TV writers, I'd be personally remiss if I didn't stand up for the quality of the craft. Second, I like playing Riviera with my old buddy, and want to make sure I keep playing the course with him whenever my travels take me in that direction.

I met Ron through our mutual friend, the late sports columnist and my colleague at the old *Los Angeles Herald Examiner* Allan Malamud, just before the release of *Bull Durham,* arguably the best sports movie ever made. With their crisp dialogue and deft storytelling, all his films since—*Cobb* (baseball), *Blue Chips* and *White Men Can't Jump* (basketball), *Tin Cup* (golf), *Play It to the Bone* (boxing), even *Blaze* (isn't politics a sport?)—have tackled sporting themes in one form or another. In his hands, they resonate with human drama and lots of divine comedy.

Tin Cup, cowritten with John Norville, himself a fine golfer, charts the improbable odyssey of Roy "Tin Cup" McAvoy from driving range pro in the obscure scrubs of Texas to the spotlight of the leader board on the final nine of the U.S. Open. In this scene, shot on his range, "Tin Cup," played by Kevin Costner, imparts the essence of his wisdom to a new pupil, played by Rene Russo. It's a golf scene, sure, but it's also a love scene—to the game itself.

Here beginneth the lesson:

TIN CUP

The first thing you gotta learn about this game, Doc, is it ain't about hitting a little white ball into some yonder hole. It's about inner demons and self-doubt and human frailty and overcoming all that crap. So . . . what kinda doctor'd you say you were?

MOLLY

I'm a psychologist—in layman's terms call me a neo-Jungian, post-modern Freudian, holistic, secularist.

TIN CUP

Damn.

SHE BEGINS UNPACKING ONE OF HER BAGS, pulling out every golf gimmick on the market—swing aid straps to pull your elbows together, a ball pendulum that hangs from your hat, a metal contraption for your feet, etc.

MOLLY

Inner demons and human frailty are my life's work. I used to practise in El Paso, but I've moved here now. . . .

TIN CUP

What're those?

MOLLY

I ordered these from the Golf Channel.

HE STARES IN DISBELIEF as she tries to wriggle into some of this stuff. He's enchanted and dismayed.

TIN CUP

That stuff's a waste of money.

MOLLY

I'm sure there are excesses and repetitions here, but I believe in the gathering of knowledge and I figured, well, there must be some truths about the golf swing illustrated by these devices—and that you'd help me sort through it.

SHE STANDS THERE with contraptions coming from every limb.

MOLLY (cont'd)

I have dozens of golf videotapes too . . . and a golf watch.

TIN CUP   (irritated, impatient)

Take it off. All of it. Now! You're a smart woman, for crissakes don't you know the work of charlatans when you see it?

SHE DEPOSITS ALL THE GOLF GIMMICK devices in a pile.

MOLLY

No. I can always tell when someone is lying to himself, but I'm quite suscepti-ble and frequently wrong when that person lies to me.

(pointing to the pile of devices)

That stuff cost me over $200. . . .

TIN CUP

Then it's $200 of shit. . . .

HE TEES A BALL, hands Molly her driver and steps back.

TIN CUP (cont'd)

Go ahead. Take a swing.

MOLLY TAKES A PITTY-PAT SWING and whiffs, and mutters under her breath with the ease of a longshoreman.

MOLLY

Aw, fuck . . .

TIN CUP

Well you talk like a golfer.

MOLLY UNLOADS A MIGHTY SECOND SWING. The club head bounces off the mat. The ball sits untouched.

MOLLY

Shit.

TIN CUP

"Fuck" . . . "Shit" . . . these are highly technical golf terms and you're using them on your first lesson—this is promising.

MOLLY

Awright, wise ass, show me.

TIN CUP TAKES THE CLUB from Molly, motions for her to step back, tees up a ball, and rockets a drive into the night.

TIN CUP

Something like that.

HE HANDS HER back the club and tees up another ball. Molly just looks at him.

MOLLY

Impressive. Y'know, I tend to process things verbally. Can you break down into words how you did that?

TIN CUP TAKES a deep breath—this is his speech.

TIN CUP

"What is the golf swing?"—by Roy McAvoy.

(beat)

The golf swing is a poem. Sometimes a love sonnet and sometimes a Homerian epic—it is organic and of a piece, yet it breaks down into elegant stanzas and quatrains. The critical opening phrase of this song is the grip, in which the thumbs and index fingers of each hand form "V" shapes that each must point to the appropriate arm pit, the back of each hand pointing in opposite directions but on line to the intended target, the club gripped with the fingers lightly, the small finger of the right hand overlapping the index and middle fingers of the left, with the exception of the Harry Vardon interlock, which we will not go into here tonight. . . .

MOLLY (to herself)

Thank God.

BUT HE'S OFF on a roll, lost in, well, poetry.

TIN CUP

Tempo is everything, perfection unobtainable, the golfer's signature is a nod to the Gods that he is fallible. . . .

MOLLY

A nod to the Gods?

TIN CUP

Yes . . . the hands cocked on the takeaway just before the weight shift pulled by the powers of the earth—it's alive, this swing, a living sculpture—down through contact with terra firma, striking the ball crisply, with character—a tuning fork goes off in your heart, your balls—such a pure feeling is the well-struck golf shot.

(beat)

And then the follow-through to finish, always on line, the reverse "C" of the Golden Bear, the steelworker's power and brawn of Carl Sandburg's Arnold Palmer, the da Vinci of Hogan, every finishing position unique, as if that is the brushstroke left to the artist, the warrior athlete who, finally and thereby, has asserted his oneness with and power over the universe through willing the golf ball to go where he wants and how and when, because that is what the golf swing is about . . .

(finally)

It is about gaining control of your life, and letting go at the same time.

MOLLY STARES BACK, exhausted and intrigued.

MOLLY

Jeez Louise . . .

TIN CUP

There is only one other acceptable theory of how to hit a golf ball.

MOLLY

I'm afraid to ask. What's the other theory?

TIN CUP

Grip it and rip it.

The Golfomaniac

BY STEPHEN LEACOCK

I had a friend in high school who, we'd joke, only excelled at the sports we never got to see him play. Canadian Stephen Leacock (1869–1944) deliciously describes what must have been my friend's ancestor in this, one of the true chestnuts of golf fiction. Leacock, himself, was a true chestnut, perhaps his country's most beloved humorist. But there was another side to Leacock. In addition to his 35 books of short stories and other comic writings, Leacock published 27 serious volumes of history, biography, economics, and politics, fitting for a fellow who spent 28 years as chairman of the Department of Economics and Political Science at McGill University in Montreal.

We ride in and out pretty often together, he and I, on a suburban train.

That's how I came to talk to him. "Fine morning," I said as I sat down beside him yesterday and opened a newspaper.

"Great!" he answered. "The grass is drying out fast now and the greens will soon be all right to play."

"Yes," I said, "the sun is getting higher and the days are decidedly lengthening."

"For the matter of that," said my friend, "a man could begin to play at six in the morning easily. In fact, I've often wondered that there is little golf played before breakfast. We happened to be talking about golf, a few of us last night—I don't know how it came up—and we were saying that it seems a pity that some of the best part of the day, say, from five o'clock to seven thirty, is never used."

"That's true," I answered, and then, to shift the subject, I said, looking out of the window:

"It's a pretty bit of country just here, isn't it?"

"It is," he replied, "but it seems a shame they make no use of it—just a few market gardens and things like that. Why, I noticed along here acres and acres of just glass—some kind of houses for plants or something—and whole fields of lettuces and things like that. It's a pity they don't make something of it. I was remarking only the other day as I came along in the train with a friend of mine, that you could easily lay out an eighteen-hole course any-where here."

"Could you?" I said.

"Oh, yes. This ground, you know, is an excellent light soil to shovel up into bunkers. You could drive some ditches through it and make one or two deep holes—the kind they have on some of the French links. In fact, improve it to any extent."

I glanced at my morning paper. "I see," I said, "that it is again ru-moured that Lloyd George is at last definitely to retire."

"Funny thing about Lloyd George," answered my friend. "He never played, you know; most extraordinary thing—don't you think?—for a man in his position. Balfour, of course, was very different: I remember when I was over in Scotland last summer I had the honour of going around the course at Dum-fries just after Lord Balfour. Pretty interesting experience, don't you think?"

"Were you over on business?" I asked.

"No, not exactly. I went to get a golf ball, a particular golf ball. Of course, I didn't go merely for that. I wanted to get a mashie as well. The only way, you know, to get what you want is to go to Scotland for it."

"Did you see much of Scotland?"

"I saw it all. I was on the links at St. Andrew's and I visited the Loch Lomond course and the course at Inverness. In fact, I saw everything."

"It's an interesting country, isn't it, historically?"

"It certainly is. Do you know they have played there for over five hun-dred years! Think of it! They showed me at Loch Lomond the place where they said Robert the Bruce played the Red Douglas (I think that was the party—at any rate, Bruce was one of them), and I saw where Bonnie Prince Charlie disguised himself as a caddie when the Duke of Cumberland's soldiers were looking for him. Oh, it's a wonderful country historically."

After that I let a silence intervene so as to get a new start. Then I looked up again from my newspaper.

"Look at this," I said pointing to a headline, *United States Navy Ordered Again to Nicaragua*. "Looks like more trouble, doesn't it?"

"Did you see in the paper a while back," said my companion, "that the United States Navy Department is now making golf compulsory at the training school at Annapolis? That's progressive, isn't it? I suppose it will have to mean shorter cruises at sea; in fact, probably lessen the use of the Navy for sea purposes. But it will raise the standard."

"I suppose so," I answered. "Did you read about this extraordinary murder case in Long Island?"

"No," he said. "I never read murder cases. They don't interest me. In fact, I think the whole continent is getting over-preoccupied with them—"

"Yes, but this case had such odd features—"

"Oh, they all have," he replied, with an air of weariness. "Each one is just boomed by the papers to make it a sensation—"

"I know, but in this case it seems as if the man was killed with a blow from a golf club."

"What's that? Eh, what's that? Killed with a blow from a golf club?"

"Yes, some kind of club—"

"I wonder if it was an iron—let me see the paper—though, for the matter of that I imagine a blow from even a wooden driver, let alone one of the steel-handled drivers—where does it say it?—pshaw, it only just says 'a blow with a golf club'. It's a pity the papers don't write these things up with more detail, isn't it? But perhaps it will be better in the afternoon paper—"

"Have you played golf much?" I inquired. I saw it was no use to talk of anything else.

"No," answered my companion, "I am sorry to say I haven't. You see, I began late. I've only played twenty years, twenty-one if you count the year that's beginning in May. I don't know what I was doing. I wasted about half my life. In fact, it wasn't till I was well over thirty that I caught on to the game. I suppose a lot of us look back over our lives that way and realize what we have lost.

"And even as it is," he continued, "I don't get much chance to play. At the best I can only manage about four afternoons a week, though of course I get most of Saturday and all of Sunday. I get my holiday in the summer, but it's only a month, and that's nothing. In the winter I manage to take a run south for a game once or twice and perhaps a little swack at it around Easter, but only a week at a time. I'm too busy—that's the plain truth of it." He sighed. "It's hard to leave the office before two," he said. "Something always turns up."

And after that he went on to tell me something of the technique of the game, illustrate it with a golf ball on the seat of the car, and the peculiar mental poise needed for driving, and the neat, quick action of the wrist (he showed me how it worked) that is needed to undercut a ball so that it flies straight up in the air. He explained to me how you can do practically anything with a golf ball, provided that you keep your mind absolutely poised and your eye in shape and your body a trained machine. It appears that even Bobby Jones of Atlanta and people like that fall short very often from the high standard set by my friend in the suburban car.

So later in the day, meeting someone in my club who was a person of authority on such things, I made inquiry about my friend. "I rode into town with Llewellyn Smith," I said. "I think he belongs to your golf club. He's a great player, isn't he?"

"A great player!" laughed the expert. "Llewellyn Smith? Why, he can hardly hit a ball! And anyway, he's only played about twenty years!"

The Charm of Golf

BY A. A. MILNE

The name A. A. Milne (1882–1956) will forever be more associated with Pooh Corner than Amen Corner, and given the quality of Milne's play on the golf course, that's probably for the best. The creator of Piglet, Eeyore, and Tigger—as well as literature's most beloved bear—was an accomplished and popular essayist, weighing in on such diverse subjects as goldfish, diaries, smoking, daffodils, thermometers, and, on occasion, the royal and ancient game. Milne included "The Charm of Golf" in his 1919 collection, *Not That It Matters.*

When he reads of the notable doings of famous golfers, the eighteen-handicap man has no envy in his heart. For by this time he has discovered the great secret of golf. Before he began to play he wondered wherein lay the fascination of it; now he knows. Golf is so popular simply because it is the best game in the world at which to be bad.

Consider what it is to be bad at cricket. You have bought a new bat, perfect in balance; a new pair of pads, white as driven snow; gloves of the very latest design. Do they let you use them? No. After one ball, in the negotiation of which neither your bat, nor your pads, nor your gloves came into play, they send you back into the pavilion to spend the rest of the afternoon listening to fatuous stories of some old gentleman who knew Fuller Pilch. And when your side takes the field, where are you? Probably at long leg both ends, exposed to the public gaze as the worst fieldsman in London. How devastating are your

1 5

emotions. Remorse, anger, mortification, fill your heart; above all, envy—envy of the lucky immortals who disport themselves on the green level of Lord's.

Consider what it is to be bad at lawn tennis. True, you are allowed to hold on to your new racket all through the game, but how often are you allowed to employ it usefully? How often does your partner cry "Mine!" and bundle you out of the way? Is there pleasure in playing football badly? You may spend the full eighty minutes in your new boots, but your relations with the ball will be distant. They do not give you a ball to yourself at football.

But how different a game is golf. At golf it is the bad player who gets the most strokes. However good his opponent, the bad player has the right to play out each hole to the end; he will get more than his share of the game. He need have no fears that his new driver will not be employed. He will have as many swings with it as the scratch man; more, if he misses the ball altogether upon one or two tees. If he buys a new niblick he is certain to get fun out of it on the very first day.

And, above all, there is this to be said for golfing mediocrity—the bad player can make the strokes of the good player. The poor cricketer has perhaps never made fifty in his life; as soon as he stands at the wickets he knows that he is not going to make fifty to-day. But the eighteen-handicap man has some time or other played every hole on the course to perfection. He has driven a ball 250 yards; he has made superb approaches; he has run down the long putt. Any of these things may suddenly happen to him again. And therefore it is not his fate to have to sit in the club smoking-room after his second round and listen to the wonderful deeds of others. He can join in too. He can say with perfect truth, "I once carried the ditch at the fourth with my second," or "I remember when I drove into the bunker guarding the eighth green," or even "I did a three at the eleventh this afternoon"—bogey being five. But if the bad cricketer says, "I remember when I took a century in forty minutes off Lockwood and Richardson," he is nothing but a liar.

For these and other reasons golf is the best game in the world for the bad player. And sometimes I am tempted to go further and say that it is a better game for the bad player than for the good player. The joy of driving a ball straight after a week of slicing, the joy of putting a mashie shot dead, the joy of even a moderate stroke with a brassie; best of all, the joy of the perfect cleek shot—these things the good player will never know. Every stroke we bad players make we make in hope. It is never so bad but it might have been worse; it is never so bad but we are confident of doing better next time. And if the next stroke is good, what happiness fills our soul. How eagerly we tell ourselves that in a little while all our strokes will be as good.

What does Vardon know of this? If he does a five hole in four he blames himself that he did not do it in three; if he does it in five he is miserable. He will never experience that happy surprise with which we hail our best strokes. Only his bad strokes surprise him, and then we may suppose that he is not happy. His length and accuracy are mechanical; they are not the result, as so often in our case, of some suddenly applied maxim or some suddenly discovered innovation. The only thing which can vary in his game is his putting, and putting is not golf but croquet.

But of course we, too, are going to be as good as Vardon one day. We are only postponing the day because meanwhile it is so pleasant to be bad. And it is part of the charm of being bad at golf that in a moment, in a single night, we may become good. If the bad cricketer said to a good cricketer, "What am I doing wrong?" the only possible answer would be, "Nothing particular, except that you can't play cricket." But if you or I were to say to our scratch friend, "What am I doing wrong?" he would reply at once, "Moving the head" or "Dropping the right knee" or "Not getting the wrists in soon enough," and by to-morrow we should be different players. Upon such a little depends, or seems to the eighteen-handicap to depend, excellence in golf.

And so, perfectly happy in our present badness and perfectly confident of our future goodness, we long-handicap men remain. Perhaps it would be pleasanter to be a little more certain of getting the ball safely off the first tee; perhaps at the fourteenth hole, where there is a right of way and the public encroach, we should like to feel that we have done with topping; perhaps—

Well, perhaps we might get our handicap down to fifteen this summer. But no lower; certainly no lower.

Stark

BY MICHAEL BAMBERGER

One of golf's more enchanting myths is the one that imparts something on the order of cosmic wisdom to any Scotsman with a wizened visage, a lilting brogue, and a knowledge of where the Old Course is. Michael Murphy built an industry in the magical character Shivas Irons from his novel *Golf in the Kingdom;* John Updike, too, walked this course in his brilliant short story, "Farrell's Caddie." On the other hand, Michael Bamberger went out to find the real thing in the second half of the golfing adventure he captured in *To the Linksland.* Now a writer at *Sports Illustrated,* he was a reporter at the *Philadelphia Inquirer* in 1991 when he took a sabbatical to caddie on the European Tour. His experiences toting journeyman Peter Teravainen's bag make up the first half of the book. The second traces his quest to find the heart of the game by playing some of the less well-known Scottish courses. It was in the pro shop at the Crieff Golf Club that Bamberger met John Stark.

T ell me precisely what it is you seek to accomplish," John Stark said. We were sitting in his crammed office, in the back of his pro shop at the Crieff Golf Club, in central Scotland. I was expecting a trim man in a tweed coat, but my expectations were wrong. Stark was a behemoth, two or three inches over six feet and a stone or two over two hundred pounds, with a deep, booming voice and a rich Scots dialect. He wore white loafers, shiny blue nylon sweat pants, and a white golf shirt a size or two too small. Around his neck hung a gold chain, and the borders of his front teeth were lined with gold, too. He had a heavy, compassionate face, and thick white hair combed off his broad forehead. He smoked a cheap cigar. He was sixty years old, and he looked it, except in his eyes—he had ageless, piercing, wise blue eyes.

"I want to get better," I said quietly.

Stark stared at me. My God, how he stared at me! I felt as if the master teacher were looking right into my golfing past: here I am in an eighth-grade gym class, my first brush with the game, whacking balls with wild, happy abandon off Astroturf mats; here I am in the summer before my freshman year of college, at the height of my modest powers, which is to say, able to beak eighty from time to time on a course I knew intimately; here I am, ten years later, at dangerous Pine Valley, in New Jersey, losing balls and putting monstrously while mentally composing a letter of apology to my host; here I am a few years later, on the practice tee of a Palm Beach resort, hearing old Mr. Hartmann say to the youth working the range, "Young sir, I am running out of time," and feeling solidarity with him. No, Stark wasn't staring at me, he was staring right through me: he saw my suffering, my dissatisfaction, my false pride, my humiliation, my longing, my urgency.

He lit his cigar and we sat in silence for a long moment. In time, he spoke; I remember the weird way his lips started moving, well before his words came out. I will tell you what he said, but before I do, I'd like to explain how I found my way to that back room, amid the boxed shoes waiting for feet, the unfinished woods waiting for paint, the naked shafts waiting for grips; I think I should tell you how I came to have an audience with Mr. J. M. Stark, golf professional, whose dangerous and powerful vision was so immediately apparent.

I had been looking for a teacher. In my mind, I was a seventies shooter in the midst of a thirteen-year slump, but in reality I had to play well to shoot 82, and more often shot 92. I could play to my handicap, twelve or thirteen, only on my good days, and that was an unsatisfying way to go through life. I longed to feel again the thrill of discovery, the thrill of improvement. I felt I needed a fresh start, and a teacher to set me on a new course. A British Ryder Cup player from the Palmer era, whom I had met in England while caddying for Teravainen, told me about Stark. "He teaches no two people the same way, and he knows the game from the outside and the inside," I was told. "He's a mystic, something of a recluse, and if you get him to take you on you'll be lucky indeed."

Intrigued, I wrote to John Stark, and inquired about becoming a pupil. He invited me in for a "little chat"—that's how he put it. So, during the weekend of the Scottish Open, after Peter had missed the cut, I went up to see Stark at the club where he has worked since 1961, in the town of Crieff, on the same latitude as St. Andrews, but far off the coast, midway between Loch Earn and the Firth of Tay. I left my clubs behind; I didn't want to appear presumptuous.

"You want to get better, a worthy goal," Stark said. "But what makes you think tuition is the way to improvement? I've seen many players ruined with instruction, I've seen instruction rob a player of all his natural instincts for the game."

Stark leaned back in his desk chair, which was too small to accommodate him. I didn't know if he wanted me to respond. The rhythms of Scottish and American conversation are different. The Scots pause more, and ask more questions, questions not always meant to be answered. I waited, and eventually Stark continued.

"When I was a boy, there was no teaching of golf in Scotland, not in a formal sense, and I don't think the quality of the play in this country was any worse for it. Your father showed you a couple of things when you played with him in the summer evenings. You caddied, and if you had a player you liked, you emulated him. If you were lucky enough to see a Henry Cotton, you didn't ask him how many knuckles of his left hand were visible at address. You'd follow him around, watch how he approached the game, watch his swing, and then you'd try to do the same. You'd fiddle around, perform experiments, amalgamate what he was doing with your own ideas, and come up with something distinctly your own."

A young shop assistant came in with instant coffee and Stark stirred it with a letter opener.

"You Americans have made the game so bloody mechanical and plodding. You've made these mechanical courses, where all you do is hit the ball from point A to point B. Target golf, aye, they got that name just right. The best of your countrymen have become good golf robots, outstanding golf robots, all swinging the club the same way. You've made us change the way we think about the game. As a result, there's virtually nobody left playing golf in the old Scottish manner: fast and unschooled. Not that long ago, Scottish golf had a style all its own—low, running hooks into the wind; quick, flat, handsy swings; wristy putting; bunker play where you nipped the ball cleanly; putting from twenty yards off the green; bump-and-run shots from *anywhere*. It was great fun, great *sport*, to play that way, but it wasn't very efficient. You could be impressive, but it didn't necessarily result in low scores. Of course, for a very long time we didn't care much about scores.

"That is another American thing, this fascination with score, always keeping track with pencil and scorecard. In the Scottish game, the only thing that mattered was your match, and you knew how that stood intuitively. Now you have all these endless first-tee discussions about handicaps and what type of wager to make and where the strokes should be allocated. Too much."

The telephone rang, and Stark made arrangements for a fishing trip.

"You showed us that there's money in golf. That had never occurred to us. The money has corrupted us, all of us, myself included. Once you start making it, it's a damn cancer, the money is. You start thinking, 'What can I do to make more money?' In my generation, we went into golf with no expectation of wealth. The golf alone sustained us. For years, we resisted thinking of golf as a business. Right through the Second World War, we had clubs with one full-time employee: he gave lessons, made clubs and sold 'em, kept the caddies in line, and mixed the drinks. The game was cheap then: you might have paid five quid for a year's worth of golf, and you got your money's worth. You played after work, until you could see the ball no more. You played every day, except Sunday; the Presbyterians wouldn't hear of golf on Sunday. But you played the six other days, and you hoped for wind to make your game interesting. Scotland was poor, and there was nothing else to do, except the pubs. Golf was the national sport. Everybody played. Your mother played. Golf was the game."

He took a long sip of coffee and stared me down, not a hint of smile on his face. He was sizing me up, trying to figure out if I knew what he was talking about. I was transfixed.

"In 1953, Scottish golf took a mortal blow, when Hogan came to Carnoustie to play in the Open. He had already won the Masters. He had won your Open. If I hadn't witnessed what he did at Carnoustie, I would not have believed it. I was playing in the championship, but I felt we were in different tournaments altogether. I remember how he played the sixth, a par-five. I was a reasonably long hitter, but I never regarded the hole as reachable in two, because of the fairway bunkers that came into play if you hit a big driver off the tee. I thought you had to play short of the bunkers. We all did. But Hogan showed us we were wrong. He found this little strip of fairway, between the rough and the bunkers, maybe ten yards wide, and he landed his drives on that strip every time, and from there the green could be fetched. Nobody else would have dared such a tee shot. We were amazed. They started calling that little landing zone 'Hogan's Alley.' I had never seen a technique like that before, a technique that could produce long shots that went so straight. None of us had. That was the beginning of the end of Scottish golf, in the classical sense. Hogan was playing a different game. Everybody was fascinated. Everybody became keen to study it. Everybody started thinking about method. What was Hogan's method? How could we achieve the ideal method?

"After Hogan's triumph at Carnoustie—and that is what it was—the shutterbug descended upon golf. Suddenly, there was this fascination with high-speed golf photography that enabled you to break down the swing into hundreds of stop-action photos. It all seemed so obvious: there was a correct position for *everything,* at all points in the swing. You just had to match yourself up with the pictures, make sure your angles, or your student's angles, matched the angles in the pictures. The swing, as a whole, was subverted. The important thing was all the hundreds of little movements. Every frame of Hogan showed the perfect position, for that split-second."

At this point, Stark produced a pad from a desk drawer and found a pen with the top chewed off and started drawing lines and curves with much more care than the sputtering pen could convey. While he drew, he talked.

"You know that a line, in mathematics, is in fact a series of points? Most people see only the line, but the mathematician can see the points. That's what happened with the golf swing. We teachers became mathematicians, seeing all these bloody points, but we lost track of the line. I was as guilty as anyone. I turned my back on the Scottish game, the game of my youth. A year after Hogan won at Carnoustie, I went to Sweden to teach golf there, and for my seven years there I taught a very technical game. Used photographs all the time. It made great sense to me then, made sense to me for years afterwards. Now I'm not so sure. With all this technical instruction, I don't see people playing better, and I certainly don't see them enjoying their golf more, not at any level. I see them enjoying it less. I see more frustration and less pleasure. That's what saddens me. If I stand for anything at this point in my life, it's to turn back the hands of time, to see if I can help people to treat golf as a game.

"You come to me and say you want to get better, that you want to take lessons from me, but I wonder if you really need them. You have been doing just the right thing, haven't you: working as a caddie, seeing up close world-class players, the Henry Cottons of your day. This is a very good thing. Think of the players you really admire. Right now, go on and think of them. Think of what makes them special to you. Adopt from them what is useful to yourself."

We again sat in silence for a moment. I thought of Teravainen, how his face got all scrunched up when he was trying to figure out the line of a putt, how hard he would try. I thought of the rhythmic pounding of Ballesteros's swing, a swing that reminded me of the crashing of a mighty Pacific roller.

"Who've you got in mind?" Stark asked.

"Peter Teravainen and Seve," I said.

"Interesting," Stark said. He relit his cigar. "And why do you particularly admire them?" I wanted to answer well; I felt that if I could show Stark that I was a student of the game, that the game was as important to me as it was to him, that I was worthy of his time, then maybe he would take me on. I knew that he would be unlike any other teacher I would find anywhere else. When he spoke of the mortal blow Hogan had dealt old-school Scottish golf it was without cynicism or despair. It was with reverence and fascination. It was with the tone Cronkite once reserved for the Apollo liftoffs. Through Stark, I felt, I could reincarnate myself as a Scottish golfer. I could have a fresh start.

I struggled to put together the words of my answer. *What is it that I particularly admire about Teravainen?*

Finally, I answered. "Everything Teravainen has accomplished in the game has come by way of physical effort."

"Yes, that's right, isn't it," Stark said. "You can see that in his scores. I've followed Teravainen for years—his Finnish name has always interested me—and I see that he is an exceptional par-shooter, regardless of the course, regardless of the weather. That tells you that he may lack brilliance, but that he is tough, that he knows how to make par hole after hole, round after round, week after week, year after year. Yes, Teravainen—interesting. And why Ballesteros—what do you particularly admire about him?"

"Ballesteros's game seems to come from inside him," I said. "He seems to produce shots by subconscious force, by will. Seve doesn't seem to be aware of what he is doing, he just does it. He is the opposite of Peter in that."

"Ah, very good, Michael. Yes, will is the thing with Seve. There is no one in his class today. Nick Faldo may be a better player, but Ballesteros is a better golfer. He may be the last of the Scottish players. I could watch him all day. He came here a few days ago to put on an exhibition for the kids. They were fascinated by him, as if he were a magician, which of course he is. He said to one boy, 'I don't like your swing, but I like how your ball goes.' In style he is completely different, but Ballesteros is the first player since Hogan that I have found totally mesmerizing. Good choices, those two. Now what have you learned from Teravainen that you can apply to your own game?"

It dawned on me that Stark was giving me a lesson. We were sitting in his office, surrounded by clubs. Though we had none in hand, he was giving me a lesson.

"Peter understands the value of every shot, he understands that all shots count equally," I said. "He never lets up, because he knows that one slipup will fast lead to another. He has this idea, which I think he got from Nicklaus, that when he stands over a shot he knows it will be the only time in his entire life that he is able to play that shot. After the shot is played, the moment is lost forever. So every shot is important, every shot is once-in-a-lifetime. He feels an obligation to make something of it. At the root of all his effort is great concentration. I very seldom can focus intensely on each shot through eighteen holes."

"Now there's your first mistake, Michael. Don't tell me what you can't do. What's past is prologue. Tell me what you *want* to do." I nodded; I understood. "You want to do like Teravainen, and concentrate on each shot. A worthy goal."

Stark clasped his thick hands behind his head. He was enjoying this discourse, I felt. "Now what about Ballesteros, what did you learn from him that you can apply to your own game?"

"Seve makes the most beautiful swings," I said, "so graceful and powerful. He's fluid, uncluttered. I would love to make swings like that. On the practice tee, you can see he thinks about a lot of technical things, but you don't see that on the course. He seems to be thinking only about the ball and the hole. I would hope someday to have a fluid swing like that."

"You will, when you come to trust yourself," Stark said. "Seve looks uncluttered because he trusts his mechanics. He trusts his mechanics because he knows they're good. He knows they're good because he's had successful results with them in the past." He paused. "Sometimes the game seems so - simple."

Stark stood up and walked awkwardly to a window—a damaged and arthritic hip and spine had robbed him of mobility, made sitting in one place for long periods painful, and ended his days of walking eighteen holes. He stayed with the game through teaching, reading, thinking, and talking. He leaned up against the window and watched a cold early July rain fall, watched the trees shake. People were playing.

"This rain keeps up, our greens will look like bloody gargoyles," Stark said. He pulled and pressed on different parts of his face to show the softness of the greens and to imitate a gargoyle. In the shop, two or three people were waiting to see Stark.

"For how long will you be in Scotland?" he asked.

"Through the end of summer," I said.

"That's good, you've given yourself enough time to discover some of our secrets."

My time with Stark was drawing to a close. I gathered my things, happy for our excellent conversation, disappointed that he seemed unwilling to take me on as a pupil.

I was standing in the doorway to his office when Stark said, "Do you know what I mean when I say *linksland?* Linksland is the old Scottish word for the earth at the edge of the sea—tumbling, duney, sandy, covered by beach grasses. When the light hits it, and the breeze sweeps over it, you get every shade of green and brown, and always, in the distance, is the water. The land was long considered worthless, except to the shepherds and their sheep and the rabbits, and to the early golfers. You see, the game comes out of the ocean, just like man himself! Investigate our linksland, Michael, get to know it. I think you'll find it worthwhile. Drop in on your travels. I'll be curious to know what you learn."

The Way the Ball Bounces

BY JOHN P. MARQUAND

One of the finest chroniclers of American manners and the monied elite, John P. Marquand (1893–1960) took great delight in scrutinizing the very Upper Crust from which he descended. His literary pokings and proddings earned a Pulitzer Prize—for his novel *The Late George Apley*—and the hearts of mystery buffs—with his invention of the Japanese detective Mr. Moto. In the late 1950s, Marquand created a fictional country club for his epistolary novel *Life at Happy Knoll,* and filled it with a bagful of the usual problems. How to keep the pro was just one of them.

A letter from Mr. Roger Horlick of the Board of Governors of the Happy Knoll Country Club to Mr. Albert Magill, President Emeritus, regarding the golf professional, Benny Muldoon.

Dear Albert:

The Board of Governors at the Happy Knoll Country Club faces a crisis right at the height of our golfing season. It suddenly looks as though we may lose our golf professional on a two weeks' notice. I know what you are going to say. You are going to say that the Board voted another thousand dollars for Benny Muldoon at one of their recent meetings, and you are also going to say that we should at least have tied Benny up on a season's contract. Well, I suppose you are right on both scores, but still, facts are facts. We have never signed Benny up on a contract because Benny has always said he loved the Club and he has always seemed to us like one of our members. Actually, one cannot help being touched by Benny's reaction because he seems more upset, if possible, by the prospect of impending change than any of his host of admirers.

You know as well as I do that Benny is a sentimentalist at heart. There is a genuine quaver in his voice when he speaks about the possibility of leaving Happy Knoll, which he says very frankly is his second home. But, as Benny says, you have got to face facts. It is like, he said when I interviewed him yesterday, the time when he was playing his second 18 at Rough Briar in the State Open. He had belted out a 300-yard drive right down the middle of the fairway. There was quite a gallery following because, frankly, he was hot as a pistol right up to the 7th. There was the green, 80 yards away, heavily trapped, but a cinch for a roll to the cup, if you aimed for the upper slope. Would he use an eight-, a nine-iron or a wedge? He had to make up his mind. He must have been thinking about all his responsibilities there because he called for the wrong club, landed in the trap and blasted out for a measly four. So you have to make up your mind, and either in match play or in life, making up your mind is a pretty tough proposition. Come to think of it, as Benny told me, and you know how philosophical Benny can get when he has the golf house to himself, life from his experience is a good deal like a game of golf. You get yourself into the rough in life just the way you do when you slice off the tee and you've got to take a wedge and some religion to get yourself squared away. Just like in life, in golf you start out with nothing but you have to come home with something.

I took the liberty of interrupting Benny at this point, telling him that in golf the less strokes you come back with the better, and that in life, too, a large income is often a source of worry.

Benny said that at the same time you had to come back with something. And these days when he came back to Patricia (that's Mrs. Muldoon), Patricia didn't feel he was bringing home enough, even if life wasn't exactly like golf. It seems that Patricia has been needling Benny Muldoon ever since he won that State Open. I told you at the time, Albert, you never should have offered to pay Benny's expenses for that occasion, and if you hadn't, I don't believe that Patricia (that's Mrs. Muldoon) would have allowed Benny to take the money out of what he calls "the kitty" for any such long shot. After all, Benny always said, previous to the State Open, that he was a teacher and not a tournament player. Well, now it's different. Benny now wants to go out to California to Pebble Beach or somewhere so that he can slug it out with "the circuit," and

Patricia (that's Mrs. Muldoon) has begun reading the sports columns, and if an unknown like Fleck could beat Hogan, why couldn't Benny beat Fleck?

It seems that Patricia is now making notes on the annual incomes of Hogan and a few others, and these figures prove that Benny is not coming home with enough. It seems that he is not thinking of the future of their two children and of the other that is on the way. Instead he only thinks about analyzing the golf swings of a lot of stingy though rich old loafers at the Happy Knoll Country Club. These are my words, not Benny's. These people, Patricia says, could never win the State Open and she could give any of them a stroke a hole and beat them herself if she weren't expecting. That's the way she is, pugnacious (I'm referring to Mrs. Muldoon). It seems that she keeps needling Benny. Only yesterday she asked him, now that he has won the State Open, why he can't go to a sporting goods store and get his name inscribed on a set of matched irons, like Mr. MacGregor? Ambition, it seems, is Patricia's middle name. It seems to me that Lady Macbeth displayed many of the same attributes on the evening that King Duncan dropped in for the night.

Well, as Benny said yesterday, that's the way the ball bounces and he is a family and not a single man and now there has come a crisis. Hard Hollow first made a bid for him and now comes Rocky River. Rocky River is willing to guarantee Benny two thousand dollars more than we are after we have met the Hard Hollow offer. Benny has been most honorable about it and is holding nothing up his sleeve because he loves Happy Knoll and everybody in it, but that's the way the ball bounces. Besides, if he turns Rocky River down, how can he tell Mrs. Muldoon? In addition, Rocky River has a golf house twice the size of ours and everybody at Rocky River loyally buys all their equipment from it. Benny doesn't mean to say anything tough about Happy Knoll members because he loves them all, but sometimes, just to save a buck, they do go to some cut-rate store in the city and come back to the Happy Knoll course with a lot of junk that he would be ashamed to handle, but that's the way the ball bounces. He has an ironclad guarantee that they never will do that at Rocky River, and they have a display room that can even handle slacks and tweeds besides caps and windbreakers. So here we have the question. What are we going to do about Benny Muldoon? I know what our deficit is, but Benny has been here for 10 years. A lot of people, including you, Albert, have to go to him regularly. How would you like it if you had to start with someone else? A golf pro, after all, is like a priest in a parish or a headmaster at school.

There are of course people who shop around among golf teachers, but these are hypochondriacs who can never cure themselves by advice from several sources. We both know this, Albert. You may recollect that some years ago I caught you sneaking out to the Hard Hollow Country Club to see whether their Jerry Scalponi could do more about your basic game than Benny Muldoon. I met you there because, frankly, I had come out for the same purpose and we were both agreed that all that results from promiscuous golf advice is unhealthy cynicism. Most professionals after diagnosing your golf ailments ask who taught you. When you tell them, they say it is too bad and all that can be done now is to start all over again and, by the way, your set of laminated woods are too heavy in the head and disturb your back swing.

I cannot bear at my time of life to face anyone else except Benny Muldoon, because he has a beautiful gift of sympathy and on the practice tee he suffers with me always. I admit it has been true lately, perhaps because Mrs. Muldoon has been suggesting that he underrates himself, that Benny seems to be cultivating a Scottish accent. The other day I thought I heard him say "Verra guid," but if Benny wants to be Sir Harry Lauder he still comforts me and leads me safely over the water hazards because his good words are with me; and I certainly ought to remember what Benny Muldoon has told me, because he says the same things over and over but then, what else is there for him to say?

You have got to be calm and collected, he says. Golf, if you will excuse his using a long word, is a psychological game. Have a mental picture in your mind, he says, of the right way of hitting through the ball and you can do it. Golf, if you will excuse his saying so, is a wee bit like religion, and a while ago a gentleman whom he doesn't think I ever knew, because Benny met him years ago at Hot Springs (but he was very important in the coal business and had a Rolls Royce and two lovely daughters) told him about a French doctor called M. Cooey or something like that. You'll have to excuse his French, but seriously, this Doctor Cooey or however you say it stated that you simply had to say a couple of thousand times every morning, "Every day in every way I am getting better and better" and, believe it or not, you did. What Benny wants you to say is simply that every day in every way your golf is getting better. Say it two thousand times and then go out and see what happens. Only recently he made this suggestion to Mrs. Falconhurst. Benny was worried so sick about Mrs. Falconhurst that when he came home at night he couldn't eat. Frankly, Mrs. Falconhurst was a lovely lady, but he couldn't teach her to hit a balloon. But then he told her about this Frenchman and you ought to see her now.

Confidence is what you need in golf. If you want it in two words, confidence and Cooey is all there is. Now of course, Benny says, golf isn't like trying to bat a baseball or anything so easy, but in the end, like batting a baseball, it's confidence. Benny says he almost lost his confidence on the long 13th in the Open up at Rocky River. It was the afternoon round and something he ate wasn't sitting well on his stomach. He was using the two-wood on the fairway, giving it everything he had, and he might have even pressed but it was probably the frankfurter he had for lunch. Anyway, instead of making the green he hooked over the third bunker. Frankly, his knees sagged and he burst into a cold sweat, but he said to himself, "I can do it, I can do it," and he came across with the sweetest wedge shot of the day. It wasn't Benny who did it. It was Doctor Cooey and that's the way the ball bounces. As Benny says, there's some other things to golf. Sweep your club head low back on the ground, make a nice pivot, hit from the inside out clean, crisp and smooth. That's another little motto: be crisp and smooth, and let the club head do the work. Don't worry where the ball goes. Just do it and Benny will be happy. Just be crisp and easy and relaxed.

Well, I have been going to Benny more often I am afraid than I go to church. I have heard everything, and in fact I now know exactly what he will say next. In spite of Doctor Cooey, my reason tells me that my golf never will greatly improve and yet I do keep going back to Benny and so does everyone else at Happy Knoll. Why? I don't know any direct answer except that Benny can always make you feel that you're going to do better sometime in the foreseeable future. After all, as Benny said when I was speaking to him yesterday, golf teaching is like being a shill in a crap game. You've got to keep the customers coming, you've got to make them feel good and if you don't—no bottle for Buster.

Yet there is another, more cogent reason, I believe, that Benny is able to hold the large and captious public that he has at Happy Knoll. It is because he universally commands a deep respect. Somehow whenever I see Benny Muldoon I know I am in the presence of greatness. In a way he is more of a doctor than a teacher, but he does not need signed certificates nor garbled language to make his point. The tee-side is different from the bedside manner. The truth is, Benny always comes across. He can invariably chip to six inches of the cup. With his left arm alone he can send the ball two hundred yards. He can slice or hook at will and can parody the play of any of his pupils, but always in a genial manner. He can also drive a ball from the top of a gold watch without damaging its mechanism and once he was prepared to drive a ball off the head of our fellow member, Mr. Featherstone, who was in one of his customarily genial moods, but the Greens Committee intervened. I have always been sorry for this because it might have been that Benny would have hit below the ball for once in his career. Somehow when Benny Muldoon wears the golf accessories that are on sale in the golf shop they always fit him; they never look ridiculous as they do on some of the rest of us—not the loudest shirts, not even tam-o'-shanters. But it is not dress, not exposition, but his unfailing kindness that I most admire. Benny knows very well that we could all be as good as he if we had had his chance to be a caddie at a New Jersey country club whose name I can never pronounce. He has a special niche in his heart for everyone, and a very long memory, too. It is true that he asked me the other day how my water on the knee was getting on, but he corrected himself immediately. He had been thinking of Mrs. Falconhurst. He meant the bursitis in my right shoulder, the same complaint from which President Eisenhower suffers, and Ike is a pretty hot golfer, considering. It is inconceivable to think of telling any more intimate golfing troubles or the more disgraceful things I have done on the Happy Knoll links to anyone except Benny Muldoon. There is a personal rapport in these matters which cannot be overlooked.

Frankly, Albert, I have not had a good year in a business sense, but the stock market has been rising in spite of the Fulbright Committee. I can, if necessary, sell something. There has been so much hat passing lately that any more might cause repercussions. I think that you and I have got to take it upon ourselves to fix this thing about Benny Muldoon. In fact, I have done so already. I have told him that I would pay half and you would pay the rest, and just remember, that's the way the ball bounces.

Sincerely,
Roger Horlick

The Long Hole

BY P. G. WODEHOUSE

By all accounts—including his own—P. (for Pelham) G. (for Grenville) Wodehouse (1881–1975) was a horrible golfer. "I never win a match," the obsessive high-handicapper once admitted. "I spend my life out of bounds. I never even count my strokes." No matter. What his spoon, his mashie, and his niblick never mastered, his pen did. Extraordinarily prolific, Wodehouse possessed an incomparable literary short game; his collections of golf stories—*Golf Without Tears, Divots,* and *Nothing Serious*—brim with gems of comic fiction, wicked in their observations, and often searching, in their heart, for love. Most feature an appearance from the meddlesome Oldest Member. Like Wodehouse's other eternal warhorses, Bertie Wooster and Jeeves, the OM is an enduring—and in his own way endearing—creation, a kind of human personification of the Nineteenth Hole. From his seat on the terrace, in the smoking room—where we find him at the beginning of this marvelous tale, first published in 1919— or wherever else he might be lurking in the clubhouse, the OM filled his purpose brilliantly, always watching, always listening, always willing to take in a confidence, and always—*always*—ready to offer his two cents, whether it was asked for or whether it wasn't.

T he young man, as he sat filling his pipe in the club-house smoking-room, was inclined to be bitter.

"If there's one thing that gives me a pain squarely in the centre of the gizzard," he burst out, breaking a silence that had lasted for some minutes, "it's a golf-lawyer. They oughtn't to be allowed on the links."

The Oldest Member, who had been meditatively putting himself outside a cup of tea and a slice of seed-cake, raised his white eyebrows.

"The Law," he said, "is an honourable profession. Why should its practitioners be restrained from indulgence in the game of games?"

"I don't mean actual lawyers," said the young man, his acerbity mellowing a trifle under the influence of tobacco. "I mean the blighters whose best club is the book of rules. You know the sort of excrescences. Every time you think you've won a hole, they dig out Rule eight hundred and fifty-three, section two, sub-section four, to prove that you've disqualified yourself by having an ingrowing toe-nail. . . . Well, take my case." The young man's voice was high and plaintive. "I go out with that man Hemmingway to play an ordinary friendly round—nothing depending on it except a measly ball—and on the seventh he pulls me up and claims the hole simply because I happened to drop my niblick in the bunker."

The Sage shook his head.

"Rules are rules, my boy, and must be kept. It is curious that you should have brought up this subject, for only a moment before you came in I was thinking of a somewhat curious match which ultimately turned upon a question of the rule-book. It is true that, as far as the actual prize was concerned, it made little difference. . . . But perhaps I had better tell you the whole story from the beginning."

The young man shifted uneasily in his chair.

"Well, you know, I've had a pretty rotten time this afternoon already. . . ."

"I will call my story," said the Sage tranquilly, " 'The Long Hole,' for it involved the playing of what I am inclined to think must be the longest hole in the history of golf."

"I half promised to go and see a man. . . ."

"But I will begin at the beginning," said the Sage. "I see that you are all impatient to hear the full details."

Rollo Bingham and Otis Jukes (said the Oldest Member) had never been friends—their rivalry was too keen to admit of that—but it was not till Amelia Trivett came to stay at Manhooset that a smouldering distaste for each other burst out into the flames of actual enmity. It is ever so. One of the poets, whose name I cannot recall, has a passage, which I am unable at the moment to remember, in one of his works, which for the time being has slipped my mind, which hits off admirably this age-old situation. The gist of his remarks is that lovely woman rarely fails to start something. In the weeks that followed her arrival, being in the same room with the two men was like dropping in on a reunion of Capulets and Montagues.

You see, Rollo and Otis were so exactly equal in their skill on the links that life for them had, for some time past, resolved itself into a silent, bitter struggle in which first one, then the other gained some slight advantage. If Rollo won the May medal by a stroke, Otis would be one ahead in the June competition, only to be nosed out again in July. It was a state of affairs which, had they been men of a more generous stamp, would have bred a mutual respect, esteem, and even love. But I am sorry to say that, apart from their golf, which was in a class of its own as far as this neighbourhood was concerned, Rollo Bingham and Otis Jukes were nothing less than a couple of unfortunate incidents. A sorry pair—and yet, mark you, far from lacking in mere superficial good looks, they were handsome fellows, both of them, and well aware of the fact; and, when Amelia Trivett came to stay, they simply straightened their ties, twirled their mustaches, and expected her to do the rest.

But here they were disappointed. Perfectly friendly though she was to both of them, the lovelight was conspicuously absent from her beautiful eyes. And it was not long before each had come independently to a solution of this mystery. It was plain to them that the whole trouble lay in the fact that each neutralised the other's attractions. Otis felt that, if he could only have a clear field, all would be over except the sending out of the wedding invitations; and Rollo was of the opinion that, if he could just call on the girl one evening without finding the place all littered up with Otis, his natural charms would swiftly bring home the bacon. And, indeed, it was true that they had no rivals except themselves. It happened at the moment that Manhooset was extraordinarily short of eligible bachelors. We marry young in this delightful spot, and all the likely men were already paired off. It seemed that, if Amelia Trivett intended to get married, she would have to select either Rollo Bingham or Otis Jukes. A dreadful choice.

It had not occurred to me at the outset that my position in the affair would be anything closer than that of a detached and mildly interested spectator. Yet it was to me that Rollo came in his hour of need. When I returned home one evening I found that my man had brought him in and laid him on the mat in my sitting-room.

I offered him a chair and a cigar, and he came to the point with com-mendable rapidity.

"Manhooset," he said, directly he had lighted his cigar, "is too small for Otis Jukes and myself."

"Ah, you have been talking it over and decided to move?" I said, de-lighted. "I think you are perfectly right. Manhooset *is* overbuilt. Men like you and Jukes need a lot of space. Where do you think of going?"

"I'm not going."

"But I thought you said. . . ."

"What I meant was that the time has come when one of us must leave."

"Oh, only one of you?" It was something, of course, but I confess I was disappointed, and I think my disappointment must have shown in my voice, for he looked at me, surprised.

"Surely you wouldn't mind Jukes going?" he said.

"Why, certainly not. He really is going, is he?"

A look of saturnine determination came into Rollo's face.

"He is. He thinks he isn't, but he is."

I failed to understand him, and said so. He looked cautiously about the room, as if to reassure himself that he could not be overheard.

"I suppose you've noticed," he said, "the disgusting way that man Jukes has been hanging 'round Miss Trivett, boring her to death?"

"I have seen them together sometimes."

"I love Amelia Trivett!" said Rollo.

"Poor girl!" I sighed.

"I beg your pardon?"

"Poor girl," I said. "I mean to have Otis Jukes hanging 'round her."

"That's just what I think," said Rollo Bingham. "And that's why we're going to play this match."

"What match?"

"This match we've decided to play. I want you to act as one of the judges, to go along with Jukes and see that he doesn't play any of his tricks. You know what he is! And in a vital match like this. . . ."

"How much are you playing for?"

"The whole world!"

"I beg your pardon?"

"The whole world. It amounts to that. The loser is to leave Manhooset for good, and the winner stays on and marries Amelia Trivett. We have arranged all the details. Rupert Bailey will accompany me, acting as the other judge."

"And you want me to go round with Jukes?"

"Not round," said Rollo Bingham. "Along."

"What is the distinction?"

"We are not going to play a round. Only one hole."

"Sudden death, eh?"

"Not so very sudden. It's a longish hole. We start on the first tee here and hole out in the doorway of the Hotel Astor in Times Square. A distance, I imagine, of about sixteen miles."

I was revolted. About that time a perfect epidemic of freak matches had broken out in the club, and I had strongly opposed them from the start. George Willis had begun it by playing a medal round with the pro, George's first nine against the pro's complete eighteen. I was extremely pleased when the pro did a sixty-two, a record for the course, thus getting home by three strokes and putting George back a matter of two hundred and fifty dollars. After that came the contest between Herbert Widgeon and Montague Brown, the latter, a twenty-four handicap man, being entitled to shout "Boo!" three times during the round at moments selected by himself. There had been many more of these degrading travesties on the sacred game, and I had writhed to see them. Playing freak golf matches is to my mind like ragging a great classical melody. But of the whole collection this one, considering the sentimental interest and the magnitude of the stakes, seemed to me the most terrible. My face, I imagine, betrayed my disgust, for Bingham attempted extenuation.

"It's the only way," he said. "You know how Jukes and I are on the links. We are as level as two men can be. This, of course, is due to his extraordinary luck. Everybody knows that he is the world's champion fluker. I, on the other hand, invariably have the worst luck. The consequence is that in an ordinary round it is always a toss-up which of us wins. The test we propose will eliminate luck. After sixteen miles of give-and-take play, I am certain—that is to say, the better man is certain to be ahead. That is what I meant when I said that Otis Jukes would shortly be leaving Manhooset. Well, may I take it that you will consent to act as one of the judges?"

I considered. After all, the match was likely to be historic, and one always feels tempted to hand one's name down to posterity.

"Very well," I said.

"Excellent. You will have to keep a sharp eye on Jukes, I need scarcely remind you. You will, of course, carry a book of the rules in your pocket and refer to them when you wish to refresh your memory. We start at daybreak, for, if we put it off till later, the course at the other end might be somewhat congested when we reached it. We want to avoid publicity as far as possible. If I took a full iron down Broadway and hit a policeman, it would excite remark."

"It would. I can tell you the exact remark which it would excite."

"We shall take bicycles with us, to minimize the fatigue of covering the distance. Well, I am glad that we have your coöperation. At daybreak to-morrow on the first tee, and don't forget to bring your rules book."

The atmosphere brooding over the first tee, when I reached it on the following morning, somewhat resembled that of a dueling ground in the days when these affairs were settled with rapiers or pistols. Rupert Bailey, an old friend of mine, was the only cheerful member of the party. I am never at my best in the early morning, and the two rivals glared at each other with silent sneers. I had never supposed till that moment that men ever really sneered at one another outside the movies, but these two were indisputably doing so. They were in the mood when men say "Pshaw!"

They tossed for the honour; and Otis Jukes, having won, drove off with a fine ball that landed well down the course. Rollo Bingham, having teed up, turned to Rupert Bailey.

"Go down on to the fairway of the seventeenth," he said. "I want you to mark my ball."

Rupert stared.

"The seventeenth!"

"I am going to take that direction," said Rollo, pointing over the trees.

"But that will land your second or third shot in the Sound."

"I have provided for that. I have a flat-bottomed boat moored close by the sixteenth green. I shall use a mashie-niblick and chip my ball aboard, row across to the other side, ship it ashore, and carry on. I propose to go across country as far as Flushing. I think it will save me a stroke or two."

I gasped. I had never before realised the man's devilish cunning. His tactics gave him a flying start. Otis, who had driven straight down the course, had as his objective the highroad, which adjoins the waste ground beyond the first green. Once there, he would play the orthodox game by driving his ball along till he reached the Fifty-ninth Street Bridge. While Otis was winding along the highroad, Rollo would have cut off practically two sides of a triangle. And it was hopeless for Otis to imitate his enemy's tactics now. From where his ball lay he would have to cross a wide tract of marsh in order to reach the seventeenth fairway, an impossible feat. And, even if it had been feasible, he had no boat to take him across the water.

He uttered a violent protest. He was an unpleasant young man, almost—it seems absurd to say so, but almost as unpleasant as Rollo Bingham; yet at the moment I am bound to say I sympathised with him.

"Where do you get that stuff?" he demanded. "You can't play fast and loose with the rules like that."

"To what rule do you refer?" said Rollo coldly.

"Well, that damned boat of yours is a hazard, isn't it? And you can't row a hazard about all over the place."

"Why not?"

The simple question seemed to take Otis Jukes aback.

"Why not?" he repeated. "Why not? Well, you can't. That's why."

"There is nothing in the rules," said Rollo Bingham, "against moving a hazard. If a hazard can be moved without disturbing the ball, you are at liberty, I gather, to move it wherever you darn please. Besides, what is all this about moving hazards? I have a perfect right to go for a morning row, haven't I? If I were to ask my doctor, he would probably actually recommend it. I am going to row my boat across the Sound. If it happens to have my ball on board, that's not my affair. I'll play it from where it lies. Am I right in saying that the rules enact that the ball shall be played from where it lies?"

"Very well, then," said Rollo, after we admitted that he was. "Don't let us waste any more time. We will wait for you at Flushing."

He addressed his ball, and drove a beauty over the trees. It flashed out of sight in the direction of the seventeenth tee. Otis and I made our way down the hill to play our second.

It is a curious trait of the human mind that, however little personal interest one may have in the result, it is impossible to prevent oneself taking sides in any event of a competitive nature. I had embarked on this affair in a purely neutral spirit, not caring which of the two won, and only sorry that both could not lose. Yet, as the morning wore on, I found myself almost unconsciously becoming distinctly pro-Jukes. I did not like the man. I objected to his face, his manners, and the colour of his tie. Yet there was something in the dogged way in which he struggled against adversity which touched me and won my grudging support. Many men, I felt, having been so outmanœuvred at the start, would have given up the contest in despair; but Otis Jukes, for all his defects, had the soul of a true golfer. He declined to give up. In grim silence he hacked his ball through the rough till he reached the highroad; and then, having played twenty-seven, set himself resolutely to propel it to New York.

It was a lovely morning, and, as I bicycled along keeping a fatherly eye on Otis's activities, I realised for the first time in my life the full meaning of that exquisite phrase of Coleridge:

Clothing the palpable and familiar
With golden exhalations of the dawn,

for in the pellucid air everything seemed weirdly beautiful, even Otis Jukes's heather-mixture knickerbockers, of which hitherto I had never approved. The sun gleamed on their seat, as he bent to make his shots, in a cheerful and almost a poetic way. The birds were singing gaily in the hedgerows, and such was my uplifted state that I, too, burst into song, until Otis petulantly desired me to refrain, on the plea that, though he yielded to no man in his enjoyment of farmyard imitations in their proper place, I put him off his stroke. And so we passed through Bayside in silence and started to cover the long stretch of road which ends in the railway bridge and the gentle descent into Flushing.

Otis was not doing badly. He was at least keeping them straight. And in the circumstances straightness was to be preferred to distance. Soon after leaving Little Neck he had become ambitious and had used his brassie with disastrous results, slicing his fifty-third into the rough on the right of the road. It had taken him ten with the niblick to get back to the car tracks, and this had taught him prudence. He was now using his putter for every shot, and, except when he got trapped in the cross-lines at the top of the hill just before reaching Bayside, he had been in no serious difficulties. He had once, so he informed me, had to fulfil an election bet by rolling a peanut down Seventh Avenue with a toothpick, and this stood him now in good stead. He was playing a nice easy game, getting the full face of the putter on to each shot.

At the top of the slope that drops down into Flushing Main Street, he paused.

"I think I might try my brassie again here," he said. "I have a nice lie."

"Is it wise?" I said.

"What I was thinking," he said, "was that with luck I might wing that man Bingham. I see he is standing right out in the middle of the fairway."

I followed his gaze. It was perfectly true. Rollo Bingham was leaning on his bicycle in the roadway, smoking a cigarette. Even at this distance one could detect the man's disgustingly complacent expression. Rupert Bailey was sitting with his back against the door of the Flushing Garage, looking rather used up. He was a man who liked to keep himself clean and tidy, and it was plain that the 'cross-country trip had done him no good. He seemed to be scraping mud off his face. I learned later that he had had the misfortune to fall into a ditch just beyond Bayside.

"No," said Otis. "On second thought, the safe game is the one to play. I'll stick to the putter."

We dropped down the hill, and presently came up with the opposition. I had not been mistaken in thinking that Rollo looked complacent. The man was smirking.

"Playing three hundred and ninety-six," he said, as we drew near. "How are you?"

I consulted my score-card.

"We have shot a snappy seven hundred and eleven," I said.

Rollo exulted openly.

Rupert Bailey made no comment. He was too busy with the alluvial deposits on his person.

"Perhaps you would like to give up the match?" said Rollo to Otis.

"Tchah!" said Otis.

"Might just as well."

"Pah!" said Otis.

"You can't win now."

"Pshaw!" said Otis.

I am aware that Otis's dialogue might have been brighter, but he had been through a trying time.

Rupert Bailey sidled up to me.

"I'm going home," he said.

"Nonsense," I replied. "You must stick to your post. Besides, what could be nicer than a pleasant morning ramble?"

"Pleasant morning ramble my number nine foot! I want to get back to civilisation and set an excavating party with pickaxes to work on me."

"You take too gloomy a view of the matter. You are a little dusty. Nothing more."

"And it's not only the being buried alive that I mind. I cannot stick Rollo Bingham much longer."

"You have found him trying?"

"Trying! Why, after I had fallen into that ditch and was coming up for the third time all the man did was simply to call to me to admire an infernal iron shot he had just made. No sympathy, mind you! Wrapped up in himself. Why don't you make your man give up the match? He can't win."

"I refuse to admit it. Much may happen between here and Times Square."

I have seldom known a prophecy more swiftly fulfilled. At this moment the doors of the Flushing Garage opened and a small car rolled out with a grimy young man in a sweater at the wheel. He brought the machine out into the road, and alighted and went back into the garage, where we heard him shouting unintelligibly to some one in the rear premises. The car remained puffing and panting against the curb.

Engaged in conversation with Rupert Bailey, I was paying little attention to this evidence of an awakening world, when suddenly I heard a hoarse, triumphant cry from Otis Jukes, and turning, I perceived his ball dropping neatly into the car's interior. Otis himself, brandishing a niblick, was dancing about the fairway.

"Now what about your moving hazards?" he cried.

That moment the man in the sweater returned, carrying a spanner. Otis sprang forward.

"I'll give you twenty dollars to drive me to Times Square," he said.

I do not know what the sweater-clad young man's engagements for the morning had been originally, but nothing could have been more obliging than the ready way in which he consented to revise them at a moment's notice. I daresay you have noticed that the sturdy peasantry of our beloved land respond to an offer of twenty dollars as to a bugle-call.

"You're on," said the youth.

"Good!" said Otis Jukes.

"You think you're darned clever," said Rollo Bingham.

"I know it," said Otis.

"Well, then," said Rollo, "perhaps you will tell us how you propose to get the ball out of the car when you reach Times Square?"

"Certainly," replied Otis. "You will observe on the side of the vehicle a convenient handle which, when turned, opens the door. The door thus opened, I shall chip my ball out!"

"I see," said Rollo. "Yes, I never thought of that."

There was something in the way the man spoke that I did not like. His mildness seemed to me suspicious. He had the air of a man who has something up his sleeve. I was still musing on this when Otis called to me impatiently to get in. I did so, and we drove off. Otis was in great spirits. He had ascertained from the young man at the wheel that there was no chance of the opposition being able to hire another car at the garage. This machine was his own property, and the only other one at present in the shop was suffering from complicated trouble of the oiling system and would not be able to be moved for at least another day.

I, however, shook my head when he pointed out the advantages of his position. I was still wondering about Rollo.

"I don't like it," I said.

"Don't like what?"

"Rollo Bingham's manner."

"Of course not," said Otis. "Nobody does. There have been complaints on all sides."

"I mean, when you told him how you intended to get the ball out of the car."

"What was the matter with him?"

"He was too—ha!"

"How do you mean he was too ha?"

"I have it!"

"What?"

"I see the trap he was laying for you. It has just dawned on me. No wonder he didn't object to your opening the door and chipping the ball out. By doing so you would forfeit the match."

"Nonsense. Why?"

"Because," I said, "it is against the rules to tamper with a hazard. If you had got into a sand-trap, would you smooth away the sand? If you had put your shot under a tree, could your caddy hold up the branches to give you a clear shot? Obviously you would disqualify yourself if you touched that door."

Otis's jaw dropped.

"What! Then how the deuce am I to get it out?"

"That," I said gravely, "is a question between you and your Maker."

It was here that Otis Jukes forfeited the sympathy which I had begun to feel for him. A crafty, sinister look came into his eyes.

"Say, listen," he said. "It'll take them an hour to catch up with us. Suppose, during that time, that door happened to open accidentally, as it were, and close again? You wouldn't think it necessary to mention the fact, eh? You would be a good fellow and keep your mouth shut, yes? You might even see your way to go so far as to back me up in a statement to the effect that I hooked it out with my . . . ?"

I was revolted.

"I am a golfer," I said coldly, "and I obey the rules."

"Yes, but . . ."

"Those rules were drawn up by"—I bared my head reverently—"by the Committee of the Royal and Ancient at St. Andrew's. I have always respected them, and I shall not deviate on this occasion from the policy of a lifetime."

Otis Jukes relapsed into a moody silence. He broke it once, crossing the Fifty-ninth Street Bridge, to observe that he would like to know if I called myself a friend of his,—a question which I was able to answer with a whole-hearted negative. After that he did not speak till the car drew up in front of the Astor Hotel in Times Square.

Early as the hour was, a certain bustle and animation already prevailed in that centre of the great city, and the spectacle of a man in a golf-coat and plus-four knickerbockers hacking with a niblick at the floor of an automobile was not long in collecting a crowd of some dimensions. Three messenger-boys, four stenographers, and a gentleman in full evening-dress who obviously possessed or was friendly with someone who possessed a large private stock formed the nucleus of it; and they were joined about the time when Otis addressed the ball in order to play his nine hundred and fifteenth by six newsboys, eleven charladies, and perhaps a dozen assorted loafers, all speculating with the liveliest interest as to which particular asylum had had the honour of sheltering Otis before he had contrived to elude the vigilance of his custodians.

Otis had prepared for some such contingency. He suspended his activities with the niblick, and calmly proceeded to draw from his pocket a large poster which he proceeded to hang over the side of the car. It read:

COME
TO
McCLURG
and MacDONALD
18 West 49th Street
for
ALL GOLFING
SUPPLIES

His knowledge of psychology had not misled him. Directly they gathered that he was advertising something, the crowd declined to look at it; they melted away, and Otis returned to his work in solitude.

He was taking a well-earned rest after playing his eleven hundred and fifth, a nice niblick-shot with lots of wrist behind it, when out of Forty-fifth Street there trickled a weary-looking golf-ball, followed in the order named by Rollo Bingham, resolute but giving a trifle at the knees, and Rupert Bailey on a bicycle. The latter, on whose face and limbs the mud had dried, made an arresting spectacle.

"What are you playing?" I inquired.

"Eleven hundred," said Rupert. "We got into a casual dog."

"A casual dog?"

"Yes, just before the bridge. We were coming along nicely, when a stray dog grabbed our nine hundred and ninety-eighth and took it nearly back to Flushing, and we had to start all over again. How are you making out?"

"We have just played our eleven hundred and fifth. A nice even game." I looked at Rollo's ball, which was lying close to the curb. "You are away, I think. Your shot, Bingham."

Rupert Bailey suggested breakfast. He was a man who was altogether too fond of creature comforts. He had not the true golfing spirit.

"Breakfast!" I exclaimed.

"Breakfast," said Rupert firmly. "If you don't know what it is, I can teach you in half a minute. You play it with a pot of coffee, a knife and fork, and about a hundredweight of scrambled eggs. Try it. It's a pastime that grows on you."

I was surprised when Rollo Bingham supported the suggestion. He was so near holing out that I should have supposed that nothing would have kept him from finishing the match. But he agreed heartily.

"Breakfast," he said, "is an excellent idea. You go along in. I'll follow in a moment. I want to buy a paper."

We went into the hotel, and a few minutes later he joined us. Now that we were actually seated at the table, I frankly confess the idea of breakfast was by no means repugnant to me. The keen air and the exercise had given me an appetite, and it was some little time before I was able to assure the waiter definitely that he could cease bringing orders of scrambled eggs. The others having finished also, I suggested a move.

We filed out of the hotel, Otis Jukes leading. When I had passed through the swing-doors, I found him gazing perplexedly up and down the street.

"What is the matter?" I asked.

"It's gone!"

"What has gone?"

"The car!"

"Oh, the car?" said Rollo Bingham. "That's all right. Didn't I tell you about that? I bought it just now and engaged the driver as my chauffeur. I've been meaning to buy a car for a long time."

"Where is it?" said Otis blankly. The man seemed dazed.

"I couldn't tell you to a mile or two," replied Rollo. "I told the man to drive to Boston. Why? Had you any message for him?"

"But my ball was inside it!"

"Now that," said Rollo, "is really unfortunate! Do you mean to tell me you hadn't managed to get it out yet? Yes, that *is* a little awkward for you. It means that you lose the match."

"Lose the match?"

"Certainly. The rules are perfectly definite on that point. A period of five minutes is allowed for each stroke. The player who fails to make his stroke within that time loses the hole. Unfortunate, but there it is!"

Otis Jukes sank down on the sidewalk and buried his face in his hands. He had the look of a broken man.

"Playing eleven hundred and one," said Rollo Bingham in his odiously self-satisfied voice, as he addressed his ball. He laughed jovially. A messenger-boy had paused close by and was watching the proceedings gravely. Rollo Bingham patted him on the head.

"Well, sonny," he said, "what club would *you* use here?"

"I claim the match!" cried Otis Jukes, springing up. Rollo Bingham regarded him coldly.

"I beg your pardon?"

"I claim the match!" repeated Otis Jukes. "The rules say that a player who asks advice from any person other than his caddy shall lose the hole."

"This is absurd!" said Rollo, but I noticed that he had turned pale.

"I appeal to the judges."

"We sustain the appeal," I said, after a brief consultation with Rupert Bailey. "The rule is perfectly clear."

"But you had lost the match already by not playing within five minutes," said Rollo vehemently.

"It was not my turn to play. You were away."

"Well, play now. Go on! Let's see you make your shot."

"There is no necessity," said Otis frigidly. "Why should I play when you have already disqualified yourself?"

"I claim a draw!"

"I deny the claim."

"I appeal to the judges."

"Very well. We will leave it to the judges."

I consulted with Rupert Bailey. It seemed to me that Otis Jukes was entitled to the verdict. Rupert, who, though an amiable and delightful companion, had always been one of Nature's fat-heads, could not see it. We had to go back to our principals and announce that we had been unable to agree.

"This is ridiculous," said Rollo Bingham. "We ought to have had a third judge."

At this moment, who should come out of the hotel but Amelia Trivett. A veritable goddess from the machine.

"It seems to me," I said, "that you would both be well advised to leave the decision to Miss Trivett. You could have no better referee."

"I'm game," said Otis Jukes.

"Suits *me*," said Rollo Bingham.

"Why, whatever are you all doing here with your golf-clubs?" asked the girl wonderingly.

"These two gentlemen," I explained, "have been playing a match, and a point has arisen on which the judges do not find themselves in agreement. We need an unbiased outside opinion, and we should like to put it up to you. The facts are as follows."

Amelia Trivett listened attentively, but, when I had finished, she shook her head.

"I'm afraid I don't know enough about the game to be able to decide a question like that," she said.

"Then we must consult the National Committee," said Rupert Bailey. "They are the fellows to give judgment."

"I'll tell you who might know," said Amelia Trivett after a moment's thought.

"Who is that?" I asked.

"My *fiancé*. He has just come back from England. That's why I'm in town this morning. I've been down to the dock to meet his boat. He is very good at golf. He won a medal at Little-Mudbury-In-The-Wold the day before he sailed."

There was a tense silence. I had the delicacy not to look at Rollo or Otis. Then the silence was broken by a sharp crack. Rollo Bingham had broken his mashie-niblick across his knee. From the direction where Otis Jukes was standing there came a muffled gulp.

"Shall I ask him?" said Amelia Trivett.

"Don't bother," said Rollo Bingham.

"It doesn't matter," said Otis Jukes.

Winter Dreams

BY F. SCOTT FITZGERALD

If, as Shakespeare surmised, a winter's tale is a sad tale, then, perhaps, a winter's dream supplies a ray of hope to warm the bittersweet winds that pervade it. F. Scott Fitzgerald (1896–1940) wrote this story between his two early masterpieces, *This Side of Paradise* and *The Great Gatsby,* and it takes aim at some similar themes: wealth, class, the outsider looking in.

Early in the story, Fitzgerald mentions playing on snow-covered courses with red golf balls. Those happen to be the brainchildren of another man of letters—Rudyard Kipling. Between 1892 and 1896, the prolific writer and his wife had settled in on an 11-acre estate in Brattleboro, Vermont. Writing in the morning, Kipling penned his beloved classics *The Jungle Books* and *Captains Courageous* here. In the afternoon, summer and winter, he liked to play golf.

The game was in its American infancy then, and courses were scarce. Kipling used his creativity to design a makeshift layout of indeterminate par that extended from the meadow beyond his front door right to the edge of the Connecticut River. His frequent golfing companion, the Rev. Charles O. Day of the local Congregationalist church, would later explain how Kipling enlisted that same resourcefulness to triumph over at least one of the hazards of golf in New England:

"We played golf over snow two feet deep, upon the crust," he wrote in 1899, "cutting holes in the snow and naturally losing the balls, until it occurred to [Kipling] to ink them red. The first day we experimented with them, we dyed the plain like some football gridiron; then we had them painted."

Golf Journal, the monthly publication of the USGA, related the tale at length some years back. Its research ascribed to Day the first known mention of painted golf balls, thus giving Kipling the credit for extending golf dreams into winter dreams, as well.

I

Some of the caddies were poor as sin and lived in one-room houses with a neurasthenic cow in the front yard, but Dexter Green's father owned the second best grocery store in Black Bear—the best one was "The Hub," patronized by the wealthy people from Sherry Island—and Dexter caddied only for pocket money.

In the fall when the days became crisp and gray, and the long Minnesota winter shut down like the white lid of a box, Dexter's skis moved over the snow that hid the fairways of the golf course. At these times the country gave him a feeling of profound melancholy—it offended him that the links should lie in enforced fallowness, haunted by ragged sparrows for the long season. It was dreary, too, that on the tees where the gay colors fluttered in summer there were now only the desolate sandboxes knee-deep in crusted ice. When he crossed the hills the wind blew cold as misery and if the sun was out he tramped with his eyes squinted up against the hard dimensionless glare.

In April the winter ceased abruptly. The snow ran down into Black Bear Lake scarcely tarrying for the early golfers to brave the season with red and black balls. Without elation, without an interval of moist glory, the cold was gone.

Dexter knew that there was something dismal about this Northern spring, just as he knew there was something gorgeous about the fall. Fall made him clinch his hands and tremble and repeat idiotic sentences to himself, and make brisk abrupt gestures of command to imaginary audiences and armies. October filled him with hope which November raised to a sort of ecstatic triumph, and in this mood the fleeting brilliant impressions of the summer at Sherry Island were ready grist to his mill. He became a golf champion and defeated Mr. T. A. Hedrick in a marvelous match played a hundred times over the fairways of his imagination, a match each detail of which he changed about untiringly—sometimes he won with almost laughable ease, sometimes he came up magnificently from behind. Again, stepping from a Pierce-Arrow automobile, like Mr. Mortimer Jones, he strolled frigidly into the lounge of the Sherry Island Golf Club—or perhaps, surrounded by an admiring crowd, he gave an exhibition of fancy diving from the springboard of the club raft. . . .

Among those who watched him in open-mouthed wonder was Mr. Mortimer Jones.

And one day it came to pass that Mr. Jones—himself and not his ghost—came up to Dexter with tears in his eyes and said that Dexter was the damned best caddy in the club, and wouldn't he decide not to quit if Mr. Jones made it worth his while, because every other damn caddy in the club lost one ball a hole for him—regularly—

"No, sir," said Dexter decisively. "I don't want to caddie any more." Then, after a pause: "I'm too old."

"You're not more than fourteen. Why the devil did you decide just this morning that you wanted to quit? You promised that next week you'd go over to the state tournament with me."

"I decided I was too old."

Dexter handed in his "A Class" badge, collected what money was due him from the caddy master, and walked home to Black Bear Village.

"The best damned caddy I ever saw," shouted Mr. Mortimer Jones over a drink that afternoon. "Never lost a ball! Willing! Intelligent! Quiet! Honest! Grateful!"

The little girl who had done this was eleven—beautifully ugly as little girls are apt to be who are destined after a few years to be inexpressibly lovely and bring no end of misery to a great number of men. The spark, however, was perceptible. There was a general ungodliness in the way her lips twisted down at the corners when she smiled, and in the—Heaven help us!—in the almost passionate quality of her eyes. Vitality is born in such women. It was utterly in evidence now, shining through her thin frame in a sort of glow.

She had come eagerly out on to the course at nine o'clock with a white linen nurse and five small new golf-clubs in a white canvas bag which the nurse was carrying. When Dexter first saw her she was standing by the caddy house, rather ill at ease and trying to conceal the fact by engaging her nurse in an obviously unnatural conversation graced by startling and irrelevant grimaces from herself.

"Well, it's certainly a nice day, Hilda," Dexter heard her say. She drew down the corners of her mouth, smiled, and glanced furtively around, her eyes in transit falling for an instant on Dexter.

Then to the nurse:

"Well, I guess there aren't very many people out here this morning, are there?"

The smile again—radiant, blatantly artificial—convincing.

"I don't know what we're supposed to do now," said the nurse, looking nowhere in particular.

"Oh, that's all right. I'll fix it up."

Dexter stood perfectly still, his mouth slightly ajar. He knew that if he moved forward a step his stare would be in her line of vision—if he moved backward he would lose his full view of her face. For a moment he had not realized how young she was. Now he remembered having seen her several times the year before—in bloomers.

Suddenly, involuntarily, he laughed, a short abrupt laugh—then, startled by himself, he turned and began to walk quickly away.

"Boy!"

Dexter stopped.

"Boy—"

Beyond question he was addressed. Not only that, but he was treated to that absurd smile, that preposterous smile—the memory of which at least a dozen men were to carry into middle age.

"Boy, do you know where the golf teacher is?"

"He's giving a lesson."

"Well, do you know where the caddy master is?"

"He isn't here yet this morning."

"Oh." For a moment this baffled her. She stood alternately on her right and left foot.

"We'd like to get a caddy," said the nurse. "Mrs. Mortimer Jones sent us out to play golf, and we don't know how without we get a caddy."

Here she was stopped by an ominous glance from Miss Jones, followed immediately by the smile.

"There aren't any caddies here except me," said Dexter to the nurse, "and I got to stay here in charge until the caddy master gets here."

"Oh."

Miss Jones and her retinue now withdrew, and at a proper distance from Dexter became involved in a heated conversation, which was concluded by Miss Jones taking one of the clubs and hitting it on the ground with violence. For further emphasis she raised it again and was about to bring it down smartly upon the nurse's bosom, when the nurse seized the club and twisted it from her hands.

"You damn little mean old *thing!*" cried Miss Jones wildly.

Another argument ensued. Realizing that the elements of the comedy were implied in the scene, Dexter several times began to laugh, but each time restrained the laugh before it reached audibility. He could not resist the monstrous conviction that the little girl was justified in beating the nurse.

The situation was resolved by the fortuitous appearance of the caddy master, who was appealed to immediately by the nurse.

"Miss Jones is to have a little caddy, and this one says he can't go."

"Mr. McKenna said I was to wait here till you came," said Dexter quickly.

"Well, he's here now." Miss Jones smiled cheerfully at the caddy master. Then she dropped her bag and set off at a haughty mince toward the first tee.

"Well?" The caddy master turned to Dexter. "What you standing there like a dummy for? Go pick up the young lady's clubs."

"I don't think I'll go out today," said Dexter.

"You don't—"

"I think I'll quit."

The enormity of his decision frightened him. He was a favorite caddy, and the thirty dollars a month he earned through the summer were not to be made elsewhere around the lake. But he had received a strong emotional shock, and his perturbation required a violent and immediate outlet.

It is not so simple as that, either. As so frequently would be the case in the future, Dexter was unconsciously dictated to by his winter dreams.

II

Now, of course, the quality and the seasonability of these winter dreams varied, but the stuff of them remained. They persuaded Dexter several years later to pass up a business course at the state university—his father, prospering now, would have paid his way—for the precarious advantage of attending an older and more famous university in the East, where he was bothered by his scanty funds. But do not get the impression, because his winter dreams happened to be concerned at first with musings on the rich, that there was anything merely snobbish in the boy. He wanted not association with glittering things and glittering people—he wanted the glittering things themselves. Often he reached out for the best without knowing why he wanted it—and sometimes he ran up against the mysterious denials and prohibitions in which life indulges. It is with one of those denials and not with his career as a whole that this story deals.

He made money. It was rather amazing. After college he went to the city from which Black Bear Lake draws its wealthy patrons. When he was only twenty-three and had been there not quite two years, there were already people who liked to say: "Now *there's* a boy—" All about him rich men's sons were peddling bonds precariously, or investing patrimonies precariously, or plodding through the two dozen volumes of the "George Washington Commercial Course," but Dexter borrowed a thousand dollars on his college degree and his confident mouth, and bought a partnership in a laundry.

It was a small laundry when he went into it, but Dexter made a specialty of learning how the English washed fine woolen golf stockings without shrinking them, and within a year he was catering to the trade that wore knickerbockers. Men were insisting that their Shetland hose and sweaters go to his laundry, just as they had insisted on a caddy who could find golf balls. A little later he was doing their wives' lingerie as well—and running five branches in different parts of the city. Before he was twenty-seven he owned the largest string of laundries in his section of the country. It was then that he sold out and went to New York. But the part of his story that concerns us goes back to the days when he was making his first big success.

When he was twenty-three Mr. Hart—one of the gray-haired men who like to say, "Now there's a boy"—gave him a guest card to the Sherry Island Golf Club for a weekend. So he signed his name one day on the register, and that afternoon played golf in a foursome with Mr. Hart and Mr. Sandwood and Mr. T. A. Hedrick. He did not consider it necessary to remark that he had once carried Mr. Hart's bag over this same links, and that he knew every trap and gully with his eyes shut—but he found himself glancing at the four caddies who trailed them, trying to catch a gleam or gesture that would remind him of himself, that would lessen the gap which lay between his present and his past.

It was a curious day, slashed abruptly with fleeting, familiar impressions. One minute he had the sense of being a trespasser—in the next he was impressed by the tremendous superiority he felt toward Mr. T. A. Hedrick, who was a bore and not even a good golfer any more.

Then, because of a ball Mr. Hart lost near the fifteenth green, an enormous thing happened. While they were searching the stiff grasses of the rough there was a clear call of "Fore!" from behind a hill in their rear. And as they all turned abruptly from their search a bright new ball sliced abruptly over the hill and caught Mr. T. A. Hedrick in the abdomen.

"By Gad!" cried Mr. T. A. Hedrick, "they ought to put some of these crazy women off the course. It's getting to be outrageous."

A head and a voice came up together over the hill:

"Do you mind if we go through?"

"You hit me in the stomach!" declared Mr. Hedrick wildly.

"Did I?" The girl approached the group of men. "I'm sorry. I yelled, 'Fore!'"

Her glance fell casually on each of the men—then scanned the fairway for her ball.

"Did I bounce into the rough?"

It was impossible to determine whether this question was ingenuous or malicious. In a moment, however, she left no doubt, for as her partner came up over the hill she called cheerfully:

"Here I am! I'd have gone on the green except that I hit something."

As she took her stance for a short mashie shot, Dexter looked at her closely. She wore a blue gingham dress, rimmed at throat and shoulders with a white edging that accentuated her tan. The quality of exaggeration, of thinness, which had made her passionate eyes and down-turning mouth absurd at eleven, was gone now. She was arrestingly beautiful. The color in her cheeks was centered like the color in a picture—it was not a "high" color, but a sort of fluctuating and feverish warmth, so shaded that it seemed at any moment it would recede and disappear. This color and the mobility of her mouth gave a continual impression of flux, of intense life, of passionate vitality—balanced only partially by the sad luxury of her eyes.

She swung her mashie impatiently and without interest, pitching the ball into a sand pit on the other side of the green. With a quick, insincere smile and a careless "Thank you!" she went on after it.

"That Judy Jones!" remarked Mr. Hedrick on the next tee, as they waited—some moments—for her to play on ahead. "All she needs is to be turned up and spanked for six months and then to be married off to an old-fashioned cavalry captain."

"My God, she's good-looking!" said Mr. Sandwood, who was just over thirty.

"Good-looking!" cried Mr. Hedrick contemptuously. "She always looks as if she wanted to be kissed! Turning those big cow eyes on every calf in town!"

It was doubtful if Mr. Hedrick intended a reference to the maternal instinct.

"She'd play pretty good golf if she'd try," said Mr. Sandwood.

"She has no form," said Mr. Hedrick solemnly.

"She has a nice figure," said Mr. Sandwood.

"Better thank the Lord she doesn't drive a swifter ball," said Mr. Hart, winking at Dexter.

Later in the afternoon the sun went down with a swirl of gold and varying blues and scarlets, and left the dry, rustling night of Western summer.

Dexter watched from the veranda of the golf club, watched the even overlap of the waters in the little wind, silver molasses under the harvest moon. Then the moon held a finger to her lips and the lake became a clear pool, pale and quiet. Dexter put on his bathing suit and swam out to the farthest raft, where he stretched dripping on the wet canvas of the springboard.

There was a fish jumping and a star shining and the lights around the lake were gleaming. Over on a dark peninsula a piano was playing the songs of last summer and of summers before that—songs from "Chin-Chin" and "The Count of Luxembourg" and "The Chocolate Soldier"*—and because the sound of a piano over a stretch of water had always seemed beautiful to Dexter he lay perfectly quiet and listened.

The tune the piano was playing at that moment had been gay and new five years before when Dexter was a sophomore at college. They had played it at a prom once when he could not afford the luxury of proms, and he had stood outside the gymnasium and listened. The sound of the tune precipitated in him a sort of ecstasy and it was with that ecstasy he viewed what happened to him now. It was a mood of intense appreciation, a sense that, for once, he was magnificently attuned to life and that everything about him was radiating a brightness and a glamor he might never know again.

A low, pale oblong detached itself suddenly from the darkness of the island, spitting forth the reverberate sound of a racing motorboat. Two white streamers of cleft water rolled themselves out behind it and almost immediately the boat was beside him, drowning out the hot tinkle of the piano in the drone of its spray. Dexter raising himself on his arms was aware of a figure standing at the wheel, of two dark eyes regarding him over the lengthening space of water—then the boat had gone by and was sweeping in an immense and pur-poseless circle of spray round and round in the middle of the lake. With equal eccentricity one of the circles flattened out and headed back toward the raft.

"Who's that?" she called, shutting off her motor. She was so near now that Dexter could see her bathing suit, which consisted apparently of pink rompers.

The nose of the boat bumped the raft, and as the latter tilted rakishly he was precipitated toward her. With different degrees of interest they recognized each other.

"Aren't you one of those men we played through this afternoon?" she demanded.

---

*Popular Broadway musicals of the day.

He was.

"Well, do you know how to drive a motorboat? Because if you do I wish you'd drive this one so I can ride on the surfboard behind. My name is Judy Jones"—she favored him with an absurd smirk—rather, what tried to be a smirk, for, twist her mouth as she might, it was not grotesque, it was merely beautiful—"and I live in a house over there on the island, and in that house there is a man waiting for me. When he drove up at the door I drove out of the dock because he says I'm his ideal."

There was a fish jumping and a star shining and the lights around the lake were gleaming. Dexter sat beside Judy Jones and she explained how her boat was driven. Then she was in the water, swimming to the floating surfboard with a sinuous crawl. Watching her was without effort to the eye, watching a branch waving or a sea gull flying. Her arms, burned to butternut, moved sinuously among the dull platinum ripples, elbow appearing first, casting the forearm back with a cadence of falling water, then reaching out and down, stabbing a path ahead.

They moved out into the lake: turning, Dexter saw that she was kneeling on the low rear of the now uptilted surfboard.

"Go faster," she called, "fast as it'll go."

Obediently he jammed the lever forward and the white spray mounted at the bow. When he looked around again the girl was standing up on the rushing board, her arms spread wide, her eyes lifted toward the moon.

"It's awful cold," she shouted. "What's your name?"

He told her.

"Well, why don't you come to dinner tomorrow night?"

His heart turned over like the flywheel of the boat, and, for the second time, her casual whim gave a new direction to his life.

III

Next evening while he waited for her to come downstairs, Dexter peopled the soft deep summer room and the sun porch that opened from it with the men who had already loved Judy Jones. He knew the sort of men they were—the men who when he first went to college had entered from the great prep schools with graceful clothes and the deep tan of healthy summers. He had seen that, in one sense, he was better than these men. He was newer and stronger. Yet in acknowledging to himself that he wished his children to be like them he was admitting that he was but the rough, strong stuff from which they eternally sprang.

When the time had come for him to wear good clothes, he had known who were the best tailors in America, and the best tailors in America had made him the suit he wore this evening. He had acquired that particular reserve peculiar to his university, that set it off from other universities. He recognized the value to him of such a mannerism and he had adopted it; he knew that to be careless in dress and manner required more confidence than to be careful. But carelessness was for his children. His mother's name had been Krimplich. She was a Bohemian of the peasant class and she had talked broken English to the end of her days. Her son must keep to the set patterns.

At a little after seven Judy Jones came downstairs. She wore a blue silk afternoon dress, and he was disappointed at first that she had not put on something more elaborate. This feeling was accentuated when, after a brief greeting, she went to the door of a butler's pantry and pushing it open called: "You can serve dinner, Martha." He had rather expected that a butler would announce dinner, that there would be a cocktail. Then he put these thoughts behind him as they sat down side by side on a lounge and looked at each other.

"Father and mother won't be here," she said thoughtfully.

He remembered the last time he had seen her father, and he was glad the parents were not to be here tonight—they might wonder who he was. He had been born in Keeble, a Minnesota village fifty miles farther north, and he always gave Keeble as his home instead of Black Bear Village. Country towns were well enough to come from if they weren't inconveniently in sight and used as footstools by fashionable lakes.

They talked of his university, which she had visited frequently during the past two years, and of the nearby city which supplied Sherry Island with its patrons, and whither Dexter would return next day to his prospering laundries.

During dinner she slipped into a moody depression which gave Dexter a feeling of uneasiness. Whatever petulance she uttered in her throaty voice worried him. Whatever she smiled at—at him, at a chicken liver, at nothing—it disturbed him that her smile could have no root in mirth, or even in amusement. When the scarlet corners of her lips curved down, it was less a smile than an invitation to a kiss.

Then, after dinner, she led him out on the dark sun porch and deliberately changed the atmosphere.

"Do you mind if I weep a little?" she said.

"I'm afraid I'm boring you," he responded quickly.

"You're not. I like you. But I've just had a terrible afternoon. There was a man I cared about, and this afternoon he told me out of a clear sky that he was poor as a churchmouse. He'd never even hinted it before. Does this sound horribly mundane?"

"Perhaps he was afraid to tell you."

"Suppose he was," she answered. "He didn't start right. You see, if I'd thought of him as poor—well, I've been mad about loads of poor men, and fully intended to marry them all. But in this case, I hadn't thought of him that way, and my interest in him wasn't strong enough to survive the shock. As if a girl calmly informed her fiancé that she was a widow. He might not object to widows, but—

"Let's start right," she interrupted herself suddenly. "Who are you, any-how?"

For a moment Dexter hesitated. Then: "I'm nobody," he announced. "My career is largely a matter of futures."

"Are you poor?"

"No," he said frankly, "I'm probably making more money than any man my age in the Northwest. I know that's an obnoxious remark, but you advised me to start right."

There was a pause. Then she smiled and the corners of her mouth drooped and an almost imperceptible sway brought her closer to him, looking up into his eyes. A lump rose in Dexter's throat, and he waited breathless for the experiment, facing the unpredictable compound that would form mysteriously from the elements of their lips. Then he saw—she communicated her excitement to him, lavishly, deeply, with kisses that were not a promise but a fulfilment. They aroused in him not hunger demanding renewal but surfeit that would demand more surfeit . . . kisses that were like charity, creating want by holding back nothing at all.

It did not take him many hours to decide that he had wanted Judy Jones ever since he was a proud, desirous little boy.

IV

It began like that—and continued, with varying shades of intensity, on such a note right up to the dénouement. Dexter surrendered a part of himself to the most direct and unprincipled personality with which he had ever come in contact. Whatever Judy wanted, she went after with the full pressure of her charm. There was no divergence of method, no jockeying for position or premeditation of effects—there was a very little mental side to any of her affairs. She simply made men conscious to the highest degree of her physical loveliness. Dexter had no desire to change her. Her deficiencies were knit up with a passionate energy that transcended and justified them.

When, as Judy's head lay against his shoulder that first night, she whispered, "I don't know what's the matter with me. Last night I thought I was in love with a man and tonight I think I'm in love with you—" It seemed to him a beautiful and romantic thing to say. It was the exquisite excitability that for the moment he controlled and owned. But a week later he was compelled to view this same quality in a different light. She took him in her roadster to a picnic supper, and after supper she disappeared, likewise in her roadster, with another man. Dexter became enormously upset and was scarcely able to be decently civil to the other people present. When she assured him that she had not kissed the other man, he knew she was lying—yet he was glad that she had taken the trouble to lie to him.

He was, as he found before the summer ended, one of a varying dozen who circulated about her. Each of them had at one time been favored above all others—about half of them still basked in the solace of occasional sentimental revivals. Whenever one showed signs of dropping out through long neglect, she granted him a brief honeyed hour, which encouraged him to tag along for a year or so longer. Judy made these forays upon the helpless and defeated without malice, indeed half unconscious that there was anything mischievous in what she did.

When a new man came to town every one dropped out—dates were automatically canceled.

The helpless part of trying to do anything about it was that she did it all herself. She was not a girl who could be "won" in the kinetic sense—she was proof against cleverness, she was proof against charm: if any of these assailed her too strongly she would immediately resolve the affair to a physical basis, and under the magic of her physical splendor the strong as well as the brilliant played her game and not their own. She was entertained only by the gratification of her desires and by the direct exercise of her own charm. Perhaps from so much youthful love, so many youthful lovers, she had come, in self-defense, to nourish herself wholly from within.

Succeeding Dexter's first exhilaration came restlessness and dissatisfaction. The helpless ecstasy of losing himself in her was opiate rather than tonic. It was fortunate for his work during the winter that those moments of ecstasy came infrequently. Early in their acquaintance it had seemed for a while that there was a deep and spontaneous mutual attraction—that first August, for example—three days of long evenings on her dusky veranda, of strange wan kisses through the late afternoon, in shadowy alcoves or behind the protecting trellises of the garden arbors, of mornings when she was fresh as a dream and almost shy at meeting him in the clarity of the rising day. There was all the ecstasy of an engagement about it, sharpened by his realization that there was no engagement. It was during those three days that, for the first time, he had asked her to marry him. She said, "Maybe someday." She said, "Kiss me." She said, "I'd like to marry you." She said, "I love you"—she said—nothing.

The three days were interrupted by the arrival of a New York man who visited at her house for half September. To Dexter's agony, rumor engaged them. The man was the son of the president of a great trust company. But at the end of a month it was reported that Judy was yawning. At a dance one night she sat all evening in a motorboat with a local beau, while the New Yorker searched the club for her frantically. She told the local beau that she was bored with her visitor, and two days later he left. She was seen with him at the station, and it was reported that he looked very mournful indeed.

On this note the summer ended. Dexter was twenty-four, and he found himself increasingly in a position to do as he wished. He joined two clubs in the city and lived at one of them. Though he was by no means an integral part of the stag lines at these clubs, he managed to be on hand at dances where Judy Jones was likely to appear. He could have gone out socially as much as he liked—he was an eligible young man, now, and popular with downtown fathers. His confessed devotion to Judy Jones had rather solidified his position. But he had no social aspirations and rather despised the dancing men who were always on tap for the Thursday or Saturday parties and who filled in at dinners with the younger married set. Already he was playing with the idea of going East to New York. He wanted to take Judy Jones with him. No disillusion as to the world in which she had grown up could cure his illusion as to her desirability.

Remember that—for only in the light of it can what he did for her be understood.

Eighteen months after he first met Judy Jones he became engaged to another girl. Her name was Irene Scheerer, and her father was one of the men who had always believed in Dexter. Irene was light-haired and sweet and honorable, and a little stout, and she had two suitors whom she pleasantly relinquished when Dexter formally asked her to marry him.

Summer, fall, winter, spring, another summer, another fall—so much he had given of his active life to the incorrigible lips of Judy Jones. She had treated him with interest, with encouragement, with malice, with indifference, with contempt. She had inflicted on him the innumerable little slights and indignities possible in such a case—as if in revenge for having ever cared for him at all. She had beckoned him and yawned at him and beckoned him again and he had responded often with bitterness and narrowed eyes. She had brought him ecstatic happiness and intolerable agony of spirit. She had caused him untold inconvenience and not a little trouble. She had insulted him, and she had ridden over him, and she had played his interest in her against his interest in his work—for fun. She had done everything to him except to criticize him—this she had not done—it seemed to him only because it might have sullied the utter indifference she manifested and sincerely felt toward him.

When autumn had come and gone again it occurred to him that he could not have Judy Jones. He had to beat this into his mind but he convinced himself at last. He lay awake at night for a while and argued it over. He told himself the trouble and the pain she had caused him, he enumerated her glaring deficiencies as a wife. Then he said to himself that he loved her, and after a while he fell asleep. For a week, lest he imagined her husky voice over the telephone or her eyes opposite him at lunch, he worked hard and late, and at night he went to his office and plotted out his years.

At the end of a week he went to a dance and cut in on her once. For almost the first time since they had met he did not ask her to sit out with him or tell her that she was lovely. It hurt him that she did not miss these things—that was all. He was not jealous when he saw that there was a new man tonight. He had been hardened against jealousy long before.

He stayed late at the dance. He sat for an hour with Irene Scheerer and talked about books and about music. He knew very little about either. But he was beginning to be master of his own time now, and he had a rather priggish notion that he—the young and already fabulously successful Dexter Green—should know more about such things.

That was in October, when he was twenty-five. In January, Dexter and Irene became engaged. It was to be announced in June, and they were to be married three months later.

The Minnesota winter prolonged itself interminably, and it was almost May when the winds came soft and the snow ran down into Black Bear Lake at last. For the first time in over a year Dexter was enjoying a certain tranquillity of spirit. Judy Jones had been in Florida, and afterward in Hot Springs, and somewhere she had been engaged, and somewhere she had broken it off. At first, when Dexter had definitely given her up, it had made him sad that people still linked them together and asked for news of her, but when he began to be placed at dinner next to Irene Scheerer people didn't ask him about her any more—they told him about her. He ceased to be an authority on her.

May at last. Dexter walked the streets at night when the darkness was damp as rain, wondering that so soon, with so little done, so much of ecstasy had gone from him. May one year back had been marked by Judy's poignant, unforgivable, yet forgiven turbulence—it had been one of those rare times when he fancied she had grown to care for him. That old penny's worth of happiness he had spent for this bushel of content. He knew that Irene would be no more than a curtain spread behind him, a hand moving among gleaming teacups, a voice calling to children . . . fire and loveliness were gone, the magic of nights and the wonder of the varying hours and seasons . . . slender lips, downturning, dropping to his lips and bearing him up into a heaven of eyes. . . . The thing was deep in him. He was too strong and alive for it to die lightly.

In the middle of May when the weather balanced for a few days on the thin bridge that led to deep summer he turned in one night at Irene's house. Their engagement was to be announced in a week now—no one would be surprised at it. And tonight they would sit together on the lounge at the University Club and look on for an hour at the dancers. It gave him a sense of solidity to go with her—she was so sturdily popular, so intensely "great."

He mounted the steps of the brownstone house and stepped inside.

"Irene," he called.

Mrs. Scheerer came out of the living room to meet him.

"Dexter," she said. "Irene's gone upstairs with a splitting headache. She wanted to go with you, but I made her go to bed."

"Nothing serious, I—"

"Oh, no. She's going to play golf with you in the morning. You can spare her for just one night, can't you, Dexter?"

Her smile was kind. She and Dexter liked each other. In the living room he talked for a moment before he said good night.

Returning to the University Club, where he had rooms, he stood in the doorway for a moment and watched the dancers. He leaned against the door post, nodded at a man or two—yawned.

"Hello, darling."

The familiar voice at his elbow startled him. Judy Jones had left a man and crossed the room to him—Judy Jones, a slender enameled doll in cloth of gold: gold in a band at her head, gold in two slipper points at her dress's hem. The fragile glow of her face seemed to blossom as she smiled at him. A breeze of warmth and light blew through the room. His hands in the pockets of his dinner jacket tightened spasmodically. He was filled with a sudden excitement.

"When did you get back?" he asked casually.

"Come here and I'll tell you about it."

She turned and he followed her. She had been away—he could have wept at the wonder of her return. She had passed through enchanted streets, doing things that were like provocative music. All mysterious happenings, all fresh and quickening hopes, had gone away with her, come back with her now.

She turned in the doorway.

"Have you a car here? If you haven't, I have."

"I have a coupé."

In then, with a rustle of golden cloth. He slammed the door. Into so many cars she had stepped—like this—like that—her back against the leather, so—her elbow resting on the door—waiting. She would have been soiled long since had there been anything to soil her—except herself—but this was her own self outpouring.

With an effort he forced himself to start the car and back into the street. This was nothing, he must remember. She had done this before, and he had put her behind him, as he would have crossed a bad account from his books.

He drove slowly downtown and, affecting abstraction, traversed the deserted streets of the business section, peopled here and there where a movie was giving out its crowd or where consumptive or pugilistic youth lounged in front of pool halls. The clink of glasses and the slap of hands on the bars issued from saloons, cloisters of glazed glass and dirty yellow light.

She was watching him closely and the silence was embarrassing, yet in this crisis he could find no casual word with which to profane the hour. At a convenient turning he began to zigzag back toward the University Club.

"Have you missed me?" she asked suddenly.

"Everybody missed you."

He wondered if she knew of Irene Scheerer. She had been back only a day—her absence had been almost contemporaneous with his engagement.

"What a remark!" Judy laughed sadly—without sadness. She looked at him searchingly. He became absorbed in the dashboard.

"You're handsomer than you used to be," she said thoughtfully. "Dexter, you have the most rememberable eyes."

He could have laughed at this, but he did not laugh. It was the sort of thing that was said to sophomores. Yet it stabbed at him.

"I'm awfully tired of everything, darling," She called everyone darling, endowing the endearment with careless, individual camaraderie. "I wish you'd marry me."

The directness of this confused him. He should have told her now that he was going to marry another girl, but he could not tell her. He could as easily have sworn that he had never loved her.

"I think we'd get along," she continued on the same note, "unless probably you've forgotten me and fallen in love with another girl."

Her confidence was obviously enormous. She had said, in effect, that she found such a thing impossible to believe, that if it were true he had merely committed a childish indiscretion—and probably to show off. She would forgive him, because it was not a matter of any moment but rather something to be brushed aside lightly.

"Of course you could never love anybody but me," she continued. "I like the way you love me. Oh, Dexter, have you forgotten last year?"

"No, I haven't forgotten."

"Neither have I!"

Was she sincerely moved—or was she carried along by the wave of her own acting?

"I wish we could be like that again," she said, and he forced himself to answer:

"I don't think we can."

"I suppose not. . . . I hear you're giving Irene Scheerer a violent rush."

There was not the faintest emphasis on the name, yet Dexter was suddenly ashamed.

"Oh, take me home," cried Judy suddenly: "I don't want to go back to that idiotic dance—with those children."

Then, as he turned up the street that led to the residence district, Judy began to cry quietly to herself. He had never seen her cry before.

The dark street lightened, the dwellings of the rich loomed up around them, he stopped his coupé in front of the great white bulk of the Mortimer Joneses' house, somnolent, gorgeous, drenched with the splendor of the damp moonlight. Its solidity startled him. The strong walls, the steel of the girders, the breadth and beam and pomp of it were there only to bring out the contrast with the young beauty beside him. It was sturdy to accentuate her slightness—as if to show what a breeze could be generated by a butterfly's wing.

He sat perfectly quiet, his nerves in wild clamor, afraid that if he moved he would find her irresistibly in his arms. Two tears had rolled down her wet face and trembled on her upper lip.

"I'm more beautiful than anybody else," she said brokenly. "Why can't I be happy?" Her moist eyes tore at his stability—her mouth turned slowly downward with an exquisite sadness: "I'd like to marry you if you'll have me, Dexter. I suppose you think I'm not worth having, but I'll be so beautiful for you, Dexter."

A million phrases of anger, pride, passion, hatred, tenderness fought on his lips. Then a perfect wave of emotion washed over him, carrying off with it a sediment of wisdom, of convention, of doubt, of honor. This was his girl who was speaking, his own, his beautiful, his pride.

"Won't you come in?" He heard her draw in her breath sharply.

Waiting.

"All right," his voice was trembling. "I'll come in."

V

It was strange that neither when it was over nor a long time afterward did he regret that night. Looking at it from the perspective of ten years, the fact that Judy's flare for him endured just one month seemed of little importance. Nor did it matter that by his yielding he subjected himself to a deeper agony in the end and gave serious hurt to Irene Scheerer and to Irene's parents, who had befriended him. There was nothing sufficiently pictorial about Irene's grief to stamp itself on his mind.

Dexter was at bottom hard-minded. The attitude of the city on his action was of no importance to him, not because he was going to leave the city, but because any outside attitude on the situation seemed superficial. He was completely indifferent to popular opinion. Nor, when he had seen that it was no use, that he did not possess in himself the power to move fundamentally or to hold Judy Jones, did he bear any malice toward her. He loved her, and he would love her until the day he was too old for loving but he could not have her. So he tasted the deep pain that is reserved only for the strong, just as he had tasted for a little while the deep happiness.

Even the ultimate falsity of the grounds upon which Judy terminated the engagement that she did not want to "take him away" from Irene—Judy who had wanted nothing else—did not revolt him. He was beyond any revulsion or any amusement.

He went East in February with the intention of selling out his laundries and settling in New York—but the war came to America in March and changed his plans. He returned to the West, handed over the management of the business to his partner, and went into the first officers' training camp in late April. He was one of those young thousands who greeted the war with a certain amount of relief, welcoming the liberation from webs of tangled emotion.

VI

This story is not his biography, remember, although things creep into it which have nothing to do with those dreams he had when he was young. We are almost done with them and with him now. There is only one more incident to be related here, and it happens seven years farther on.

It took place in New York, where he had done well—so well that there were no barriers too high for him. He was thirty-two years old, and, except for one flying trip immediately after the war, he had not been West in seven years. A man named Devlin from Detroit came into his office to see him in a business way, and then and there this incident occurred, and closed out, so to speak, this particular side of his life.

"So you're from the Middle West," said the man Devlin with careless curiosity. "That's funny—I thought men like you were probably born and raised on Wall Street. You know—wife of one of my best friends in Detroit came from your city. I was an usher at the wedding."

Dexter waited with no apprehension of what was coming.

"Judy Simms," said Devlin with no particular interest: "Judy Jones she was once."

"Yes, I knew her." A dull impatience spread over him. He had heard, of course, that she was married—perhaps deliberately he had heard no more.

"Awfully nice girl," brooded Devlin meaninglessly, "I'm sort of sorry for her."

"Why?" Something in Dexter was alert, receptive, at once.

"Oh, Lud Simms has gone to pieces in a way. I don't mean he ill-uses her, but he drinks and runs around—"

"Doesn't she run around?"

"No. Stays at home with her kids."

"Oh."

"She's a little too old for him," said Devlin.

"Too old!" cried Dexter. "Why, man, she's only twenty-seven."

He was possessed with a wild notion of rushing out into the streets and taking a train to Detroit. He rose to his feet spasmodically.

"I guess you're busy," Devlin apologized quickly. "I didn't realize—"

"No, I'm not busy," said Dexter, steadying his voice. "I'm not busy at all. Not busy at all. Did you say she was—twenty-seven? No, I said she was twenty-seven."

"Yes, you did," agreed Devlin dryly.

"Go on, then. Go on."

"What do you mean?"

"About Judy Jones."

Devlin looked at him helplessly.

"Well, that's—I told you all there is to it. He treats her like the devil. Oh, they're not going to get divorced or anything. When he's particularly outrageous she forgives him. In fact, I'm inclined to think she loves him. She was a pretty girl when she first came to Detroit."

A pretty girl! The phrase struck Dexter as ludicrous.

"Isn't she—a pretty girl, any more?"

"Oh, she's all right."

"Look here," said Dexter, sitting down suddenly. "I don't understand. You say she was a 'pretty girl' and now you say she's 'all right.' I don't understand what you mean—Judy Jones wasn't a pretty girl, at all. She was a great beauty. Why, I knew her. I knew her. She was—"

Devlin laughed pleasantly.

"I'm not trying to start a row," he said. "I think Judy's a nice girl and I like her. I can't understand how a man like Lud Simms could fall madly in love with her, but he did." Then he added: "Most of the women like her."

Dexter looked closely at Devlin, thinking wildly that there must be a reason for this, some insensitivity in the man or some private malice.

"Lots of women fade just like *that*," Devlin snapped his fingers. "You must have seen it happen. Perhaps I've forgotten how pretty she was at her wedding. I've seen her so much since then, you see. She has nice eyes."

A sort of dullness settled down upon Dexter. For the first time in his life he felt like getting very drunk. He knew that he was laughing loudly at something Devlin had said, but he did not know what it was or why it was funny. When, in a few minutes, Devlin went he lay down on his lounge and looked out the window at the New York skyline into which the sun was sinking in dull lovely shades of pink and gold.

He had thought that having nothing else to lose he was invulnerable at last—but he knew that he had just lost something more, as surely as if he had married Judy Jones and seen her fade away before his eyes.

The dream was gone. Something had been taken from him. In a sort of panic he pushed the palms of his hands into his eyes and tried to bring up a picture of the waters lapping on Sherry Island and the moonlit veranda, and gingham on the golf links and the dry sun and the gold color of her neck's soft down. And her mouth damp to his kisses and her eyes plaintive with melancholy and her freshness like new fine linen in the morning. Why, these things were no longer in the world! They had existed and they existed no longer.

For the first time in years the tears were streaming down his face. But they were for himself now. He did not care about mouth and eyes and moving hands. He wanted to care, and he could not care. For he had gone away and he could never go back any more. The gates were closed, the sun was gone down, and there was no beauty but the gray beauty of steel that withstands all time. Even the grief he could have borne was left behind in the country of illusion, of youth, of the richness of life, where his winter dreams had flourished.

"Long ago," he said, "long ago, there was something in me, but now that thing is gone. Now that thing is gone, that thing is gone. I cannot cry. I cannot care. That thing will come back no more."

Mr. Frisbie

BY RING LARDNER

One of the first American sportswriters to break out of the pack, Ring Lardner (1885–1933) was also, of course, a maestro of short fiction. His best stories— "Alibi Ike," "Baseball Hattie," "The Haircut," and, certainly, the 1928 ace of a tale "Mr. Frisbie"—are as funny as they are cynical. A satirist at his core—how could he not be after the dark doings of the 1919 World Series?—Lardner loved to shoot holes through pretense when he wasn't out shooting at flagsticks with friends like Grantland Rice. As in his most celebrated work, the epistolary novel *You Know Me, Al,* Lardner revels in the language of the common man to create the chauffeur and caddie Mr. Frisbie so relies on, a factotum who can read his boss much better than Mr. Frisbie can read a green . . . or himself.

I am Mr. Allen Frisbie's chauffeur. Allen Frisbie is a name I made up because they tell me that if I used the real name of the man I am employed by that he might take offense and start trouble though I am sure he will never see what I am writing as he does not read anything except the American Golfer but of course some of his friends might call his attention to it. If you knew who the real name of the man is it would make more interesting reading as he is one of the 10 most wealthiest men in the United States and a man who everybody is interested in because he is so famous and the newspapers are always writing articles about him and sending high salary reporters to interview him but he is a very hard man to reproach or get an interview with and when they do he never tells them anything.

That is how I come to be writing this article because about two weeks ago a Mr. Kirk had an appointment to interview Mr. Frisbie for one of the newspapers and I drove him to the station after the interview was over and he said to me your boss is certainly a tough egg to interview and getting a word out of him is like pulling turnips.

"The public do not know anything about the man," said Mr. Kirk. "They know he is very rich and has got a wife and a son and a daughter and what their names are but as to his private life and his likes and dislikes he might just as well be a monk in a convent."

"The public knows he likes golf," I said.

"They do not know what kind of a game he plays."

"He plays pretty good," I said.

"How good?" said Mr. Kirk.

"About 88 or 90," I said.

"So is your grandmother," said Mr. Kirk.

He only meant the remark as a comparison but had either of my grandmothers lived they would both have been over 90. Mr. Kirk did not believe I was telling the truth about Mr. Frisbie's game and he was right though was I using real names I would not admit it as Mr. Frisbie is very sensitive in regards to his golf.

Mr. Kirk kept pumping at me but I am used to being pumped at and Mr. Kirk finally gave up pumping at me as he found me as closed mouth as Mr. Frisbie himself but he made the remark that he wished he was in my place for a few days and as close to the old man as I am and he would then be able to write the first real article which had ever been written about the old man. He called Mr. Frisbie the old man.

He said it was too bad I am not a writer so I could write up a few instance about Mr. Frisbie from the human side on account of being his caddy at golf and some paper or magazine would pay me big. He said if you would tell me a few instance I would write them up and split with you but I said no I could not think of anything which would make an article but after Mr. Kirk had gone I got to thinking it over and thought to myself maybe I could be a writer if I tried and at least there is no harm in trying so for the week after Mr. Kirk's visit I spent all my spare time writing down about Mr. Frisbie only at first I used his real name but when I showed the article they said for me not to use real names but the public would guess who it was anyway and that was just as good as using real names.

So I have gone over the writing again and changed the name to Allen Frisbie and other changes and here is the article using Allen Frisbie.

When I say I am Mr. Frisbie's chauffeur I mean I am his personal chauffeur. There are two other chauffeurs who drive for the rest of the family and run errands. Had I nothing else to do only drive I might well be turned a man of leisure as Mr. Frisbie seldom never goes in to the city more than twice a week and even less oftener than that does he pay social visits.

His golf links is right on the place an easy walk from the house to the first tee and here is where he spends a good part of each and every day playing alone with myself in the roll of caddy. So one would not be far from amiss to refer to me as Mr. Frisbie's caddy rather than his chauffeur but it was as a chauffeur that I was engaged and can flatter myself that there are very few men of my calling who would not gladly exchange their salary and position for mine.

Mr. Frisbie is a man just this side of 60 years of age. Almost 10 years ago he retired from active business with money enough to put him in a class with the richest men in the United States and since then his investments have increased their value to such an extent so that now he is in a class with the richest men in the United States.

It was soon after his retirement that he bought the Peter Vischer estate near Westbury, Long Island. On this estate there was a 9 hole golf course in good condition and considered one of the best private 9 hole golf courses in the United States but Mr. Frisbie would have had it plowed up and the land used for some other usage only for a stroke of chance which was when Mrs. Frisbie's brother came over from England for a visit.

It was during while this brother-in-law was visiting Mr. Frisbie that I entered the last named employee and was an onlooker when Mr. Frisbie's brother-in-law persuaded his brother-in-law to try the game of golf. As luck would have it Mr. Frisbie's first drive was so good that his brother-in-law would not believe he was a new beginner till he had seen Mr. Frisbie shoot again but that first perfect drive made Mr. Frisbie a slave of the game and without which there would be no such instance as I am about to relate.

I would better explain at this junction that I am not a golfer but I have learned quite a lot of knowledge about the game by cadding for Mr. Frisbie and also once or twice in company with my employer have picked up some knowledge of the game by witnessing players like Bobby Jones and Hagen and Sarazen and Smith in some of their matches. I have only tried it myself on a very few occasions when I was sure Mr. Frisbie could not observe me and will confide that in my own mind I am convinced that with a little practise that I would have little trouble defeating Mr. Frisbie but will never seek to prove same for reasons which I will leave it to the reader to guess the reasons.

One day shortly after Mr. Frisbie's brother-in-law had ended his visit I was cadding for Mr. Frisbie and as had become my custom keeping the score for him when a question arose as to whether he had taken 7 or 8 strokes on the last hole. A 7 would have given him a total of 63 for the 9 holes while a 8 would have made it 64. Mr. Frisbie tried to recall the different strokes but was not certain and asked me to help him.

As I remembered it he had sliced his 4th. wooden shot in to a trap but had recovered well and got on to the green and then had taken 3 putts which would make him a 8 but by some slip of the tongue when I started to say 8 I said 7 and before I could correct myself Mr. Frisbie said yes you are right it was a 7.

"That is even 7s," said Mr. Frisbie.

"Yes," I said.

On the way back to the house he asked me what was my salary which I told him and he said well I think you are worth more than that and from now on you will get $25.00 more per week.

On another occasion when 9 more holes had been added to the course and Mr. Frisbie was playing the 18 holes regular every day he came to the last hole needing a 5 to break 112 which was his best score.

The 18th. hole is only 120 yards with a big green but a brook in front and traps in back of it. Mr. Frisbie got across the brook with his second but the ball went over in to the trap and it looked like bad business because Mr. Frisbie is even worse with a niblick than almost any other club except maybe the No. 3 and 4 irons and the wood.

Well I happened to get to the ball ahead of him and it laid there burred in the deep sand about a foot from a straight up and down bank 8 foot high where it would have been impossible for any man alive to oust it in one stroke but as luck would have it I stumbled and gave the ball a little kick and by chance it struck the side of the bank and stuck in the grass and Mr. Frisbie got it up on the green in one stroke and was down in 2 putts for his 5.

"Well that is my record 111 or 3 over 6s," he said.

Now my brother had a couple of tickets for the polo at Meadowbrook the next afternoon and I am a great lover of horses flesh so I said to Mr. Frisbie can I go to the polo tomorrow afternoon and he said certainly any time you want a afternoon off do not hesitate to ask me but a little while later there was a friend of mine going to get married at Atlantic City and Mr. Frisbie had just shot a 128 and broke his spoon besides and when I mentioned about going to Atlantic City for my friend's wedding he snapped at me like a wolf and said what did I think it was the xmas holidays.

Personally I am a man of simple tastes and few wants and it is very seldom when I am not satisfied to take my life and work as they come and not seek fear or favor but of course there are times in every man's life when they desire something a little out of the ordinary in the way of a little vacation or perhaps a financial accommodation of some kind and in such cases I have found Mr. Frisbie a king amongst men provide it one uses discretion in choosing the moment of their reproach but a variable tyrant if one uses bad judgment in choosing the moment of their reproach.

You can count on him granting any reasonable request just after he has made a good score or even a good shot where as a person seeking a favor when he is off his game might just swell ask President Coolidge to do the split.

I wish to state that having learned my lesson along these lines I did not use my knowledge to benefit myself alone but have on the other hand utilized same mostly to the advantage of others especially the members of Mr. Frisbie's own family. Mr. Frisbie's wife and son and daughter all realized early in my employment that I could handle Mr. Frisbie better than anyone else and without me ever exactly divulging the secret of my methods they just naturally began to take it for granted that I could succeed with him where they failed and it became their habit when they sought something from their respective spouse and father to summons me as their adviser and advocate.

As an example of the above I will first sight an example in connection with Mrs. Frisbie. This occurred many years ago and was the instance which convinced her beyond all doubt that I was a expert on the subject of managing her husband.

Mrs. Frisbie is a great lover of music but unable to perform on any instrument herself. It was her hope that one of the children would be a pianiste and a great deal of money was spent on piano lessons for both Robert the son and Florence the daughter but all in vain as neither of the two showed any talent and their teachers one after another gave them up in despair.

Mrs. Frisbie at last became desirous of purchasing a player piano and of course would consider none but the best but when she brooched the subject to Mr. Frisbie he turned a deaf ear as he said pianos were made to be played by hand and people who could not learn same did not deserve music in the home.

I do not know how often Mr. and Mrs. Frisbie disgust the matter pro and con.

Personally they disgust it in my presence any number of times and finally being a great admirer of music myself and seeing no reason why a man of Mr. Frisbie's great wealth should deny his wife a harmless pleasure such as a player piano I suggested to the madam that possibly if she would leave matters to me the entire proposition might be put over. I can no more than fail I told her and I do not think I will fail so she instructed me to go ahead as I could not do worse than fail which she had already done herself.

I will relate the success of my plan as briefly as possible. Between the house and the golf course there was a summer house in which Mrs. Frisbie sat reading while Mr. Frisbie played golf. In this summer house she could sit so as to not be visible from the golf course. She was to sit there till she heard me whistle the strains of "Over There" where at she was to appear on the scene like she had come direct from the house and the fruits of our scheme would then be known.

For two days Mrs. Frisbie had to console herself with her book as Mr. Frisbie's golf was terrible and there was no moment when I felt like it would not be courting disaster to summons her on the scene but during the 3rd. afternoon his game suddenly improved and he had shot the 1st. 9 holes in 53 and started out on the 10th. with a pretty drive when I realized the time had come.

Mrs. Frisbie appeared promptly in answer to my whistling and walked rapidly up to Mr. Frisbie like she had hurried from the house and said there is a man at the house from that player piano company and he says he will take $50.00 off the regular price if I order today and please let me order one as I want one so much.

"Why certainly dear go ahead and get it dear," said Mr. Frisbie and that is the way Mrs. Frisbie got her way in regards to a player piano. Had I not whistled when I did but waited a little longer it would have spelt ruination to our schemes as Mr. Frisbie took a 12 on the 11th. hole and would have bashed his wife over the head with a No. 1 iron had she even asked him for a toy drum.

I have been of assistance to young Mr. Robert Frisbie the son with reference to several items of which I will only take time to touch on one item with reference to Mr. Robert wanting to drive a car. Before Mr. Robert was 16 years of age he was always after Mr. Frisbie to allow him to drive one of the cars and Mr. Frisbie always said him nay on the ground that it is against the law for a person under 16 years of age to drive a car.

When Mr. Robert reached the age of 16 years old however this excuse no longer held good and yet Mr. Frisbie continued to say Mr. Robert nay in regards to driving a car. There is plenty of chauffeurs at your beckon call said Mr. Frisbie to drive you where ever and when ever you wish to go but of course Mr. Robert like all youngsters wanted to drive himself and personally I could see no harm in it as I personally could not drive for him and the other 2 chauffeurs in Mr. Frisbie's employee at the time were just as lightly to wreck a car as Mr. Robert so I promised Mr. Robert that I would do my best towards helping him towards obtaining permission to drive one of the cars.

"Leave it to me" was my bequest to Mr. Robert and sure enough my little strategy turned the trick though Mr. Robert did not have the patience like his mother to wait in the summer house till a favorable moment arrived so it was necessary for me to carry through the entire proposition by myself.

The 16th. hole on our course is perhaps the most difficult hole on our course at least it has always been a variable tartar for Mr. Frisbie.

It is about 350 yards long in length and it is what is called a blind hole as you can not see the green from the tee as you drive from the tee up over a hill with a direction flag as the only guide and down at the bottom of the hill there is a brook a little over 225 yards from the tee which is the same brook which you come to again on the last hole and in all the times Mr. Frisbie has played around the course he has seldom never made this 16th. hole in less than 7 strokes or more as his tee shot just barely skins the top of the hill giving him a down hill lie which upsets him so that he will miss the 2d. shot entirely or top it and go in to the brook.

Well I generally always stand up on top of the hill to watch where his tee shot goes and on the occasion referred to he got a pretty good tee shot which struck on top of the hill and rolled half way down and I hurried to the ball before he could see me and I picked it up and threw it across the brook and when he climbed to the top of the hill I pointed to where the ball laid the other side of the brook and shouted good shot Mr. Frisbie. He was overjoyed and beamed with joy and did not suspect anything out of the way though in realty he could not hit a ball more than 160 yards if it was teed on the summit of Pike's Peak.

Fate was on my side at this junction and Mr. Frisbie hit a perfect mashie shot on to the green and sunk his 2d. put for the only 4 of his career on this hole. He was almost delirious with joy and you may be sure I took advantage of the situation and before we were fairly off the green I said to him Mr.

Frisbie if you do not need me tomorrow morning do you not think it would be a good time for me to learn Mr. Robert to drive a car.

"Why certainly he is old enough now to drive a car and it is time he learned."

I now come to the main instance of my article which is in regards to Miss Florence Frisbie who is now Mrs. Henry Craig and of course Craig is not the real name but you will soon see that what I was able to do for her was no such childs play like gaining consent for Mr. Robert to run a automobile or Mrs. Frisbie to purchase a player piano but this was a matter of the up most importance and I am sure the reader will not consider me a vain bragger when I claim that I handled it with some skill.

Miss Florence is a very pretty and handsome girl who has always had a host of suiters who paid court to her on account of being pretty as much as her great wealth and I believe there has been times when no less than half a dozen or more young men were paying court to her at one time. Well about 2 years ago she lost her heart to young Henry Craig and at the same time Mr. Frisbie told her in no uncertain turns that she must throw young Craig over board and marry his own choice young Junior Holt or he would cut her off without a dime.

Holt and Craig are not the real names of the two young men referred to though I am using their real first names namely Junior and Henry. Young Holt is a son of Mr. Frisbie's former partner in business and a young man who does not drink or smoke and has got plenty of money in his own rights and a young man who any father would feel safe in trusting their daughter in the bands of matrimony. Young Craig at that time had no money and no position and his parents had both died leaving nothing but debts.

"Craig is just a tramp and will never amount to anything," said Mr. Frisbie. "I have had inquirys made and I understand he drinks when anyone will furnish him the drinks. He has never worked and never will. Junior Holt is a model young man from all accounts and comes of good stock and is the only young man I know whose conduct and habits are such that I would consider him fit to marry my daughter."

Miss Florence said that Craig was not a tramp and she loved him and would not marry anyone else and as for Holt he was terrible but even if he was not terrible she would never consider undergoing the bands of matrimony with a man named Junior.

"I will elope with Henry if you do not give in," she said.

Mr. Frisbie was not alarmed by this threat as Miss Florence has a little common sense and would not be lightly to elope with a young man who could hardly finance a honeymoon trip on the subway. But neither was she showing any signs of yielding in regards to his wishes in regards to young Holt and things began to take on the appearance of a dead lock between father and daughter with neither side showing any signs of yielding.

Miss Florence grew pale and thin and spent most of her time in her room instead of seeking enjoyment amongst her friends as was her custom. As for Mr. Frisbie he was always a man of iron will and things began to take on the appearance of a dead lock with neither side showing any signs of yielding.

It was when it looked like Miss Florence was on the verge of a serious illness when Mrs. Frisbie came to me and said we all realize that you have more influence with Mr. Frisbie than anyone else and is there any way you can think of to get him to change his status toward Florence and these 2 young men because if something is not done right away I am afraid of what will happen. Miss Florence likes you and has a great deal of confidence in you said Mrs. Frisbie so will you see her and talk matters over with her and see if you can not think up some plan between you which will put a end to this situation before my poor little girl dies.

So I went to see Miss Florence in her bedroom and she was a sad sight with her eyes red from weeping and so pale and thin and yet her face lit up with a smile when I entered the room and she shook hands with me like I was a long lost friend.

"I asked my mother to send you," said Miss Florence. "This case looks hopeless but I know you are a great fixer as far as Father is concerned and you can fix it if anyone can. Now I have got a idea which I will tell you and if you like it it will be up to you to carry it out."

"What is your idea?"

"Well," said Miss Florence, "I think that if Mr. Craig the man I love could do Father a favor why Father would not be so set against him."

"What kind of a favor?"

"Well Mr. Craig plays a very good game of golf and he might give Father some pointers which would improve Father's game."

"Your father will not play golf with anyone and certainly not with a good player and besides that your father is not the kind of a man that wants anyone giving him pointers. Personally I would just as leaf go up and tickle him as tell him that his stance is wrong."

"Then I guess my idea is not so good."

"No," I said and then all of a sudden I had a idea of my own. "Listen Miss Florence does the other one play golf?"

"Who?"

"Young Junior Holt."

"Even better than Mr. Craig."

"Does your father know that?"

"Father does not know anything about him or he would not like him so well."

Well I said I have got a scheme which may work or may not work but no harm to try and the first thing to be done is for you to spruce up and pretend like you do not feel so unkindly towards young Holt after all. The next thing is to tell your father that Mr. Holt never played golf and never even saw it played but would like to watch your father play so he can get the hang of the game.

And then after that you must get Mr. Holt to ask your father to let him follow him around the course and very secretly you must tip Mr. Holt off that your father wants his advice. When ever your father does anything wrong Mr. Holt is to correct him. Tell him your father is crazy to improve his golf but is shy in regards to asking for help.

There is a lot of things that may happen to this scheme but if it should go through why I will guarantee that at least half your troubles will be over.

Well as I said there was a lot of things that might have happened to spoil my scheme but nothing did happen and the very next afternoon Mr. Frisbie confided in me that Miss Florence seemed to feel much better and seemed to have changed her mind in regards to Mr. Holt and also said that the last named had expressed a desire to follow Mr. Frisbie around the golf course and learn something about the game.

Mr. Holt was a kind of a fat pudgy young man with a kind of a sneering smile and the first minute I saw him I wished him the worst.

For a second before Mr. Frisbie started to play I was certain we were lost as Mr. Frisbie remarked where have you been keeping yourself Junior that you never watched golf before. But luckily young Holt took the remark as a joke and made no reply. Right afterwards the storm clouds began to gather in the sky. Mr. Frisbie sliced his tee shot.

"Mr. Frisbie," said Young Holt, "there was several things the matter with you then but the main trouble was that you stood too close to the ball and cut across it with your club head and besides that you swang back faster than Alex Smith and you were off your balance and you gripped too hard and you jerked instead of hitting with a smooth follow through."

Well, Mr. Frisbie gave him a queer look and then made up his mind that Junior was trying to be humorous and he frowned at him so as he would not try it again but when we located the ball in the rough and Mr. Frisbie asked me for his spoon young Holt said Oh take your mashie Mr. Frisbie never use a wooden club in a place like that and Mr. Frisbie scowled and mumbled under his breath and missed the ball with his spoon and missed it again and then took a midiron and just dribbled it on to the fairway and finally got on the green in 7 and took 3 putts.

I suppose you might say that this was one of the quickest golf matches on record as it ended on the 2d. tee. Mr. Frisbie tried to drive and sliced again. Then young Holt took a ball from my pocket and a club from the bag and said here let me show you the swing and drove the ball 250 yards straight down the middle of the course.

I looked at Mr. Frisbie's face and it was puffed out and a kind of a purple black color. Then he burst and I will only repeat a few of the more friendlier of his remarks.

"Get to hell and gone of my place. Do not never darken my doors again. Just show up around here one more time and I will blow out what you have got instead of brains. You lied to my girl and you tried to make a fool out of me. Get out before I sick my dogs on you and tear you to pieces."

Junior most lightly wanted to offer some word of explanation or to demand one on his own account but saw at a glance how useless same would be. I heard later that he saw Miss Florence and that she just laughed at him.

"I made a mistake about Junior Holt," said Mr. Frisbie that evening. "He is no good and must never come to this house again."

"Oh Father and just when I was beginning to like him," said Miss Florence.

Well like him or not like him she and the other young man Henry Craig were married soon afterwards which I suppose Mr. Frisbie permitted the bands in the hopes that same would rile Junior Holt.

Mr. Frisbie admitted he had made a mistake in regards to the last named but he certainly was not mistaken when he said that young Craig was a tramp and would never amount to anything.

Well I guess I have rambled on long enough about Mr. Frisbie.

Dressing the Part for Golf

BY GLENNA COLLETT VARE

They called her "the female Bobby Jones," and with good reason: she dominated the game in her time. Glenna Collett Vare (1903–1989)—whose name is inscribed on the trophy that the LPGA presents each year to the golfer with the lowest scoring average—won a record six U.S. Women's Amateur titles, and once strung together an unimaginable 16 consecutive tournament victories, five *more* than Byron Nelson's unimaginable 1945 streak. Her exuberance, confidence, personality, and style are etched into every paragraph of her 1929 memoir, *Ladies in the Rough*. The first important golf book written by a woman, it was part memoir and part instructional, very smart, often funny, sweetly acerbic, and in the final wish of the chapter that follows, heartbreakingly poignant. It is the golfing equivalent of the observation that Ginger Rogers had to do everything Fred Astaire did—only backward and in high heels.

Sometimes I wish I were a man. There would be so much more fun in golf—and so many more fewer strokes. After all, the most satisfying rounds, although not always the most enjoyable, are those that cost the fewest strokes. At least, that is true when you have become golf-conscious and are striving for par figures.

Occasionally you encounter a fair duffer who is utterly oblivious of Old Man Par, like the one who came puffing in at the end of the eighteen-hole qualifying round of a recent tournament and declared she had had 135 of the most interesting shots she had ever played!

Such a round may be highly interesting, but you would hardly consider it satisfying in this sporting age, when the competitive spirit has gripped women as well as men. So when I say: "Sometimes I wish I were a man," I am thinking of my cards. Women break eighty now and then, but men break seventy frequently.

There are many reasons for this substantial difference, some of which can be overcome. But the chief reason is insurmountable. A woman needs more strokes because she is a woman.

The margin between the sexes on the links is not wholly one of muscle. There have been comparatively short drivers among the men who have won national championships, and long drivers who failed to qualify. Even in the women's ranks the palm of victory does not always go to her who hits the longest ball. Strength is an asset on the links, but it is not indispensable.

If a golfing Amazon were to appear miraculously on the sports horizon, I should not look with too much confidence for her to defeat the male champion. She might possess the tremendous tee-shots of Cyril Tolley, the irons of Tommy Armour, and the putting touch of Bobby Jones—but it would make no difference. Being a woman, she would take more strokes than she should.

There is the matter of costume, for one thing. This may not impress the male golfer as being of great moment, but I assure you that it is.

The last national open championship introduced the prize for the best-dressed golfer. Johnny Farrell won the prize, and, although he did not win the championship, he made a most respectable showing. Later he won several tournaments in the same prize-winning costume. The point is that it didn't make much difference what he wore. The smartest plus fours do not interfere with stance.

Ted Ray, the English star, prefers to play in long trousers, and he seems to prefer them somewhat worn and baggy. He was never a contender for the best-dressed golfer's prize, but he has many cups. Clothes do not make the golfer; that is, if you limit the statement to men golfers.

A woman cares as much about her appearance as she does about her score. And, from a purely technical standpoint, the best-looking costume is not always the most helpful; nor is the "sensible" costume most becoming. The wide-hemmed skirts that permit the attitudes necessary in striving for a two-hundred-yard drive, or chipping from the face of the bunker, do not hang gracefully on the feminine form.

Frankly, they are dangerously close to dowdiness, and it is a tribute to woman's passionate devotion to golf that she will wear this "sensible" skirt, knowing that, while it adds yards to her drives, it detracts much from her charm.

Thousands have refused to yield fully to the necessities. The circumference of the hem of their golfing skirts is not the maximum required for a wide stance. They are a little fuller, to be sure, than they like, but there is a limit even to the pursuit of par.

Miss Cecil Leitch, one of the world's finest golfers, has her skirt just wide enough to hold her widest stance. This permits her to set herself firmly for the tremendous drives and hard-hit iron-shots that won her the British ladies' championship on several occasions. Another famous woman star, an American, has skirts just wide enough to fit her putting stance. Most have adopted a style between these extremes, but very few go to the lengths—or wouldn't it be more accurate to say the widths?—in golfing costumes that Miss Leitch sets in England.

This is not due to vanity. The feminine golfer's costume is a compromise, not alone for appearance' sake, but for utility as well. The wide-hemmed skirt is best for driving or for any stroke where one must play from a wide stance and put all one's strength into the swing.

But there are just as many strokes that are interfered with by the flapping folds of the full-hemmed skirt. They are whipped into the path of the stroke, and if the day is a bit breezy, they make steadiness impossible. Even if there is no actual interference with the stroke, they are distracting when a delicate shot must be played.

Clothes are not in the slightest degree a matter of concern with men, but they can play havoc at times with women golfers. Once I won an important match because of the handicap of dress—my opponent's dress. The story of Miss Ada Mackenzie's knitted skirt has been told in chapter viii. Ordinarily a knitted skirt is an excellent golfing costume—almost ideal. It stretches to fit the widest stance and falls back into place. But, as Miss Mackenzie's experience shows, it is worse than useless on a rainy day.

The plus fours of the male are an ideal costume. Feminine ingenuity has devised no costume so perfect for golf. Some women have worn them in tournaments. There is much to be said for knickers. All that can be said against them is that the average woman does not look well in them, and well she knows it. Their undoubted utility can never outweigh their obvious futility as a means of adornment.

Such is the decision of thousands of women golfers. And that is that, for golf is not everything. If men could play golf more efficiently in skirts, we might confidently expect to see them so garb themselves; but the ladies, unfortunately for their golfing reputations, will not wear plus fours. And it is probably just as well, for the resulting snickers at the women in knickers would so disconcert them that they would lose whatever gain in athletic efficiency the innovation would bring.

Feminine golf carries another handicap that is not so marked in the men's ranks. A woman is easily flustered by a variety of little things to which she should give no notice. Psychologists undoubtedly can give adequate reasons for the lady golfer's jumpy nerves; we know it as "tournament nervousness." It explains why so many women score a thirty-seven on one round and a forty-seven on the next.

When a man plays golf, he can forget everything except the business in hand. He lays aside his business problems and steels himself with concentration. He remembers only to keep his head down and his eye on the ball. He resolutely puts out of his mind everything that could possibly add to his score.

A woman has no such capacity for concentration. A golf professional once told me that was his most aggravating problem—to teach his fair duffers to concentrate.

In the midst of a match the woman golfer will think of and dwell on many things that have not the slightest bearing on the game. Did she order the roast for dinner? Heavens, no! And there goes a slice. Why did she invite the Browns for Friday, when the cook is off? In contemplation of that situation she tops her mashie.

In the midst of the serious business of lining up the putt, if her tortured mind permits her at length to reach the green, she suddenly remembers that Junior went to school that morning without a handkerchief. So the putt runs past the cup, and coming back, she is short.

A man would consider such things trifles, of no importance, or else easily remedied. But a woman cannot forget trifles. Her life is made up of trifles. She must give thought to other matters even when she is playing golf, else her score as a wife would not break a hundred.

But let us suppose that our Amazonian golfer, in addition to her manlike muscle, is endowed with a certain amount of grim determination. She approaches the first tee with the male champion, her mind on the golf match and nothing else.

He winds up vigorously and gives the ball a ride. The hypothetical lady prepares to drive—and another innate feminine weakness is disclosed. She wonders if she presents a graceful appearance, decides that she might end up in some awkward posture if she, too, attempted to give the ball a ride. So she shortens her swing, sacrificing distance to decorum.

A man does not care whether he is awkward-looking. A long tee-shot soothes any hurt to his pride. But a woman, unfortunately, cannot so forget herself. She has a duty more important than golf—the age-old feminine duty never to look ridiculous if she can help it.

With the last putt sinking into the eighteenth cup, the men are prepared for their round the next day. But the ladies, because complexion is more important to most than par golf, must first retire to their boudoirs and apply cold creams and lotions.

These are some of the reasons why a woman cannot compete on even terms with a man at golf, even supposing she is his equal in strength and skill. The handicaps for the ordinary woman are still more numerous.

She does not have nearly so many opportunities to play. The busy broker can slam his desk shut at three o'clock, call a crony, and drive to the links, where they quiet their consciences by pretending to discuss business affairs. In fact, it is a male proverb that many big deals are made on the golf-links.

Women have not yet figured out a method of running the household from the links. You cannot well take the cook and maid and children's nurse with you for a foursome—deciding the menu on the first green, planning the spring housecleaning as you proceed along the fairway of the five-hundred-yard dog-leg hole, and deciding Junior's program while blasting out of a trap.

If a husband is late for dinner, he passes it off lightly by blaming the fussy foursome ahead; but imagine the dialogue that would follow a wife's attempt to offer the same explanation for a late dinner! I do not contend that these matters should not be as they are. Still, they do make it difficult at times for a woman to give proper attention to her game.

The etiquette of golf calls for certain formulas that are not found in any book of instructions. There is one expletive for a topped drive; milder ones for hooks and slices. For putts that rim the cup there are several recognized expletives. Also, it is part of the ritual that the caddie, the greens committee, the gallery, or your opponent can be held responsible for any lack of perfection in your play. That is to say, these things are permissible if you are a man. And undoubtedly they are an aid in keeping down blood-pressure. But the most that is allowed women is an apologetic, half-swallowed "Damn!" under the most trying circumstances. Women, gentle creatures, are not expected to utter harsh oaths, and that is too bad. There are probably occasions when oaths are helpful if not proper.

George Bernard Shaw has a naïve theory that women are only human beings who, by force of habit and convention, wear skirts instead of trousers. He is not in favour of coddling them. The American golfing male dissents. He is chivalrous—would not have her dainty ears shocked by man's robust golfing conversation. He guards her by telling her to stay off the links.

More and more clubs are barring women, or limiting their hours of play. Many reasons are given, but at bottom it is because the presence of women limits the vocabulary. One club in the New York district announced restrictions on women's play and frankly admitted that the men were complaining. It seemed that every time a prominent banker swore a blue streak, he was embarrassed by a ladies' foursome appearing over the brow of a hill, timidly crying "Fore!"

There are many things that hold a woman back in golf that are not common to the two other popular sports—tennis and swimming. I know of no tennis clubs that bar women, and there are no restrictions at all on the use of the ocean. In tennis and swimming the only handicaps are the woman's smaller endowment of strength and stamina.

The woman tennis-player is not hampered by dress. The sleeveless, short-skirted costume of light material permits full freedom of movement. Also the action is fast and furious, not deliberate as in golf, so the feminine weaknesses of self-consciousness and a tendency to distraction are not an important factor.

I have the word of Mary K. Browne that in skill, finesse, and tactics Suzanne Lenglen is the equal of William T. Tilden. Yet, when they met a few years ago in an informal match, Tilden won 6–0, 6–0, with the loss of not more than a dozen points.

The best man golfer could never defeat the best woman golfer by any such margin. Man's par on the average course will total about seventy-two strokes as compared with eighty-two for women. That is a difference of ten strokes, which supposes that man's golfing efficiency is about twelve per cent greater than woman's. But it is quite theoretical. The best women players can go around an eighteen-hole course within something less than ten strokes of the best men players' score.

For the past three years a series of men-versus-women matches has been held on the country-club course at Fairfield, Connecticut. The course measures slightly more than six thousand five hundred yards, and par is seventy-one for men and eighty-three for women.

The women are allowed seven bisques, which does not at all equalize the difference of twelve strokes in the pars. Nevertheless, in the eight matches played in 1926 and 1927 the women won three and halved one.

The layout of this Fairfield Country Club course, with men's and women's par, is as follows:

Hole		Men's Par	Women's Par
1	360 yards	4	5
2	445 yards	4	5
3	530 yards	5	6
4	327 yards	4	4
5	150 yards	3	3
6	415 yards	4	5
7	445 yards	4	5
8	175 yards	3	3
9	397 yards	4	5
10	395 yards	4	5
11	367 yards	4	5
12	230 yards	3	4
13	485 yards	5	5
14	350 yards	4	4
15	405 yards	4	5
16	320 yards	4	4
17	530 yards	5	6
18	205 yards	3	4
	6,531 yards	71	83

The majority of the holes are around four hundred yards long. Under the arbitrary yardage systems a four-hundred-yard hole is par four for men and par five for women. The good male golfer can drive two hundred yards from the tee and put his iron second shot close enough to the hole to get down with two putts; but the woman needs three strokes to span the four hundred yards from tee to green and the customary two putts.

There are not many women who can drive two hundred yards from the tee, and even if they could they must use a wooden club for the second shot on a four-hundred-yard hole. In such a match with a man, the woman must press to have the slightest chance of holding her own, and it is not possible to press and play steady golf.

If she does not press, but is content to play the course in her own par figures, the woman is beaten anyway.

If she played the Fairfield course in perfect women's par, and her male opponent equalled men's par, the woman would lose the match on the twelfth green by the overwhelming score of eight and seven.

On six of these holes—the fourth, fifth, eighth, thirteenth, fourteenth, and sixteenth—men's and women's pars correspond. On the other twelve the woman is one down before she tees her ball.

If she played up to her par, and her opponent played to men's par, her seven bisques would be exhausted at the tenth hole. Playing perfect golf from that point on, she would still lose the match on the sixteenth green, four and two.

That is the theoretical result of the match. Actually, it has been somewhat different. In the matches played last July, Francis Ouimet defeated Miss Bernice Wall three and two; Richard Jones, Jr., defeated Louise Fordyce four and three; Miss Maureen Orcutt defeated Roland Mackenzie one up; and I defeated Jess Sweetser three and one. The year previous, Jones defeated Miss Fordyce three and two; Mackenzie defeated Miss Wall one up; Miss Orcutt and Lauren Upson finished square; and I defeated Max Marston four and two. Both years it happened that I was "on my game" and used only four of my seven bisque handicaps.

If the matches were played on a woman's course, such as that of the Women's National Golf and Tennis Club at Glen Head, Long Island, it is likely the woman could do very well with three or four bisques instead of the seven they need at Fairfield. The Women's National course measures 5,777 yards and the par is seventy-one for women. Men's par would be sixty-eight or sixty-nine. There are but three holes four hundred yards or more in length, so it would be fairly easy for the best men players, while the women would have to play perfectly to get par figures.

Playing over such a short course would bore men, for the test would be one of accuracy rather than long driving. But if mixed matches are to have any real value, they should be played under conditions that recognize the fundamental fact that a woman cannot hit a golf-ball as fair as a man.

A great many experts say a woman cannot putt; some say she putts better than a man. Some say she is weak on iron-shots; others say they are the strongest feature of her game. I think the facts are that a woman putts as well as a man, and is just as adept with her irons, up to the limit of her strength. From the tee she is outdistanced from fifty to seventy-five yards, and therein lies her only inferiority.

Jess Sweetser and I played as a team in a foursome at Fairfield, Connecticut, and, playing the same ball, established an amateur record of seventy for the course. I drove from the first tee, and Jess from the second, and so on. As he drove well down the fairway, I was able to get the second shots fairly close to the hole, and his long iron-shots made up for my shorter drives from the tees. This match proved two things that are fundamental in comparing the ability of men and women as golfers. A woman is outdistanced through the fairway; once she is within a reasonable distance of the green, she can play as well as a man.

I do not wish I were a man, expect sometimes, when my drives only come within a full shot of my opponent's. I envy him his spirit of freedom, his independence of trifles, his disdain of convention, his disregard of appearances, and his childlike conviction, if he is a golfer, that golf is the most important thing on this bunkered sphere.

Over the Wire Is Out of Bounds

BY PAT WARD-THOMAS

Golfers have been known to go to epic lengths to play through all kinds of trouble, but it's pretty hard to imagine a more heroic stand than the one made by Pat Ward-Thomas (1913–1982), eminent golf correspondent for the *Guardian* and *Country Life* magazine. Before beginning what turned into a long and honored career in journalism—which actually began as a direct result of the remarkable experiences he unfolds in the following excerpt from his 1981 memoir *Not Only Golf*—Ward-Thomas served in the RAF as a pilot during World War II. On the trip home from a bombing run over Berlin in late 1940, his plane was shot down over enemy territory. Ward-Thomas bailed out. He was captured by the Germans, and spent the rest of the war in a series of POW camps.

He was eventually transferred to Stalag Luft III, the German's model internment camp for Allied air force officers. While the prisoners were allowed to play sports, see movies, read books, and receive mail, life in the camp was certainly no country club . . . until, in the summer of 1943, Ward-Thomas, an ardent golfer before the war, used some ingenuity—and the help of a lot of friends back home—to turn it into one. By the way, the escape facilitated by that wooden horse that stood near the sixth "green" is the same escape that inspired Billy Wilder's classic World War II movie *Stalag 17*.

Meanwhile, while Ward-Thomas was playing golf—albeit with some adjustments—behind enemy lines, the game continued to be played back in England, with some adjustments there as well. Golf may be perfectly willing to acknowledge when there's a war on, but it still insists on its right to play through. During the bombings, Major G. L. Edsell, secretary of St. Mellons Golf Club, set up these emergency rules to accommodate play during the conflagration. They were both adopted and adapted by clubs throughout the nation.

1. Players are asked to collect the bomb and shell splinters to save these causing damage to the mowers.
2. In competitions, during gunfire or while bombs are falling, players may take shelter without penalty for ceasing play.
3. The positions of known delayed-action bombs are marked by red and white flags placed at reasonably, but not guaranteed, safe distance from the bombs.
4. Shell and/or bomb splinters on the greens may be moved without penalty. On fairways or in bunkers within a club's length of a ball they may be moved without penalty and no penalty shall be incurred if a ball is thereby caused to move accidentally.
5. A ball moved by enemy action may be replaced as near as possible to where it lay, or if lost or destroyed, a ball may be dropped no nearer the hole without penalty.
6. A ball lying in any crater may be lifted and dropped not nearer the hole, preserving the line to the hole, without penalty.
7. A player whose stroke is affected by the simultaneous explosion of a bomb or shell, or by machine-gun fire, may play another ball from the same place. Penalty one stroke.

To an outsider the camp on a high summer day would have presented an astonishing spectacle. Everywhere men, as scantily clad as was decent, were throwing, hitting or kicking balls from morning until sunset. Many of us became almost totally immersed in playing, thinking or talking about games. However humorous or trivial they might appear in retrospect the activity involved was healthy, amusing and above all a distraction, an escape from the ever lurking threat of anxiety, foreboding and depression.

From my viewpoint, and that of many others, the most significant happening during this period was the appearance of a hickory-shafted lady's mashie. It came into the possession of Sydney Smith, a journalist of repute with the *Daily Express*. I came upon him one day as he was chipping a peculiar-looking ball back and forth. He had made it by winding wool and cotton round a carved piece of pine and covering it with a laboriously sewn bit of cloth. Although the ball bore no resemblance to a real one, and would travel only about sixty yards, it gave us a wonderful echo of golf. Hour after hour we would play, objects of incredulous stares. When others wanted to take part Sydney would say, 'make a ball and then you can'. His words heralded a revolution beyond our imagining.

In almost no time men were making much improved balls, more durable and tighter-wound than the original. Then one crafty fellow wound strands of rubber round his ball and straightaway was the longest hitter in the camp. Within a few weeks a score of people were involved, including several good players. The best of these were Danny O'Brien, a Scottish schoolboy international, and Ronnie Morgan, a Worcestershire county player who reached the last eight of the first English Championship after the war. George Murray Frame, who had a low handicap at Troon, and Oliver Green, now Director of the Woburn Country Club, probably were next in the ranking.

The Sagan golf club was born but we needed a course. To say that we laid out one is something of an overstatement. All we did was choose places for tees and suitable objects to hit for holes. These included tree stumps, poles, an incinerator door and a tiny fir tree about eighteen inches high. As the poles were quite high many a hole in one was recorded a dozen feet or more from the ground.

When the membership had grown to twelve we had our first competition, a knockout, and Hugh Falkus, well known after the war for his nature broadcasts, and I reached the final. Falkus, no golfer then but gifted with strong hands and a deadly aim, was expert at hitting the 'holes', such as they were. The fir tree caused some discussion because we thought that its little trunk had to be hit, whereas Falkus would claim to have holed out if his shot whistled yards past the tree but grazed a leaf in passing. Fortunately Falkus was not as deadly as usual in our match and I became the first Open champion of Sagan.

As interest grew evolution was swift. An eighteen-hole course was planned and in such a confined space involved some dangerous if fascinating shots. One blind shot over the kitchen hut, controlled by the Germans, had its perils and the fire pool made a splendid hazard for the 18th. It was deep and filthy but this did not deter two madmen from diving in to retrieve a ball on a freezing winter day. The air was alive with balls of all manner and shapes whistling about the camp. Our activities were watched with interest, scorn and at first tolerance, but it was soon obvious that the course would have to be smaller. Hole after hole was played over tiny gardens, a few yards square, where it was possible to coax vegetables into life. The horticulturists were far from amused when a golf ball decapitated a cherished tomato plant. Sunbathers were also in danger. One man was hit on the bare body with a full shot from no great range and was furious when the striker exploded with laughter. One unfortunate creature's peaceful morning shave in front of his window was in-terrupted when a half-topped tee shot crashed through the glass. On another occasion a German *Unteroffizier's* morning constitutional in the abort at the end of the kitchen buildings was disturbed by the crash of glass all around him accompanied by the inevitable mirth. Someone had shanked. No action was taken save we were asked to move the tee. Such incidents were fairly frequent and we feared that a serious complaint might be laid against us.

Meanwhile the first green or rather 'brown' had been fashioned by Norman Thomas. With the loan of a spade from the Germans this did not take long. An area of about eight by ten yards was cleared of stones, stumps and roots and the ground levelled, covered with good yellow sand and kept smooth with a home-made squeegee. The surfaces were fairly true and quite fast after rain. Eventually we had browns for all nine holes of the new and shorter course which measured some 850 yards. The longest hole was 140 and the par 29. The course record still stands at 57 and is unlikely to be broken.

At first the Germans regarded the shaping of little banks and bunkers with suspicion until they realised that there was nothing ulterior in our motives. Mistakenly, they thought otherwise after Eric Williams and his two companions had achieved the only successful escape from our camp by means of the famous Wooden Horse. The tunnel was discovered later the same night but the German attempt to hold an identity check was frustrated by deliberate fusing of the lights in one hut. This made them more angry than usual and clearly they decided on a show of strength. The next day the whole camp was assembled and surrounded by some 200 soldiers with machine guns at the ready. Had there been further signs of insurrection I think they would have fired. Fortunately they calmed down and the only victim was the golf course which seemed an obvious means of dispersing sand from the tunnel. This was understandable because for months the Wooden Horse had stood between the wire and our sixth 'brown'. The course was flattened but a few weeks later the Germans were persuaded that it was innocent, which it was, and head brownkeeper Timmy Biden and his helpers restored the course. The excavation of yellow sand was forbidden; the browns be-came almost blacks and their surfaces not so true.

The planning of the course was a natural development, the evolution of ball manufacture truly remarkable. Once rubber had been introduced it became one of the most precious commodities in the camp and the fervent golfers would make all manner of sacrifices to get it. Prisoners were allowed quarterly clothing parcels from home and many was the plea for gym shoes, air cushions, tobacco pouches and the like which were ripped to shreds on arrival. The man with rubber to spare or to exchange was every golfer's friend. The effect on our golf was no less than the Haskell banishing the gutty forever. The age of the string ball was dead.

Within no time ball-making had become almost an art form. The Scottish craftsmen of old would have nodded approvingly at the ingenuity, skill and patience we devoted to the task. Most of the balls had a solid rubber core, some hollowed to hold a small bit of lead. Several feet of rubber were necessary. This was stretched and cut with razor blades or scissors into very narrow strips which were wound round the core as in an ordinary ball. Experience alone taught one the correct tension. Too tight a winding produced a wooden effect when the ball was struck or would cause the rubber to snap. If too slack the ball was like a pudding. At the same time we strove to make the ball 1.62 inches in diameter and 1.62 ounces in weight. Delicate experiment usually made this possible.

The earlier balls of string and wood were covered with cloth, or Elastoplast coaxed from the officer in charge of medical supplies, but this process was soon abandoned. The new covers were made of leather cut into two figures of eight, similar to those covering a baseball. These were carefully sewn with thread or twine, which was not readily available, or strands of cotton strengthened with wax or German boot polish.

The leather, often obtained by cutting good shoes into pieces, varied in thickness and quality. It was usually advisable to soak and stretch it before cutting the figures of eight according to tin patterns, cut to a fraction of a millimetre of the right size. These had been shaped by one of the experts, possibly Norman Ryder who produced a detailed thesis on ball-making for the benefit of the embryo practitioners. Very soon balls of astonishing quality were appearing from the, so to speak, benches of Ryder and others. An Australian, Samson, was highly skilled and one example of his work is in the Royal and Ancient museum at St Andrews. It is precisely the same weight and size as a real golf ball, perfectly symmetrical, with cover stitching that would do credit to a machine.

I did not rank with Ryder, Samson, Graham Hogg and others as a ball-maker but mine were fairly close to the true mark. Shortly after the war Reginald Whitcombe and Alfred Perry played an exhibition match at Stockport, then my home club. I asked them to hit the balls I had brought back; they did so with drivers and both flew some 200 yards. Years later I asked Nicklaus to try one. He refused for fear that it might burst, but to this day the one I have still bounces well. The other is in the Museum of the United States Golf Association in New Jersey.

Such is my incompetence in matters domestic that my wife Jean still finds it hard to believe that the balls really were my own work. As far as I can recall making one took me about six hours as against Ryder's estimate of four. Many a man laboured long over his ball and sometimes, within moments of going on to the course, saw it soar out of bounds over the wire. If he were lucky a passing guard might throw it back, and the guards on the watch towers occasionally used their field glasses to aid the search, but if the ball were lost there was ample time to make another.

The perimeter of the camp was protected by a high double-stage barbed wire fence. Any attempt to climb this could be met with a bullet but inside the main fence was a strip of no man's land bordered by a low tripwire. Entering this area was forbidden but so many balls from the incessant games went in that the Germans provided a few white jackets. Donning one of these was tantamount to giving parole that no attempt to escape would be made and the balls could be retrieved.

During these early months of golf the little mashie, often in the hands of strong, unskilled players, must have hit several hundred thousand shots. That it survived was a rare tribute to the quality of the hickory and the firm of Patrick of Levin who, I think, were the makers. In the confusion when we were suddenly evacuated as the Russians advanced early in 1945 someone may have taken it with him. I hope so: it deserved a place of honour in a museum. I brought back the first steel-shafted club to reach the camp. It bore the name of Gilbert Heron of Oslo and mighty useful it proved as an aid during our march in the snow, lasting a week, to Luckenwalde, the final camp for most of us.

As the golfers wrote to various countries pleading for clubs a good supply was forthcoming. Norman Thomas and I had been adopted, in a manner of speaking, by a most attractive Danish girl, Doreen Wessel, who wrote to us and sent parcels. One of these consisted of ten clubs. Sadly, I never met the angelic Doreen, who married an American and went to live in Grosse Pointe, Michigan.

Our joy at the arrival of these clubs can be imagined. All were hickory but in good condition and the pressure on the little mashie was greatly eased. Such had been the demand for clubs as the golfing fever spread that home-made affairs began to appear. Some were extraordinary contraptions fit for a museum but their creation revealed remarkable skill and patience. The shafts usually were carved from ice-hockey sticks and the heads fashioned from sections of water jugs or stovepipes melted down. The latter were found to be strong enough without being too heavy, and were not constantly breaking, but the Germans objected to their use and that source was abandoned. Of the clubs that survived regular use one was the work of a Canadian, Don Elliott, a useful golfer and of necessity a powerful one. His club, known as 'Abort Annie', weighed about twenty ounces but the best of these efforts was made by Lee Usher, an American from Iowa. As I recall his club was well balanced and strong.

In the autumn of 1943 I wrote to the Royal and Ancient at St Andrews, giving a brief account of our golf and asking if they could spare a few clubs and balls. A copy of the letter was sent to Bernard Darwin who wrote of our efforts in one of his *Country Life* commentaries. He mentioned instances of golf in unusual places in the First War including a prison camp where young airmen were armed with cleeks. 'So erratic were their shots that on one occasion the German commandant, a portly and pompous old colonel, advanced to the middle of the playground, possibly to protest, and was driven into highly undignified flight. The airmen were no respecters of persons and pursued him relentlessly with a creeping barrage of cleek shots. He did not apparently bear any malice; so there must have been one German colonel for whom something good could be said'. We ventured no such liberties at Sagan, at least not intentionally.

Darwin ended his article by assuring readers that arrangements had been made by the R. and A. to send clubs and balls through the Red Cross. They arrived and among them was the steel-shafted driver. Naturally its use was forbidden except for practise swinging but I used to feel it longingly and wonder whether I would ever hit a shot with it. The chance came one bitter winter day when everyone was inside and the camp deserted. I went to a far corner, almost trembling with anticipation, and teed one of the real golf balls which had come with the clubs from St Andrews.

The driver had an extremely whippy shaft like those which Bing Crosby used and was quite unsuitable for me. However, I made a good contact with the ball which soared away out of sight in a great slice over the kitchen building. Anxiously I waited for any indication that it might have hit something and then came the inevitable plonk and tinkle of broken glass. The ball had crashed full pitch through a window and so startled the people in the room that they flung themselves to the floor. In the deep winter silence they thought that a bullet was responsible. Greatly embarrassed I went to apologise, prepared to face any anger if I could reclaim the precious ball. It was given back to me but my stroke was the first and last ever hit with a driver at Sagan.

By 1944 pleas for clubs had borne rich fruit. They came from many countries, mostly neutral. One man received several new steel-shafted irons and eventually we had about 100 clubs. Real golf balls were considered too dangerous to use except on special occasions such as an exhibition match when the course was cleared and the camp warned. And so in the naive belief that the balls would be less hurtful leather was substituted for the gutta-percha covers. Miraculously, no one was seriously hurt even though it was quite common for people to hit shots back and forth to one another, within a few yards of passers-by on their circuits of the camp.

Within a few months of the golf starting over 300 people had played the course. Although the number on it at any one time had to be controlled the fever did not abate. All day long men were swinging clubs, practising or talking golf. O'Brien and Morgan particularly, and other lesser experts, were much in demand for giving lessons and several prisoners, who had never previously touched a club, were quite competent golfers when they returned home. After all they had reasonable tuition in the basics of grip, stance and arc of swing and opportunity for practice. It was amusing to hear embryo golfers talking of draw and fade, weight transference, backspin and so on, within a few weeks of starting to play.

Hitting approaches of up to 100 yards or more to the minute browns was splendid training and I remember my first round or two on a proper course after the war. The greens looked enormous and I wondered how anyone could possibly miss them, but that illusion did not last long. Nevertheless many learned a great deal about the game and had also grown accustomed to playing in front of crowds. Quiet and well-behaved though they were when an important match was in progress one was always aware of critical eyes and that, as most golfers will agree, is a great aid to concentration.

Competitions of all kinds and challenge matches were frequent. In one such O'Brien and Samson challenged any pair in the camp to a 36-hole foursome and two 36-hole singles for a stake of fifty pounds. The backers chose Morgan and Frame to play for them but after winning the foursome they lost both singles.

In writing an account of this match for the camp newspaper (a few sheets pinned to a notice board), I began to think that reporting games was the profession for me. Later that summer I wrote the story of the golf in our camp. Several of us thought it might be of interest at home but had no idea where to send it, then someone suggested Henry Longhurst.

Everyone enjoyed his book, *It Was Good while It Lasted* and he looked an amiable soul from his pictures. First it had to be censored by the Germans and some unfortunate fellow had to plough through 14,000 words. Only one part, where I had made an oblique reference to the Wooden Horse, was deleted. The Germans probably thought the story reflected a contented life for the prisoners; it may have done. There was no point in my being critical of the conditions if the story was to reach England. It was duly mailed to Longhurst care of his publishers but little did I imagine that it would be a step towards fulfilling a dream.

September 20, 1913

BY AL LANEY

The day that 20-year-old caddie Francis Ouimet won the U.S. Open changed golf—and the way Americans perceived the game—forever. What's so fascinating about Al Laney's recollection of that day is how personally significant Ouimet's improbable quest became to a sprouting, 18-year-old newspaperman who had never held a golf club in his hands. As Laney (1895–1988) relates it, the day itself vibrates so vividly that it's hard to believe he retrieved the memories some 60 years after the fact for this chapter in what would become his fine, posthumous collection of reminiscences, *Following the Leaders.*

After World War I, Laney settled in with the American ex-pats in Paris. He was hired by the *Paris Herald,* covered international sports for its big brother, the *New York Herald-Tribune,* and enlisted in the brigade of volunteers who regularly read aloud to James Joyce, who was slowly losing his eyesight. Returning to the United States in the '30s, Laney remained a linchpin—tennis and golf were his beats—on a *Trib* sports staff that included Red Smith and Roger Kahn until the paper folded in 1966.

"Thousands of dripping rubber-coated spectators massed about Ouimet, who was hoisted to shoulders while cheer after cheer rang out in his honor. Excited women tore bunches of flowers from their bodies and hurled them at the youthful winner; hundreds of men strove to pat him on the back or shake his hand."—From the *New York Times,* Sept. 21, 1913.

"If I lived a thousand lives I should never again be spectator to such an amazing, thrilling and magnificent finish to a championship. . . . You tell me that a child like this has beaten our Vardon and Ray for a real championship? When we can go for week-end golfing trips to Jupiter and Mars, I will perhaps believe that your little Ouimet has won today. There will never be another like it. When we are old men little golfing children will ask us to tell them again the romantic story of the 20th of September in 1913."—Henry Leach, English golf correspondent, writing in the *New York Times,* Sept. 21, 1913.

★   ★   ★

There had been rain that Saturday in Brookline, Mass., but the day was hot and humid 2,000 miles away in Pensacola, and a faint lazy breeze came in off the Gulf of Mexico. About the time the scenes described above were unfolding to astonish, delight, and dismay, I, a teenage lad, was making my slow way through the heat toward the office of the Pensacola *Journal,* to which I had been apprenticed for after-school and Saturday-night service.

I wore, more than likely, the common uniform of the teenager of the day—flat, peaked cap; straight, tapered pants ending just below the knees; homemade cotton blouse with tight neckband for collar; long, ribbed black stockings held up by elastic bands; and either high-laced shoes or white sneakers called easywalkers. Knickerbockers for boys were just coming in, and I stopped to admire a suit in the window of White and White's store. It was a beautiful gray suit with a belted Norfolk jacket, but the tag said $10, an enormous price that I knew was forever beyond me. Only a few of these suits with knickers had appeared in the town or in school, and most boys of my acquaintance would jump right over knickers into long pants, the badge of manhood if not of maturity. I was, in fact, already saving up to buy my own first pair of long pants.

Under the overhanging balconies and upper stories of the building that shaded the sidewalks of the main street and gave an effect of a covered arcade, it was a little cooler, and my dawdling progress would have seemed aimless to an observer. There were few to observe, however. As I dawdled, I wrestled with a puzzle to which I was not to find the answer for many years. Why, I wondered, was I giving up a rare and precious free afternoon? Saturdays were grand, the only completely free time when I was really on my own, since all the news sources I usually checked after school were closed. The time could have been devoted to any number of pleasant schoolboy pursuits, such as sailing a boat, exploring any one of the many inlets and bayous off the harbour, or swimming at Bayview Park where many boys and girls gathered for fun and games. Actually, this particular Saturday afternoon had been set aside for a long, uninterrupted session of tennis that I had anticipated eagerly.

I could explain to myself no more than to my deserted companions why I had to disrupt our plans. They thought I'd suddenly gone strange, for they did not at all understand why I was leaving them in the lurch, reducing four to three and disrupting a carefully planned schedule of alternating singles and doubles play. Tennis partners were not so easy to come by at that time, and after the start of school I was available only on Saturdays. It seemed crazy to them and a little that way to me, too.

I tried to explain, but I could not tell them because I did not know why overnight it had become so terribly important to me to know what was happening in Brookline, Mass., and why I was driven by this necessity to know the outcome of a largely unfamiliar game played so far away by characters whose very names I had not known a few days earlier.

Much the same thing that had happened to me was happening to many others in many cities and towns on that Saturday afternoon, but I was not to know of this until long after. A certain compulsion, no doubt a certain destiny, was at work here. I was troubled by a vague uneasiness, a feeling almost of guilt or wrongdoing, as I moved slowly through the heavy shade with the brilliant white light just beyond in the street. Once you set yourself to remember such a special occasion, it all gradually comes back—the look on the faces of people you met; individual gestures; what you thought at the time; what somebody said; the hollow clop, clop of horses' hooves on the brick pavement; the faint hissing of ceiling fans, with blades as big as airplane propellers, inside the wide-open fronts of the stores; the distant screech of trolley wheels turning from Palafox into Wright Street half a mile away.

I had progressed as far as Romano Street when I saw coming toward me Mr. Sheppard, a kind, gray man who had a drugstore full of fascinating smells why down below Zaragosa Street on the edge of what was called the Red Light district, much frequented by sailors from ships in the harbor. Mr. Sheppard, a well-educated man and something of an intellectual in a community rather barren of culture, had been a good and stimulating friend of my late father, and I knew he would ask me where I was going. I knew, too, that he would not understand, and if there had been time before he saw me, I would have ducked to avoid encounter and question.

"What you doing downtown on Saturday, Boy?" he demanded to know. Mr. Sheppard never called me anything but Boy, even after I put on long pants. The reply that I was going to the newspaper office brought a "What for?", and my further explanation that I wanted to know if Ouimet had beaten the Englishmen brought a puzzled expression to the druggist's face.

I pronounced it "We-May." I was in high school and taking French, and it was not until years later that I learned that the name was pronounced "We-Met," accent on the first syllable.

"What in thunderation are you talking about, Boy?" Mr. Sheppard said, and the attempted explanation sent him on his way chuckling with amusement over schoolboy aberrations.

I leaned against an iron column supporting a balcony and thought about this reaction as I watched a round watering cart pulled by two mules. Its two arched umbrella-like jets spurting out behind sent up little gusts of smoke as the water hit the dirty roadway and ran in dusty rivulets. Did anyone else care about what was happening at Brookline? Was it perhaps a little odd to care so much?

Behind the cart came one of the town's curiosities named Leopold in one of those old seagoing hacks that were the only means of public transport other than the trolley lines. Leopold also was a friend, and he called to the driver to pull up to the sidewalk, which was raised about two feet above the roadway. Leopold wanted to tell me how things were going down at City Hall, where they humored him with a desk and a large bunch of keys fitting nothing, and he did nothing to disturb the illusion that he was running the city. He kept regular hours there, riding back and forth in an open hack whatever the weather, bowing and lifting his hat to everyone as a prince to his subjects. He belonged to one of the first families and was a rather charming and harmless man of indeterminate age.

Leopold was of the opinion that chicanery was continually on the prowl and but for his own watchfulness would conquer. He could not distinguish between man and teenager and, since I gave him contact with the power of the press, he looked upon me as a personage of almost equal importance with himself in this community. Together we would overcome the rampant forces of evil. On my daily calls to City Hall he would give me vague information of corruption in high places and direct me to "put it in the paper." Since he could not read, he always assumed that it had been done. Leopold and I enjoyed a very solid friendship. He understood instantly why I was going to the shop so early. His world was either black or white and nothing puzzled him. He was a completely happy man, never angry, always smiling even when misguided small boys would tease him. He gave me a blessing which cheered me greatly and bade me hurry lest I be late.

I paused a bit before the wide-open front of an oasis called the Kandy Kitchen where my closest and dearest schoolboy friend, Dwight Anderson, would be thumping out popular songs on the piano for the late-Saturday-afternoon crowd before moving on to render the same service at the town's one picture show in a a vacant store down by Government Street. He was going to conquer the wold as musician, I as writer. It also gave me comfort to know that Dwight would understand about this Saturday afternoon, although sports subjects did not move him in the way I thought they should.

I had about decided to go inside for a nickel's worth of cooling drink when a shout from the street made me turn.

"Hey! Where you going? Come on and ride around East Hill."

This invitation came from the only passenger on an open street car with seats running crosswise, a boy who sat just behind the motorman. This was Ralph Scholls, called Gus, a boy of my own age who was coming from somewhere down by the waterfront where there were fascinating things to attract teenagers. Gus was the best roller skater in the whole town, and he had jumped off a picnic boat in the middle of the bay that same summer to save a girl who had fallen in. They said he was going to get a medal for it partly because of the way I had written it up for the paper. The motorman slowed the car with a sudden twirling of the handle of a hand brake shaped like a goose neck to see if I'd come aboard. Riding the complete circuit of the longest trolley line was a favorite pastime whenever you had a spare nickel. I was tempted because it was about the coolest thing you could do on such a day. I waved him on, wondering if he would understand. Probably not. Gus was strictly a baseball man, as we all were, for that matter. Later I heard that after high school he had become a linotype operator and joined the ranks of the itinerant printers of that day who worked from shop to shop across the country. He even worked for a while for the Pensacola *Journal* but that was long after I had begun my own wanderings.

As the trolley clanged and clattered away, the conductor, swinging along the running board, waved to me. His name was Bud Booker and we had a business deal going. In exchange for free copies of the paper and such out-of-town papers as I could pick up around the shop, he would give me free rides all the way around East Hill and back, a journey that consumed more than an hour and took you way out into the woods where there were hardly any houses. This was for pleasure, but it became a money-saving deal whenever Bud was transferred to North Hill, where I lived.

I turned left off Palafox a little way along Intendencia Street to a tiny thoroughfare named De Luna Alley running through to Government Street and the Opera House on the corner of the Plaza Ferdinand, named in the old days for the husband of Columbus' friend, Isabella of Spain. Here the flags of five nations had flown, and they told us in school not to accept the statement that St. Augustine was older than Pensacola.

On the corner across the alley from the newspaper was the Curio Shop of Mrs. Neisius, a widow lady whose son Vincent was the *Journal's* pressman. You could find very interesting things in Mrs. Neisius's shop, like live turtles and snakes and a barrel full of sawdust where alligator eggs would hatch out. You could watch the process if you happened by at the right time. There was also a full-sized stuffed alligator wired to stand on its hind legs at the entrance.

Vince had been trying for months to persuade me to get into the mechanical side of newspapering where I would have a trade, but I was firmly committed upstairs. I knew already what I wanted to do, and I have never done any other work except when forced to by circumstance.

I had, of course, arrived too early, and I realized it when I climbed the dark stairs to the dingy and cluttered editorial room that was connected by a door with the editor's large office across the front of the building, above the business office on the ground floor. I was not exactly sure when the news wire would open on Saturday for the first of two periods. It usually had opened and closed when I arrived after an early supper, and the bulk of the day's news was there to be handled by me and two other somewhat more professional employees, one of whom was the editor himself. On such a small city daily at that time, everybody did everything and anything there was to do from reporting to copy-reading, proof-reading, and makeup, as well as handling whatever pictures there were and writing captions. I still remember one caption, or cutlines, as we called them, from the year before when we printed a big picture of the Titanic after she hit the iceberg. "Titanic in Name and Size, She Ended Her Only Voyage in a Titanic Tragedy." I was very proud of that one and carried it around in my pocket until it was in tatters.

My job was that of a sort of super copy boy, but I had to do a lot of rewriting, which I liked most. They told me, the other two, that, if I wanted to write later on, nothing was better training than doing newspaper rewrite, thereby getting me to do it more eagerly. I always looked forward to these Saturday nights, for I considered this real newspaper work, a cut above collecting small bits of local news here and there about the town. And there was always what seemed to me good newspaper talk to listen to in this room where I would continue to work part-time until I set out one day on a long trail leading through larger shops in larger cities, leading also to the playing fields, especially the golf courses of many lands.

The place was deserted now and very hot. It had been silly to come so early, but something had drawn me to the only place in town where the word would come. There was early activity in back and down below where linotype and press were, but I did not go there. As I sat waiting through the dragging minutes, I tried once more to figure out why this particular golf event should be so vital an occurrence to a schoolboy who had never swung a club. It was understandable on no logical grounds. I suppose I was able to "identify" with Ouimet, although that word had not yet come into the teenage vocabulary. Francis was not yet able to vote and, moreover, he was from the wrong side of the tracks. Francis was the son of a workingman and lived across the street from the exclusive club where he had caddied since he was old enough to tote a bag. He had become a pretty good golfer, too, by imitation, although he had to work at summer jobs all through his school years. He was good enough to enter the U.S. Amateur championship that year, but he did not plan to play in the Open at the club where he had been a caddie so recently. He was persuaded to send in his entry just to get the experience. The 1913 Open was expected to be an exciting one. All the leading American players were in it, but American golf had an inferiority complex long before Vardon and Ray, the top two British players, came over in 1913. They were held in awe by all. One of them would, of course, win the title, and the one who didn't would finish second.

Everything went about as expected. At the end of playing the regulation seventy-two holes, the two Britishers were in front, tied at 304. All those who had figured to press them had faded away. Ouimet had not. Nobody had paid any attention to him. Nobody outside Massachusetts had heard of him, and anyhow, amateurs weren't expected to figure in the Open. On the afternoon of the final round, the scoreboard showed that Ouimet, still out on the course, had a chance to catch them. A slim chance. He would have to play the last six holes in 22 strokes, four pars and two birdies. That was just about impossible. Inexperienced kids do not do such things under the pressure of the final round of a national championship.

Francis did not know this, so he set out to do it. He got his first birdie at the 13th and struggled for his pars on the next three holes. Now he had to save a stroke on one of the last two holes, which were among the most difficult on the course. The whole crowd had joined him now, and among them were Vardon and Ray. The tension of this golfing drama had seized them all, and only the boy who had to do it remained calm. Francis measured his 20-foot, downhill-sidehill putt on the 17th green. He stroked it firmly. The ball hit the back of the cup and dropped. As it clicked on the bottom, the staid old club heard a roar from its staid old members and witnessed such joyous antics as have rarely been duplicated. Ten minutes or so later, when the final putt dropped on the 18th green in the late-afternoon shadows of the stately old clubhouse, another terrific outburst took place. The local boy, the ex-caddie, had done it. He had made his par 4 and had tied Vardon and Ray.

Everyone forgot for the moment that the dragons were not yet slain. Francis would have to play off the tie with the great men the next day, Saturday, September 20th.

I had handled the short but exciting wire story of the event the day before, and it had been working as a ferment in me ever since. Caught by the excitement of it, I had taken a few mild liberties to make it even more dramatic than the straightforward story the wire copy told. I couldn't go too far, not knowing anything about golf, but I thought I'd added a few nice touches. I had told, I thought movingly, how the local lad from across the street had tied Harry Vardon, the greatest shotmaker in the game's history, and Ted Ray, the longest hitter ever known, at The Country Club, just about the most élite environment imaginable. This was a typically American development, and it was, in a word, tremendous. Now today, Saturday, Ouimet was playing off the tie with the celebrated Britishers, and a small miracle was taking place.

On the Saturday before this one, sports editors of the nation had looked upon golf as a pleasant recreation of the rich rather than a game whose results were important to many. Now, on this Saturday, front pages were being held up, newspaper publishers as well as sports editors were standing by for a big story to break, and papers around the country were demanding special service out of Brookline. All this, of course, I did not know then, but suddenly, as I sat musing, the phone rang with a clamor that startled me out of my reverie. It was our own small Country Club down along the bayshore. Everyone there wanted to know if there was any news and would I please call when there was. It cheered me to know that I was not alone in my local vigil.

Communications in 1913 were not as rapid or as urgent as they would become with the start of World War I a year later. I did not know how long a round of golf in a championship playoff might be expected to take, nor where exactly Brookline was. It was late afternoon when the telegraph operator, who took the stuff over the wire each day, came up the stairs, his personal telegrapher's key in a little cloth bag he carried in his hand. He was not surprised to see me because of my excitement the day before. I think he was borrowed from either the Western Union or Postal office to take what was called a "pony" or condensed report of the day's top news stories out of the Southern Bureau of the Associated Press in Atlanta. There always were these early and supplementary files on Saturday because the Sunday paper was much larger than the slim affair of weekdays.

I do not remember the operator's name although I saw him daily for many months. Everybody called him Spec, and that may be all I ever did know. He plugged his key into the connection on the table by the window where we all worked, and sat down to wait for the clicks that would tell him that the wire was open. He, too, wanted to know why I was so interested in "this here golf," but I did attempt to tell him.

By now the wait began to seem interminable. Across the alley in a room above the curio shop, someone was playing a grama-phone, its huge morning-glory horn faintly visible behind window curtains moving slowly in the sticky heat. Sousa marches came floating across endlessly. Ever since that day, whenever the name of Ouimet has come up or the 1913 Open at Brookline has been mentioned, there in the background echoing faintly I could hear "The Washington Post March" and "The Stars and Stripes Forever" followed by the monotonous announcement, "Played by the Edison Concert Band . . . Edison Rek-kord."

Spec took off his sweaty shirt, sitting bare from the waist up, and rolled himself another cigarette from the sack of Bull Durham he had placed on the table. He was very deft at it, and I observed carefully because up to then my own efforts had not been very successful. Seeing me watching the operation, he offered to teach me, but I was still a secret user of what our elders called "coffin nails." I decided to pass up an opportunity I felt I could hardly afford to waste, since this ability to roll a proper cigarette carried a certain distinction, and not many adults dared to teach a boy the art in those days. As a matter of fact, I never did learn to roll a proper cigarette. This was the period when smokers were changing over from roll-your-own to "tailor-made" under the influence of a pre–Madison Avenue national advertising campaign, and my real addiction came after experience with such then popular brands as Piedmonts, Home Runs (pack of twenty for a nickel), Picayunes, Sweet Caporals and some fancy things called Egyptian Deities.

At last, almost at evening's fall, the telegraph key began to click out its jerky cadences. Now there would be news. But it was exasperatingly long in coming. There was a long period of standing behind the operator and watching as he slowly transferred the unintelligible noises to the typewriter page. The day of the visible typewriter had not yet arrived in our shop. On this one, the keys struck upward on the concealed underside of the roller through a ribbon two inches wide, and you had to swing the whole carriage upright to see what had been written.

Spec seemed painfully slow as he tapped out endless unimportant news items. Now and then he stopped altogether to chat with the man at the other end of the wire in the jargon of Morse Code that the old operators employed when gossiping. Spec never went back to work without rolling himself another butt, which he let hang plastered to his lower lip while typing. It seemed impossible to wait any longer when at last he half-turned and said without removing the cigarette, "Here it comes now, Dateline Brookline, Mass." Then, after a few more clicks and a few more taps on the typewriter, "Your boy did it. You better go home now and get something to eat before you have to come back here."

All over the country at this moment, the wires were clicking out the incredible story, a story that would have been rejected immediately if thought up by a fiction writer. But who would dare contrive a hero who had been born across the street from the scene of his triumph, who had learned the game as a caddie on that same course?

Just a few paragraphs came to us down on the Gulf to give us some sense of the excitement and scores. Wholly inadequate, I thought. I felt personally cheated and felt that someone had misjudged the news value of the event. I was right, too. It was much bigger than that. I had been expecting a long, detailed account from Brookline, although I ought to have known better. Now I would have to wait for the New York papers to learn all about it, and that would not be before Wednesday. There was enough detail, though, for me to do a fairly long piece for the paper.

Of course, everyone knows what the news was, because it was the most dramatic story in the long history of golf. Ouimet beat Vardon and Ray by five and six strokes respectively. He was the first amateur to win the U.S. Open. The details can be found in the record books and old newspaper files. What you cannot find there is the effect of the victory, because, tremendous as it was from a competitive point of view, historically it was even more significant. The cheers from Brookline shook the country. Ouimet became a national sports hero, and he made America golf-conscious. In 1913, golf was generally regarded as the exclusive pastime of the wealthy, the aged and the British-born. Now young men everywhere, I among them, began to think about playing the new game. If an ex-caddie, a young man not much older than myself could do this, then golf could not be such an exclusive game. Ouimet's victory popularized the game, took the curse off it, so to speak, and put it on Page One.

It also moved thousands who had hardly considered playing golf before to try the game. It reached farther than that, farther than anyone could know at the time. It reached down to Atlanta and touched an eleven-year-old boy named Bobby Jones, who had also waited that Saturday afternoon for word from Brookline. The wave reached out to Texas to a couple of infants just recently born to the Hogan and Nelson families, and likewise into the Virginia hills to another infant named Samuel Jackson Snead. And it touched the lives of thousands yet unborn, such as Arnold Palmer and Jack Nicklaus. Historians, at odds on many things, are unanimous in declaring that this September Saturday in 1913 was the day when golf first caught the imagination of the American people.

And, finally, it reached into the dingy little office in De Luna Alley where I had waited for the word. Ouimet put golf on the front page of the Pensacola *Journal* all right. I saw to that, and the effect of experiencing it and putting it there after the long period of waiting would last a lifetime. If Francis were alive today, he would be more than eighty years old. He is not only dead, he has entered mythology. At Brookline in 1913, spectator golf in this country was born. That is where the game first began to be a big thing for the modern mercenaries of the multimillion-dollar tours.

Little of the future success of golf could have been imagined so far away and so long ago, but, walking home through the silent town after midnight when work was done, I think I must have had a premonition that my journalistic ambition, already set in a certain mold, could be changed. This would not be the last golf story I would handle. I was dreaming the sort of waking dreams that adolescents are forever dreaming.

Reality was the usual nightly stop at the Busy Bees Cafe where Angelo would just be taking the buns and donuts from the oven and would respond as always to a tap on the side door to the kitchen. The bun, all steaming from the oven, was fair exchange for the newspaper hot from the press, and both carried the thrill of things newly born. The smell of bread fresh from the oven has still the power to bring back the approaching dawn of the September day that was a prelude to golfing and newspaper adventures when, just lurching out of boyhood, life was all anticipation, shimmering with the promise of wonderful things, and when time was an invention of the elderly. An age was ending, the innocent period before 1914. An affluent, confident, and, in a way, complacent era in American life was about to turn into the hell of trench warfare, poison gas, and other horrors let loose.

The Greatest of Golfers:
A Tribute to the Rare Skill of Miss Joyce Wethered

BY ROBERT T. JONES, JR.

How enormous a shadow did Bobby Jones cast over the game he came to epitomize? When word of his death reached the Old Course at St. Andrews—site of the 1930 British Amateur, the first leg of his Grand Slam—the flag on the clubhouse was dropped to half staff, and all play immediately called on account of darkness. Golfer, lawyer, gentleman, legend, Jones (1902–1971) dominated the sport in several ways. On the field of play, he was certainly an icon, and remained a deity throughout his life. But Jones was no prop on a pedestal; he stayed active in the game. Instrumental in the founding of Augusta National and the Masters, he was also one of his game's most courtly writers and ambassadors. Between 1927 and 1935, he penned two instructional columns a week, which he eventually collected into the seminal volume *Bobby Jones on Golf.* He also contributed regularly to his friend Grantland Rice's *American Golfer.* This gracious recollection of his round with Joyce Wethered appeared in the magazine's pages in 1930.

A word on Wethered. If her swing was good, her focus was better. Ten years before playing with Jones, she reached the final match of the first of the many Ladies' British Open Amateur Championships she would play in. As she prepared to take what would become the crucial putt of the match on the 17th green, a train thundered by. Without so much as a pause, she holed the putt, and went on to win the match, marking the first of her five straight titles in the event.

When asked afterward whether the train had interfered with her concentration, she quickly responded—in true championship form—"What train?"

115

Ordinarily I would never take advantage of a friendly round of golf by making the play of a person, kind enough to go around with me, the subject of an article. I realize that everyone likes to play occasionally a round of golf when reputations can be forgotten, with nothing more at stake than the outcome of the match and a little friendly bantering afterwards.

Just before the British Amateur Championship at St. Andrews, Miss Joyce Wethered allowed herself to be led away from her favorite trout stream in order to play eighteen holes of golf over the Old Course in company with her brother, Roger, Dale Bourne, then recently crowned English Champion, and myself. At the time, I fully appreciated that Miss Wethered had not had a golf club in her hand for over a fortnight, and I certainly should have made no mention of the game had she not played so superbly.

We started out by arranging a four-ball match—Roger and Dale against Miss Wethered and myself—on a best and worst ball basis. I don't know why we didn't play an ordinary four-ball match, unless we fancied that the lady would be the weakest member of the four, and that in a best-ball match her ball would not count for very much. If any of us had any such idea at the start of the match, it is now quite immaterial, for there is not the slightest chance that we should admit it.

We played the Old Course from the very back, or the championship tees, and with a slight breeze blowing off the sea. Miss Wethered holed only one putt of more than five feet; took three putts rather half-heartedly from four yards at the seventeenth after the match was over, and yet she went round St. Andrews in 75. She did not miss one shot; she did not even half miss one shot; and when we finished, I could not help saying that I had never played golf with anyone, man or woman, amateur or professional, who made me feel so utterly outclassed.

It was not so much the score she made as the way she made it. Diegel, Hagen, Smith, Von Elm and several other male experts would likely have made a better score, but one would all the while have been expecting them to miss shots. It was impossible to expect that Miss Wethered would ever miss a shot—and she never did.

To describe her manner of playing is almost impossible. She stands quite close to the ball, she places the club once behind, takes one look toward the objective, and strikes. Her swing is not long—surprisingly short, indeed, when one considers the power she develops—but it is rhythmic in the last degree. She makes ample use of her wrists, and her left arm within the hitting area is firm and active. This, I think, distinguishes her swing from that of any other woman golfer, and it is the one thing that makes her the player she is.

Men are always interested in the distance which a first-class woman player can attain. Miss Wethered, of course, is not as long with any club as the good male player. Throughout the round, I found that when I hit a good one I was out in front by about twenty yards—by not so much when I failed to connect. It was surprising, though, how often on a fine championship course fine iron play by the lady could make up the difference. I kept no actual count, but I am certain that her ball was the nearest to the hole more often than any of the other three.

I have no hesitancy in saying that, accounting for the unavoidable handicap of a woman's lesser physical strength, she is the finest golfer I have ever seen.

Back to Cherry Hills

BY HERBERT WARREN WIND

Like superior athletes, superior writers have a knack for getting themselves up for the game. The better the event, the better the prose that flows from them. The 1960 U.S. Open at Cherry Hills was certainly one of the better events. In the long history of golf, it's never been matched for the mix of its high drama, the star quality of its main protagonists, and the generational clash that played out on its stage. Thankfully, Herbert Warren Wind was there to record it.

But, then, Wind always seemed to be there. Other than the few years he devoted to the launch of *Sports Illustrated,* he was a staff writer at *The New Yorker* from 1947 until his retirement in 1984. In addition to crafting elegant pieces on golf and tennis for the magazine, Wind wrote such essential golf books as *The Story of American Golf, The Complete Golfer,* and *Following Through,* and, with Ben Hogan, cowrote *Five Lessons: The Modern Fundamentals of Golf.* It remains, some 45 years later, the best-selling instructional ever.

"Back to Cherry Hills" appeared in *The New Yorker* following the 1978 U.S. Open, which Wind winds up dismissing in a single clause of a single sentence. He had much more on his mind when he returned to the site of Arnold Palmer's lone U.S. Open title. The venue led Wind on a walk down the fairways of memory lane and, with the luxury of perspective, gave him this literary mulligan on the epic occurrences of 18 years before.

On a gray Saturday in mid-September of 1913, when a continuous drizzle fell on the already rain-soaked course of The Country Club, in Brookline, Massachusetts, what was perhaps the most momentous round in the history of American golf took place: in a three-man playoff for the United States Open championship, Harry Vardon and Ted Ray, the celebrated English professionals who had come to this country for an exhibition tour, were defeated by Francis Ouimet, a twenty-year-old amateur who had grown up across the street from The Country Club and had caddied there for several years. Outside the Boston area, few people had ever heard of Ouimet, and even those who had were stunned to learn that this young fellow, the son of a gardener, had defeated the famous Englishmen and, furthermore, had come within a stroke of tying their best ball. The significant thing was that the news of his victory was read not only by the small number of well-to-do Americans who then played golf but also by millions of other Americans, of all strata, who weren't the least bit interested in golf. They read about Ouimet's victory because newspaper editors throughout the country thought that the story deserved to be run on the front page and put it there. The repercussions were enormous. A young man like Ouimet was someone whom the average American could empathize with, and thousands upon thousands proceeded to look into golf, many took it up avidly, and a large percentage of them converted their friends to their new passion. In 1913, fewer than three hundred and fifty thousand Americans played golf. Ten years later, two million did.

Ouimet's epic triumph, besides igniting the biggest boom a new game had ever enjoyed in this country, set the people who followed sports to following tournament golf. It made them particularly conscious of the United States Open, our national championship, which had been inaugurated in 1895, thirty-five years after the first British Open was played. The Open remains our most important tournament, and it is generally regarded as the most important tournament in the world—an eminence it gained toward the end of the nineteen-twenties, when it became apparent that Bobby Jones, Walter Hagen, Gene Sarazen, and the other top American golfers were clearly superior to the best players produced in Britain, the land that, ever since golf was invented, in Scotland in around the twelfth century, had been unrivalled in all aspects of the game.

While it is unarguable that no other tournament can compare with the Masters in the abundance of stirring finishes it has been blessed with, our Open has certainly not lacked for drama, despite the fact that prior to 1965 it was customary for the last two rounds of the championship to be played on the same day. (This meant that the men who were in the lead or close to it after the third, or morning, round were not necessarily grouped together in the last pairs to go out, after lunch, in the fourth round; they are so grouped now, of course, in the final round of a four-day, seventy-two-hole tournament, the standard format for a dozen years.) In any event, ever since the landmark championship of 1913 a third of our Opens have resulted in playoffs, and a good many others have come down to the last green before the outcome was decided. Fred Corcoran, the veteran golf entrepreneur who died last year, was fond of pointing out that no one had ever won the Open by sinking a long putt on the last green, but that is the only form of excitement the Open has failed to provide. For example, Tommy Armour in 1927, and Bobby Jones in 1929—to name two memorable golfers and Opens—had to hole a sizable putt on the seventy-second green to tie the leader and force a playoff (which both won, by the way). Down through the years, the championship has treated us to an endless variety of glittering stretch drives that have changed what had ap-peared to be an inevitable outcome. There was Billy Casper's great rush in 1966 at the Olympic Club, in San Francisco, in which he caught Arnold Palmer by making up seven shots on the last nine holes. The next day, Casper went on to win the playoff after again trailing Palmer at the end of the first nine, though this time by only two strokes. More recently, on the gnarled old course of the Oakmont Country Club, near Pittsburgh, Johnny Miller, who few savants felt had a chance to win when he started the fourth round six strokes behind the leaders, turned the 1973 championship inside out and won it with a closing 63—a score that seems a form of sacrilege at Oakmont, even taking into consideration that a heavy rain had made it possible for the players to shoot right for the flagstick. The course has long been notorious for its frighteningly hard-surfaced greens, which, when dry and cut short, are as slip-pery as glass to putt on.

The Open has also produced some unforgettable instances of sustained heroics, such as Ken Venturi's performance at the Congressional Country Club, outside Washington, in winning the championship in 1964—the last Open in which the field played two rounds on the final day. That day turned out to be a scorcher, the temperature climbing high into the nineties. At the end of the morning round, on which Venturi had shot a 66—four under par—despite missing tap-in putts on the seventeenth and eighteenth greens, he was only two strokes off the pace, but he had been close to collapse from the heat on the last four holes, and it was questionable whether he would be able to play the fourth round. A doctor examined him. He was allowed to continue, but the doctor walked the final eighteen holes with him, just to make sure. Venturi, who had played a succession of well-thought-out and sharply struck shots in the morning, continued his beautiful golf in the afternoon, matching par for the round and winning by the comfortable margin of four strokes. Many Open aficionados consider Venturi's Open the most thrilling since Ouimet's, and I must say that I thoroughly agree with them.

What, you ask, has brought on this nostalgic walk down the old Open fairways? Very simply, the fact that the venue of the 1978 championship, which Andy North won last month, was the Cherry Hills Country Club, on the outskirts of Denver. Cherry Hills has now been the scene of three Opens. The first of these, in 1938, was the first Open held in the Western part of the country. Ralph Guldahl ran away from the field that year, finishing six strokes ahead of the second man, Dick Metz. I missed that Open, but I was on hand in 1960, the second time Cherry Hills put on the championship—surely one of the great Opens of all time. Denver was a much smaller city then than it is now. Today, it has a National Football League team called the Broncos, which went to the last Super Bowl, and an excellent National Basketball Association team called the Nuggets, which went to the semifinals of the championship playoffs this year, and if Bowie Kuhn and Charlie Finley ever finish their squabbling, it may get a major-league baseball team, the financially beleaguered Oakland A's. But in 1960 one thought of Denver principally as the Mile High City—an old Western town slowly growing up, a town that was the home of the Brown Palace, and that offered a visitor intoxicatingly clean air, bright sunshine, and a view of the easternmost range of the Rockies. (In mid-June, Open time, the tallest peaks are still covered with snow.) In short, it retained the ambience of an earlier and vasty appealing America. Fresh in my memory are the young boys operating their lemonade stands beneath the cottonwoods and Chinese elms bordering the perimeter of the golf course. A large drink cost a dime, a small one a nickel. *O tempora! O mores! O denarii!*

Few clubs were as well organized to put on the U.S. Open as Cherry Hills was in 1960. There was, however, one unfortunate difficulty: the course was not long enough to be a bona-fide championship test. Designed by Bill Flynn, the able golf-course architect from Philadelphia, it measured 7,004 yards, but in the thin air a mile above sea level the flight of a golf ball was increased seven per cent. For example, on the seventeenth hole, a 548-yard par 5 on which the green was on an island in a large pond, Jack Nicklaus—he was still in college—flabbergasted everyone by reaching the green in a practice round with a drive and a 7-iron. It was the first nine, though, that caused most of the concern. At 3,316 yards, it was much shorter than the second nine and no match for the power-hitting pros. After walloping a big drive on most of the par-4 holes on this nine, they had just a short pitch left to the green. As it turned out, the vulnerability of this first nine accounted for the *Sturm und Drang* that took place on the final afternoon.

Up to that final round, Mike Souchak, a burly young man who had played end for Duke, had dominated the championship. On the opening day, he moved into the lead with a 68, three under par. He had used only twenty-six putts, which was remarkable, inasmuch as the greens were so dried out by the sun and afternoon winds that they had to be watered at night. On the second day, Souchak added a 67, and his 135 broke the record low total for the first thirty-six holes of the Open by three strokes. After the morning round on Saturday, the third and last day, Souchak was still out in front, but his lead was down to two strokes. It had been four strokes on the tee of the eighteenth, or fifty-fourth, hole, an exacting 468-yard par 4 on which a golfer had to hit a long drive over the lake to reach the left side of the heaving fairway. Souchak, intent on hitting a safe tee shot, shoved it much farther to the right than he had meant to, and the ball bounced out of bounds—a two-stroke penalty.

A two-stroke lead is not a four-stroke lead. Souchak's costly error had brought the field back to him and revived many hopes. One of the men whose eyes took on a new gleam was Palmer. At this stage of his career, Arnie was regarded as a fine golfer, but the admiration he inspired was much more restrained than it would later become. While he had already won three major championships—the 1954 United States Amateur and the 1958 and 1960 Masters—and was enjoying a big season, no one as yet spoke about his charisma or imitated the way he hiked up his trousers or used his method of putting from an exaggerated knock-kneed stance, but golf fans knew how strong he was and loved his aggressive tactics. In any event, at Cherry Hills he had played so-so rounds of 72, 71, and 72, which placed him seven strokes behind Souchak with eighteen holes to go, and so his name never came up at midday on Saturday when one discussed the probable challengers. Shortly before he was due on the first tee at one-forty-five to begin his final round, Palmer said to Bob Drum, an old friend of his, "I may shoot a 65 out there. What'll that do?" Drum replied, "That'll do nothing. You're too many shots back."

The first hole at Cherry Hills in 1960 was 346 yards long—a straight-away hole with an elevated tee. To make certain that no one drove the green, a stretch of the fairway just before the green had been allowed to grow up into tangled rough. On his final round, Palmer threw every last ounce of power into his opening tee shot and hit a huge drive that hopped out of this barrier of rough and onto the green, twenty feet from the pin. He missed his putt for his eagle, but his birdie did wonders for him. During his top years, Palmer's state of mind under tournament stress was different from that of most great golf champions: he really did depend to quite a large extent on the emotional lift he gained from pulling off a daring shot or holing a monstrous putt in a critical situation. Then, feeling that the ball was running for him, his confidence grew and grew, and frequently there was no stopping him. In that fourth round at Cherry Hills, buoyed up by his opening birdie, he smashed another long drive down the second, a 410-yard par 4, but he misgauged his pitch, and the ball finished on the fringe of the green, thirty-five feet from the pin. He ran his chip into the cup for a second birdie. On the third hole, a 348-yard par 4 that bent to the left, he hit another big drive and put his approach, a wedge flip, a foot from the stick. Three under par for the round so far. On the fourth, 426 yards long, he needed only a wedge for his second. He played a rather ordinary shot, but rapped in a putt of eighteen feet for his fourth consecutive birdie.

If there was any one hole on the front nine you would have picked Palmer to birdie, it was the fifth—the only par 5 on that side. It was moderately long—538 yards—but in the thin mountain air a top professional could get home with two solid shots. Palmer hurried his timing on his drive a fraction, however, and when his ball ended up in a poor lie in the matted rough on the left, he had to be satisfied with a par. The sixth hole was a somewhat tricky par 3 of 174 yards. The green sloped down from back to front, and most players tended to be cautious with their putts. Palmer's 7-iron shot left him with a sidehill putt of twenty-five feet. He hit it with evident assurance and holed it. (In recent years, when Palmer's putting has been the least dependable part of his game, some sports followers have tended to forget that during his best years he possibly made more important long putts than any other tournament golfer in history over a similar span of time.) He had five birdies in six holes now. He picked up another on the seventh, a 411-yard par 4, where he stopped a soft wedge six feet from the pin.

As Palmer stood on the tee of the eighth hole, he was surrounded by an exuberant, swelling gallery for the first time; it had taken a little while for the news of his dash to get around. He deliberated longer than usual before deciding on the club he wanted to use on that hole, a 233-yard par 3, on which the pin was set on the left side of the green, tight behind an intimidating front bunker. Perhaps the wise decision would have been to play conservatively, for the center of the green, but now, attacking with every shot, Palmer went straight for the pin with a 2-iron. He had the ball dead on line, and as he squinted at it in the distance, you could sense that he had hit precisely the shot he meant to, and that he felt it might end up close to the hole. No, the ball caught the far edge of the front bunker; he had underestimated the distance by about three feet. He played a first-rate sand shot a yard from the cup but then failed to sink the putt. Back to five under par for the round. He made the turn in 30 after parring the ninth.

At that point, it was far from a foregone conclusion that Palmer would go on to win. He had an excellent chance, of course, but muffing that short putt on the eighth had changed things. Generally, if a golfer stumbles into a bogey after a hot streak like Palmer's—birdie, birdie, birdie, birdie, par, birdie, birdie—it is not easy for him to regain his momentum, or the conviction that destiny is watching over him and has programmed a historic winning round stroke by stroke. There was another highly relevant matter to consider, too: Palmer's brilliant burst hadn't exactly scattered the field. An hour after he had started his round, no fewer than eleven other players had a reasonable crack at winning the championship. Souchak was still out in front, but Julius Boros, Dow Finsterwald, and Jack Nicklaus were only one stroke behind him, Ben Hogan was only two behind, and Jack Fleck and Jerry Barber (along with Palmer) were only three behind. Don Cherry, an amateur, still had a chance. There was no reliable news about Dutch Harrison, who had gone out early and was somewhere on the second nine, but he was rumored to have a terrific round going. Moreover, it was too early to write off two players who were among the last starters that afternoon—Billy Casper and Ted Kroll. As it turned out, Kroll began his round with a stream of figures almost as incredible as Palmer's: he birdied five, parred one, and bogeyed one of the first seven holes. Fleck had got off just as fast, with five birdies and one bogey on the first six holes.

Halfway through that final afternoon at Cherry Hills, more players were validly in the running than in any other U.S. Open I can think of. (It was impossible to know how all the contenders stood at any given moment, because there were only a few small scoreboards out on the course, and they were operated in such a haphazard manner that several of the men clustered near the lead were not even listed on some boards, and the data on those who were were often late in being posted and frequently varied from board to board. This was the only serious flaw at Cherry Hills in the staging of the Open—one of the most complex events in all of sport.) The only previous U.S. Open that could be compared with this one for sheer congestion was the 1925 Open, at the Worcester Country Club, in Massachusetts, when seven players came to the seventy-second tee with a chance to win or to tie for first. The finishing hole at Worcester, a typical Donald Ross product, was a 335-yard par 4 to a two-level plateau green guarded by an array of bunkers but in the main by a deep, gleaming pit cut directly in front of and below the green. The first of the seven contenders to tackle it was Leo Diegel, one of the most talented golfers of all time and, because of his high-strung temperament, one of the unluckiest. He needed a 4 for a total of 292. He took an 8. He was followed by Johnny Farrell. Farrell's approach ended up a fair distance from the pin, set on the lower level of the green, not far from the commanding front bunker. He two-putted for his 4. This gave Farrell a total of 292 and made him what most sportscasters now call "the leader in the clubhouse." In the good old days of 1925, he was probably referred to more sensibly as the golfer who had so far brought in the lowest seventy-two-hole score. Gene Sarazen came next. He got his par 4, but he had needed a 3 for 292. Then came Bobby Jones. A 4 would give him a total of 291 and the lead. He was on nicely in two and down nicely in two for his par. Shortly afterward, Willie Macfarlane came to the eighteenth. A tall, slim, scholarly-looking Scot from Aberdeen, Macfarlane could tie Jones if he finished with a par. Macfarlane's approach ended on the upper level of the green, but, fortunately for him, his playing partner, Francis Gallett, was a few inches outside him. Macfarlane, with the advantage of being able to watch Gallett putt first, gained a good idea of the speed and break of the green. Gallett had gone yards by, but Macfarlane lagged his approach putt a foot short of the hole and made his par to go into a tie with Jones. Two contenders later came to the eighteenth, each with a chance to join Jones and Macfarlane at the top if he could come up with a birdie 3. The first was Francis Ouimet. He had to be satisfied with a 4. (To protect himself from the wicked sun, Ouimet wore an Indian topee, and, as further protection, had placed a large leaf of lettuce inside it on top of his head—all this on the advice of a friend who had spent a few weeks east of Suez.) The second was Walter Hagen. A great short-iron player, Hagen tried to feather a delicate pitch inches over the front bunker to give himself a reasonable crack at the birdie he had to get. His pitch, which looked as if it might be just what he wanted, caught the high face of the bunker. In their playoff the next day, Jones and Macfarlane were tied after eighteen holes, so another round was ordained for the afternoon. Trailing by four strokes after nine holes, Macfarlane won by coming home in 33. He had two 2s on the two par 3s, and that did it.

Back to Cherry Hills and the 1960 Open. As was perhaps inevitable with so many players bunched so tightly, when things started to pop it was impossible to keep up with them. At four o'clock, Souchak and two challengers were tied for the lead at five under par for the tournament. Only minutes later, after Souchak had bogeyed the ninth, he lost his share of the lead and was never again in the battle. At about ten minutes after four, Nicklaus, all of twenty years old, was out in front by himself, five under par for the tournament, after going out in 32 and then starting back with three well-played pars. Ten minutes later, after taking three putts from ten feet on the thirteenth, Nicklaus had fallen back to four under and into a triple tie with Boros, playing a hole behind him, and Palmer, two holes behind him. On the fourteenth green, with a difficult hogback to cross, Nicklaus again three-putted, surrendering the lead to Boros and Palmer, and slipping back into a tie for second with his playing partner, Hogan, a slightly older man, two months short of turning forty-eight. There is little question that one of the elements that made the 1960 Open a championship to savor was that Hogan, the finest golfer of his time, and Palmer and Nicklaus, the finest of theirs, all had something to say about the winning and losing of it. They are to be cherished, these occasions when circumstance contrives for the graying heroes of a departing era to be locked in combat with the bright-faced young men who are moving up to take their places. The 1920 Open, at Inverness, in Toledo, had been one of those rare championships. Jones and Sarazen, both eighteen, and Diegel, a little older, had made their débuts in the big event that year, and Vardon, who was fifty—an old fifty—had come over from England for a final shot at our Open, which he had won way back in 1900. Had a severe storm off Lake Erie not swept over the course when Vardon was playing the last seven holes, he might well have won at Inverness, but the storm was too much for him, and he finished in a tie for second, a stroke behind his countryman Ray. Ray was forty-three, incidentally—the oldest player ever to win our Open.

Throughout the long, enervating double round on Saturday at Cherry Hills in 1960, Hogan, enveloped in his customary cocoon of concentration, had produced immaculate golf. When, only one stroke off the lead, he walked onto the tee of the fifteenth (or sixty-ninth) hole, a 196-yard par 3, he had hit the green on each of the thirty-two holes he had played that day in the regulation stroke. On the fifteenth, he made it thirty-three straight holes, whistling a 3-iron twenty feet past the pin. Had he been able to make just a few of the many holeable putts that his fastidious iron play had set up, he would have been out in front by several shots, but his putting stroke was no longer what it once was, and he had got down only one putt of any length all day. Here on the fifteenth, his lips set in that familiar half smile, he rolled in his twenty-footer for a 2. Now, if one could trust the information arriving via the grapevine, Hogan was tied for the lead. On the sixteenth, a medium-length par 4, he had a twelve-foot putt for his birdie but missed it. Still, he was in splendid shape as he came walking down the seventeenth, the 548-yard par 5 with the green on a small island that is separated from the fairway by about twenty feet of water. Two of the three contenders playing behind him had fallen off the pace: Boros had dropped a couple of strokes by finding bunkers on two holes, and Fleck had dropped a couple because of some errors in the green area. The only player holding up was Palmer; thus far on the in-nine he had collected one more birdie and, for the rest, a string of pars. However, it should be repeated that out on the course at this point in the late afternoon reliable information on the standing of the leaders was not readily available.

On the seventeenth, a light breeze was blowing against the golfers, and both Hogan and Nicklaus laid up short of the water with their second shots. Hogan's ball finished on the left side of the fairway, about fifty-five yards from the pin, which was positioned in the front right-hand corner of the green, some fifteen feet from the bank at the edge of the water. According to the reports that reached Hogan and Nicklaus via the walkie-talkie operator accompanying their group, several players behind them were still in the hunt. Since he felt that one of them would almost certainly birdie the seventeenth, Hogan, who never gambled in a tight situation, decided that this time he had to. The picture is as clear in my mind as if it were yesterday—Hogan getting the feel of his wedge in his hands as he studied the strip of water dividing the fairway and the green, only too well aware that in order to stop the ball close to the pin he would have to try to carry the water hazard by just two or three feet, since the surface of that corner of the green was extremely hard and a player could not count on getting any backspin on his pitch regardless of the precision with which he made contact with the ball. Hogan laid back the face of his wedge and, cutting crisply under the ball, sent up a soft, spinning pitch that had perfect line and looked to have perfect length. It was a foot too short. There was a gasp from the gallery as the ball slapped against the bank before the green and slid back into the water. Hogan subsequently exploded it out of the hazard and two-putted for a 6. Nicklaus, who had played superlatively well and who ultimately finished second, remembers glancing over at Hogan after he had failed by inches to bring off that crucial pitch and being struck by the instant change in Hogan's demeanor: he looked utterly drained. Hogan finished with a 7 on the home hole, hooking his first drive into the lake and finally taking three to get down from the edge of the green. In retrospect, this proved to be Hogan's last serious challenge to win the Open for a fifth time.

Palmer, as you will remember, was playing about two holes behind Hogan and Nicklaus. When he arrived at the seventeenth, he knew exactly what had happened and what he had to do: pars on the last two holes would win for him. On the seventeenth, he laid up short of the water with his second and made sure of his par 5. On the eighteenth, that tough par 4, he pulled his 4-iron approach slightly, a yard or two off the green, but then played a pretty running chip about four feet below the cup. He knocked the putt into the center of the hole and in almost the same motion, unleashing all his feeling, scaled his visor jubilantly across the green. His score for the round—30 out and 35 back, for a total of 65—was the lowest that had ever been shot by an Open winner on the last round. It gave him a total of 280, two strokes lower than Nicklaus's.

Day of Glory for a Golden Oldie

BY RICK REILLY

The keeper of *Sports Illustrated*'s back-page column, Rick Reilly possesses an undeniably facile short game, but he was born to go long. As entertaining, clever, witty, and, at times, irate as his rants and raves at the end of each week's issue can be, it's the perceptiveness and bravura wordsmithing that he displays in his feature pieces that best exhibit why he's considered one of the best sportswriters of our time. If his columns have a way of poking readers in the ribs, the longer stories—this stunning chronicle of Jack Nicklaus's sixth victory at Augusta, remarkably penned on tight deadline is certainly one—have a penchant for taking our breath away.

April 21, 1986—That arm. Who could forget that arm? In the roar of roars at the 18th green, from behind a Masters scoreboard glittering with the names of golf's power brokers—BALLESTEROS and WATSON and LANGER and KITE—under the sign that said No. 18, beside the huge black letters that read NICKLAUS, next to a red 9, came the arm that had put that number there, the arm that seconds before had placed a red 8 next to NORMAN, and that arm was pumping furiously.

No head, no body, no shoulder, just an arm belonging to the leaderboard man, pumping and pumping for pure, wallowing joy. To hell with employee objectivity. Jack Nicklaus had just won the Masters, once again, and that arm just couldn't help itself. If it was Old St. Nick who had delivered the goodies; if it was the Ancient One who had posted that birdie at 17, then parred 18, while Greg Norman had taken out his Fore!-iron and mailed the gallery a souvenir on the same hole; if it was the Olden Bear who had mystically come from five shots and a couple of decades back to hijack the Masters golf tournament, then it was that arm behind the scoreboard that was telling us what it meant.

Can't you see? That red 9 set off an avalanche of history. Jack Nicklaus, a 46-year-old antique, had won his 20th major golf championship, his first green jacket in 11 years, his sixth over three decades and all in this, the 50th, and arguably the best, Masters.

How complete, how whole this was for Nicklaus. Hadn't he been duped out of that 20th long ago? Hadn't Tom Watson's chip taken the U.S. Open from him at Pebble Beach in 1982 and broken his spirit? How many times had he led a major only to have his pocket picked at the end? Now the spikes were on the other foot. Here was Nicklaus, in one swell swoop, reaching down from another era and snatching a major championship from the reigning czars of this one. It is a trick no other golf god has pulled, not Palmer or Hogan or Snead or Sarazen. Nicklaus had beaten young men at a young man's game on young men's greens and beaten them when they were at their youthful best. As Tom Kite, destiny's orphan, put it, "I hit nearly every shot the way I dreamed about it today. But that's the strange thing about golf. You don't have any control about what your opponent does."

And just in the Nicklaus of time, too. Who else but Jack could save us from the woeful, doleful bowl full of American Express (do-you-know-me?) golf winners of late? And who else could play John Wayne, riding in to rescue the Yanks from golf's rampaging foreign legion: the dashingly handsome Seve Ballesteros of Spain; the stone-faced Bernhard Langer of West Germany; Australia's Norman, he of the colossal swing and larger-still reputation, more unfulfilled now than ever; and Zimbabwean–South African–Floridian Nick Price, who on Saturday broke the course record that had gone unsurpassed for 46 years, then on Sunday recoiled in the giant shadow of what he had done.

Here had come Nicklaus, an American legend still under warranty, armed with a putter the size of a Hoover attachment, denting the back of Augusta's holes with 25-foot putts at an age when most guys are afraid to take the putter back. Here had come Nicklaus, sending such a deluge of decibels into the Georgia air that lakes rippled and azaleas blushed; starting such a ruckus that grown men climbed trees, children rode on shoulders, concession-stand operators abandoned their posts, all just to tear off a swatch of history. Was that Jack in the checked pants and yellow shirt? Hmmmm. Yellow goes nice with green, doesn't it, Jack? You devil.

Maybe that was it. Maybe Nicklaus had drawn up a contract with Lucifer for one last major, for that slippery 20th that had eluded him since 1980, for a sixth green blazer. In exchange, Nicklaus would do pro-ams in Hades the rest of his days.

What else could explain it? How else to explain the guy in 160th place on the money list, just one spot behind Don Halldorson, winning the Masters? How else to explain a man who hadn't won in two years charging back the last day, going seven under for the final 10 holes, sculpting a 30 that tied the Masters record for the back nine—winding up with a sporty 65 as he roared past eight players and won? This is a guy who missed the cut at the Honda, for the love of Hogan. In fact, Nicklaus missed the cut in three of seven tournaments this year and withdrew from a fourth. Of the ones he finished, his most impressive showing was a tie for 39th at the Hawaiian Open, which didn't exactly throw a scare into Corey Pavin, who won. The $114,000 for winning the Masters means he's up to $148,404 for the year. Nicklaus goes through more than that in limo tips.

The man is older than Pete Rose, for crying out loud. He has played in more Masters (28) than Pavin has lived years (26). When Nicklaus won his first Masters, in 1963, Norman was eight years old, Ballesteros and Langer five. Nicklaus either signed his soul away or is angling for an endorsement contract with Efferdent.

"I read in the Atlanta paper this week that 46-year-olds don't win Masters," said Nicklaus. "I kind of agreed. I got to thinking. Hmmm. Done, through, washed up. And I sizzled for a while. But I said to myself, I'm not going to quit now, playing the way I'm playing. I've played too well, too long to let a shorter period of bad golf be my last."

More remarkable in all this comeback talk was the fact that rumors were flying that Nicklaus had been missing some serious greens, and not just the kind you take a Toro to. "My company was a mess," Nicklaus says.

In an effort to improve the fortunes of his own company, Golden Bear International, Nicklaus let the contract of his chief executive officer, Chuck Perry, lapse seven months ago and assumed day-to-day control of the business himself. "Chuck worked very hard for me," says Nicklaus, "but he wanted to build an empire. He was sending out p.r. releases talking about a $300 million empire and all that stuff. But I don't want an empire. What am I going to do with an empire? I've got five kids, a beautiful wife and I'm hoping on some grandkids. That's what I care about."

Nicklaus admits that he has been distracted by business worries, in particular about a couple of his many golf-course and real-estate deals. But he says he is not in a financial crunch, which makes it just a coincidence that he recently signed as a spokesman for Nabisco Brands and is in negotiation with ABC-TV to appear on golf specials for five years. "The ABC contract is with the lawyers right now," Nicklaus says.

With his business dealings weighing heavily on his shoulders, to say nothing of his checkbook, it was no wonder he was floundering on the golf course. His irons and woods were still Jack Be Nimble, but his putter had been pure Tip O'Neill. Take Thursday's opening round, for instance. He had 11 putts inside 15 feet and made one. On Sunday's front nine he missed two four-footers. "If I could just putt," he said Friday, "I might just scare somebody. Maybe me."

But that seemed fanciful, and it wasn't just newspaper writers typing him off. CBS analyst Ken Venturi told *USA Today,* "Jack's got to start thinking about when it is time to retire."

After all, who could take Nicklaus seriously after his opening rounds of 74 and 71? Besides, by Saturday, the leader board was doubly stocked with people you had actually heard of. One was a certain swashbuckling Spaniard who has been out of work much of this year, what with his father's recent death and his sword-fighting with PGA Tour commissioner Deane Beman. Coming into the Masters, Ballesteros had played only nine competitive rounds in all and had made precious little money. "Ninety dollars," he joked. "All on practice-round bets with [Ben] Crenshaw and [Gary] Player."

Still, Ballesteros's rapier hardly looked rusty, and when he opened with a convincing 71–68 and a one-shot lead, nobody could make him less than the favorite for his third coat. "They ought to name this place after him," said Price. "He hits it so long and so high and draws it so well and is so imaginative around the greens that I don't think he'll ever finish out of the top five here."

Price's game isn't all that ill-fitting, either. On a windless Saturday that Watson said left the course as "defenseless as I've ever seen it," Price's 63 was a course record, a Jackson Pollock splash of birdies—nine in a series of 12 holes—that broke the course record of 64, set in 1940 by Lloyd Mangrum and equaled by Nicklaus and four others. That left him at five under. And when Seve got heavy on Saturday, turning a one-shot lead at 17 into a one-shot deficit by the time he hit the clubhouse, Price found himself tied with Ballesteros, Langer and Donnie Hammond, one shot behind Norman.

Everybody genuflect. It's Sunday morning in the cathedral of golf, and the high priests are all here. Norman leading, with Price, Langer, Ballesteros, Watson, Tommy Nakajima of Japan and Kite all within two shots, not to mention an altar boy, Hammond. Nicklaus, with a Saturday 69 ("The first time I've broken 70 since I can't remember when," he said), was looking surprised but quite harmless at four back.

"My son Steve called me at the house we're renting this morning," Nicklaus said, "and he asked me, 'Well, Pop, what's it going to take?' And I said, 'Sixty-six will tie and 65 will win.' And he said, 'Well, go ahead and do it.' "

But as Sunday's round began, Nicklaus looked as if he was going to keep on doing what he had been doing, which was knocking the ball tight and putting loose. He missed four-footers at the 4th and the 6th, and when he got to the 9th tee, he was right where he started—two under. He was also five shots behind Norman.

Then, suddenly, all heaven broke loose.

Playing two groups ahead of Ballesteros and Kite, four ahead of Price and Norman, Nicklaus finally got a birdie putt to drop, an 11-footer. Four shots back.

At the 10th, he birdied from 25 feet, which should have put him three back, except for an odd set of goings-on at No. 8, where both Kite and Ballesteros had left the hole without ever pulling their putters. Kite had holed a wedge from 81 yards for an eagle, followed by Ballesteros from 40 for another eagle. Not only did that speed up play considerably, but it also kept Nicklaus four back of the leader, now Ballesteros.

But when Ballesteros bogeyed No. 9 and Nicklaus answered with a birdie at the portal to Amen Corner, No. 11, Augusta National began to overheat like a $99 Impala. Two back.

Then Nicklaus did something that got him cooking. He made a bogey 4 at the 12th hole. Three back.

"I don't know why, but it really got me going," he said, "I knew I couldn't play defensive with the rest of the course. I knew I needed to be aggressive coming in."

On to the par-5 13th, the Curtis Strange Memorial Hole, where the Masters is often lost and rarely won and where Nicklaus bent a three-wood so precariously close to the woods that his part-time caddie and full-time son, Jackie, thought he had put it in the creek on the left-hand side. "Shots like that are a little too much for a 24-year-old heart, Dad," he told him. Dad hit a 210-yard three-iron over Rae's Creek and to within 30 feet, then two-putted for birdie. Two back.

Now it was Ballesteros's turn at 13, only he did it better, letting a six-iron drift lazily in left to right and sinking an eight-footer, his second eagle of the day and third of the tournament. At this rate, with the par-5 15th still to come, the Spaniard looked as if he could radio ahead with his sleeve length.

Nicklaus was four behind him, two back of Kite. See you at the awards stand, Seve.

Desperate, at the 15th, Nicklaus let loose a mammoth drive, 298 yards, so big it surprised even him. He had changed his swing (less hands) and his diet (more food). He had gone on the Eat to Win Diet and lost. "I was down to 170 pounds and I realized I couldn't play golf at 170," he said. He's up to 190 and hitting it farther than ever. Fat Jack is truly back.

With 202 yards to go at 15 and the tournament in the balance, Nicklaus turned to Jackie and said, "You think a three would go very far here?" To which Jackie said, "let's see it."

Obligingly, Nicklaus hit his four-iron to 12 feet and made the eagle putt for exactly that—a three. The crowd's yelp was downright frightening. Two back.

As Nicklaus walked from the 15th green to the 16th tee, one had the odd feeling of being indoors at, say, an overtime Kentucky basketball game, yet all the while being outdoors. That's loud.

And wild. Six-figure executives were slapping high fives. Women in $400 dresses were sprinting ahead to get a vantage point. "He's hot! He's hot! He's hot!" one man kept shrieking, perhaps about to ignite himself.

"The noise was deafening," said Nicklaus, "I couldn't hear anything. I mean, nothing! I wasn't trying to think about the leader board. All I knew was that I was putting the ball on the green and making birdies and I was going to keep doing it."

As Ballesteros was walking up the 15th fairway after a King Kong–like drive, Nicklaus was pulling out a five-iron at the par-3 16th. "I nailed it," he said. But he couldn't see it. "I could hear the gallery at the green starting to rumble and I said, 'Oops, I've hit it close.' "

Oops, he had come within inches of a hole in one, the ball skittering three feet by the pin. The eruption from the gallery may have been the most resounding in Masters history, next to, of course, the one that greeted the putt that came next. One back.

What does one feel like when all around you, a golf course, a state, a country, are coming unglued and you are the only person keeping them from imploding entirely? Ballesteros surely found out as he stood over his four-iron, 200 yards from the 15th green, his ears ringing. What he felt like when he hit it is unknown since he was off the Augusta property within minutes of the finish of his round. But to watch your Masters chances go kerplunk in green-dyed water as his did cannot be good for your est training.

"He had an awkward lie up on a knob, but he hit his last few iron shots heavy," Kite said. "It was a tough situation: the lie, the circumstances, what Nicklaus was doing, the noise. It was so noisy you couldn't even hear each other."

"I wasn't under pressure," Ballesteros said on Monday. "It's just that I hit too easy a swing with a four-iron. I should have hit a hard five. I played very good. Just one bad shot, that's all."

Now Nicklaus had reeled in Ballesteros but not Kite, who would birdie 15. That made it a three-way tie at eight under par. Meanwhile, Norman had quickly recovered from a double bogey at 10 and was sitting two back.

Nicklaus tried to get ready to drive at the par-4 17th but had a small problem. "I kept getting tears in my eyes," he said. "It happened to me once at Baltusrol. But here, it happened four or five times. I had to say to myself, Hey, you've got some golf left to play."

After driving into the left rough he hit a 125-yard pitching wedge to 11 feet. He drained the putt. "Dead center." Nicklaus leads. One up over Ballesteros and Kite.

Moments later, Ballesteros, shaken, three-putted at 17 for bogey, but Kite made par from the back of the green and Norman was stormin', too, making birdies at 15 and 16. Still one up, now over Kite and Norman.

Eighteen surrendered without incident for Nicklaus. He hit onto the front of the tiered green, almost precisely where the pin traditionally has been set for the final round. This year, the green had been redesigned, and the pin was now set on the back level. He nearly holed out from 40 feet, dropped it in for the par, then hugged Jackie.

"I was getting choked up with all the people cheering on every hole. I was so proud of him," Jackie said. "Finally, when he putted out on 18 I told him, 'Dad, I loved seeing you play today. It was the thrill of my lifetime. I mean, that was awesome.' "

Father and son walked arm in arm to the scorer's tent and then to the Bob Jones cabin to wait and see.

What they saw first was Kite at 18 lining up a 12-foot putt for birdie and a tie. Would Kite, so long denied, finally have a chance at a major?

"I made that putt," said Kite. "It just didn't go in. Honest to God . . . I made it so many times in the practice rounds—seven or eight times—and it never broke left once." It broke left. Still one up.

Now the only obstacle between Nicklaus and perhaps his most re-markable major of all was Norman.

"We heard the roar [for Nicklaus] on 15 and then another roar and another," Norman recalled. "By that time, Nicky [Price] and I were back there with about 50 people following us. So I said to Nicky, 'Let's do something to wake these people up.' "

Out of an impossible divot lie on 17, Norman somehow made a pitch-and-run shot over a hill that stopped 12 feet from the hole, then sank the putt. Tie. Nine under par.

With pandemonium all around him, Norman chose to hit a three-wood from the 18th tee. The shot was fine and straight, except that it left him holding his four-iron, which in Norman's hands lately works about like a waffle iron. It was the four-iron he had hit into the gallery at 10 to set up the double bogey.

He sliced it this time into the gallery ringing the 18th green, and couldn't get up and down for par, his 16-footer missing left. "I just basically spun out and pushed it to the right," Norman explained. "I was trying to hit it too hard and too high. . . . I was going for the flag. I was going for the birdie and the win. It was the first time all week I let my ego get the best of me."

Your usual, Jack, 42 regular?

"This," said Nicklaus in triumph, "was maybe as fine a round of golf as I've ever played."

He drove down Magnolia Lane and out the iron gates in green for a preposterous sixth time. He had won at Augusta in 1963, when Sam Snead finished two strokes back, and '65, '66, '72, '75 and now, '86. That's a 23-year span between his first and last fitting. His original jacket was a 44 long. "It fits me like a tent," he said. "I wore [New York Governor] Tom Dewey's jacket for years, and finally I had my own jacket made."

His record of longevity and dominance is unequaled. And that includes his victories in five PGA Championships (1963, '71, '73, '75, '80), four U.S. Opens ('62, '67, '72, '80), three British Opens ('66, '70, '78) and two U.S. Amateurs ('59 and '61). He has now won three majors in his 40s, which is another first.

All of which says, truly, once and for all, that if there ever was a better golfer than Jack William Nicklaus, then Woody Allen can dunk.

"I finally found that guy I used to know on the golf course," Nicklaus told his wife, Barbara. "It was me."

So welcome back.

The Carry

BY GEORGE PLIMPTON

George Plimpton's most famous raid into the world of participatory journalism was, of course, *Paper Lion,* his stunning report, from the mid-'60s, on his short, preseason exploits as a last-string quarterback for the Detroit Lions. He teed it up on the links soon after; his month of playing in PGA pro-ams resulted in his book *The Bogey Man.* Here, paired with professional Bob Bruno in what was then the Crosby Clambake—now the more prosaic AT&T Pebble Beach National Pro-Am—Plimpton is about to have a whack at one of golf's most breathtaking challenges.

The 16th at Cypress Point is one of the famous golf holes of the world, certainly one of the most difficult and demanding par 3's. In the 1952 Crosby the average score of the entire field on the hole was 5, an average bolstered by Lawson Little getting a 14 and Henry Ransom an 11. Ben Hogan got a 7. The golfer stands on a small elevated tee facing the Pacific Ocean that boils in below on the rocks, its swells laced with long strands of kelp. Occasionally, a sea lion can be seen lolling about, turning lazily, a flipper up, like a log in a slow current. It would be a clear shot to the horizon if it weren't for a promontory that hooks around from the golfer's left. On the end of the promontory, circled by ice plant, is the green, a 210-yard carry across the water.

The green in shallow, with some traps behind, and then the ice plant, and beyond that, ready to receive a shot hit a touch too powerfully, the Pacific Ocean. There is a relatively safe approach to the 16th, which is to aim to the left of the green and carry a shot 125 yards or so across the water onto the wide saddle of the promontory. A lonely storm-bent tree stands in the fairway, and it is in its vicinity that one drops one's first shot. From there the golfer must chip to the green and sink his putt to make his par.

Many players are critical of the 16th at Cypress. Gardner Dickinson told me that he thought it was no sort of golf hole at all. His point was that risking a direct carry to the green, particularly if any sort of wind was blowing in the golfer's face, was ill-advised and "cotton-pickin' stupid," and the sensible golfer was penalized for the shot he *should* make—that is to say, to the fairway on the saddle of the promontory, from where he must get down in two for his par. The chances of birdieing the hole playing it that way are, of course, almost nil. Dickinson himself would not try the long shot. (One's whole daily score could be affected; Jerry Barber got a 10 on the hole the year that he was PGA champion.) He always chose the safer route, cutting across as much ocean as he dared with an iron, aiming for the promontory saddle, all the while mumbling and carrying on and pinching up his face in disgust as if the kelp surging back and forth below him in the sea were exuding a strong odor.

The spectators loved the hole, though. They gathered on the wooded bluff above the tee, some perched on the wide cypress branches, squat-shaped, like night herons. When a player motioned—somewhat theatrically, one always felt—to his caddy for a wood, and the caddy, warming to the drama, removed the woolen cover with a flourish, there would be a stirring in the trees, like a rookery at dawn, and a stretching forward, since the spectators up there knew the golfer was going to "go for it."

And it was a wonderful thing to hear the click of the club and see the ball soar off over the ocean—as senseless an act, at first glance, as watching someone drive a ball off the stern of a transatlantic liner—the ball rising up against the wind currents and high above the line of the horizon beyond. Then, with its descent, one realized the distant green had become available, until it was a question of *distance*—whether the ball would flash briefly against the cliffs that fronted the green and plummet into the ocean, or whether the green itself would suddenly be pocked by the whiteness of the ball, the feat done, accented by a roar and clatter rising out of the trees behind the tee.

Here was the distinction of this ocean hole at Cypress: it epitomized the feat of golf—excessively, Dickinson would say—namely, the hitting of a distant target with accuracy, a shot so demanding that it was either successful or, with the ocean circling the hole on three sides, emphatically a disaster.

When our foursome reached the 16th tee the wind was slight. Amid a stir of excitement, Bob Bruno went for the green with a wood. He made one of his best shots of the day, it seemed to me, and behind us the cries came out of the treetops. Bruno wasn't so sure. The ball had landed on an area of the green that we couldn't see from the tee. He thought he had "come off" the ball somewhat, a bit "fat," he thought, and that as a result the shot might have caught the ice plant. Not being at all convinced that the hole was secure for our team, he suggested that I play my shot safe and short for the promontory and, done with his advice, he walked away and stood looking moodily out at the sea. I think I would have played it that way in any case. A 210-yard carry into that slight wind would have created sufficient pressure that I would have missed the shot in some way.

I motioned for a wood, a three wood, a club I had been feeling comfortable with that day, and again there was a hum of expectation and interest among the spectators. Abe, my caddy, coming forward with the golf bag, said, "You going for it? You'll be needing a driver. Maybe *two* drivers."

He was speaking loudly enough for some of the spectators to overhear.

"I'll take the wood, Abe," I insisted.

I reached for the wood and handed him back the woolen cover.

"You're up," Bruno said from the edge of the tee, still staring out to sea. He was impatient to check the lie of his ball.

I set the ball on the tee and did what I had been intending to do all along—I hit a good easy wood across the short neck of water to the saddle, just what Dickinson would have done, except he would have used a five iron, possibly a six, but if it took me a wood to feel comfortable and get the ball there, well, that was wise golf, too.

There was an odd stir and fidget in the trees and in the crowd around the tee. I could imagine an elderly man, sitting on a golfing stick, saying impetuously and sharply: "You see that? That big fellow takes out a wood. He's going for it. So what does he do but hit a tiny little wood over yonder . . . Shortest wood I ever saw without it being topped."

The thing to do was hurry off the tee as quickly as one could.

They Might Be Giants

BY JOHN PAUL NEWPORT

One of the miracles of golf is the way the game constantly kills us with hope. Some years after John Paul Newport rivetingly captured the flavor of golf's minor leagues for *Men's Journal* in the piece that follows, he went out, in his mid-30s with a 3-handicap, to test his own game by playing the circuit and trying to qualify for the tour. He chronicles his adventures—and misadventures—in *The Fine Green Line,* a title that refers to the abstract, invisible, and uncrossable marker that keeps golf's aristocracy on one side and those who can post the occasional 69—or better, even—on the other.

The hardest-working man on the Space Coast Tour is Gene Jones, Jr., a.k.a. Gene the Machine. Granted, that's not saying an awful lot, since many of Jones's peers, especially the youngsters, spend as much time honing their personalities as honing their games. Unlike on the PGA Tour, where wit and colorful behavior are relics of the past, in bush-league professional golf personality counts for a lot. That's because most of the players are just giving the pro game a shot for a few years before moving on to their true life's work: conducting golf seminars for the plaid-pants crowd at backwater country clubs or selling universal life-insurance products for Prudential.

Jones is like the nerd in your college lit class who always read every assignment. After a tournament round, he will pound balls at a driving range, go home to videotape his swing in the search for tiny flaws and then practice putting and chipping for an hour or two. On days when the Space Coast Tour doesn't stage an event, he finds another tournament to enter. On Sundays he practices some more and then usually takes his ten-year-old daughter, Amberly, out for a round of golf. What drives Jones to pursue golf so maniacally is a matter of considerable speculation among his fellow competitors. But obviously, he's very serious about the game.

I first encountered him as I was standing near the scoreboard during the first round of the DeBary Plantation tournament, north of Orlando, last fall. Around me, young Space Coast cadets were offering preposterous excuses for why they had scored so poorly. "I'd have shot a sixty-eight if I hadn't triple-bogeyed number eight," a curly-haired fellow from Colorado assured me, explaining his round of 77. Another player, this one from Georgia, pointed toward the neat, handwritten row of 4s, 6s and 7s that appeared after his name on the scoreboard and complained, "How could someone as studly as me have shot a dip-shit round like that?" He didn't seem overly upset, however, as he lounged in his golf cart, feet on the dash, guzzling a Coors. He was young and good-looking, he had a rich sponsor somewhere paying all his bills, and there would always be tomorrow.

This was when Jones drove up, making the turn after nine holes of play, his eyes scanning the scoreboard like antiaircraft sensors. At thirty-five, he is a short, sturdy-looking man, with blond hair, plump cheeks and a forlorn, distracted air. In baggy black shorts, a Nike cap and saddle-oxford golf shoes, he looked more like a schoolboy than the tour's leading money winner. Nevertheless, his arrival silenced the cadets.

"What's the low score?" he asked in a taut North Carolina accent.

The question was precisely worded. Not "Who's in the lead?" because Jones didn't care about the person attached to the score. Not "What's in the money?" because finishing high enough to earn a check is not the issue; Jones almost always does. Rather, simply, "What's the low score?" What number precisely did he have to beat to take the lead?

"Uh, three under, Gene," someone said.

"Thanks," Jones replied and gunned the cart up the path. No one dared ask after his score, which happened to be even par.

After a pause, the banter resumed. "No one can play well *all* the time," my pal with the Coors continued in defense of his dip-shit round. But then he added, with a none-too-friendly edge in his voice, "Unless your name is frigging Gene the Machine."

The Spalding Space Coast Tour is golf's version of Bull Durham baseball. Most of the players are in their twenties, and every one thinks he is on the brink of

Big Tour stardom. Pitted against them is a handful of cagey veterans and downward-spiraling former tour pros with names like Tony Cerda and Doug Weaver. The latter group almost always cleans up.

The biggest difference between Bull Durham–style minor-league baseball and the Space Coast Tour is that in baseball the players earn a living. On the Space Coast Tour, which operates most of the year except for the hot summer months, probably fewer than a dozen golfers actually support themselves out of winnings. The rest, mostly the young guys, hit up Mom and Dad for cash transfusions, wangle financial-sponsorship deals from wealthy sportsmen who might otherwise back a racehorse, hustle amateurs at the approximately 140 Orlando-area golf courses or work part time.

The Space Coast Tour is essentially an open-air golf casino: Players put down their bets in the form of $300 to $350 entry fees, and the top few finishers walk off with most of the loot. The Spalding Company, hoping to curry favor with the club professionals of tomorrow, kicks in $100,000 a year to the kitty. And the house—in the person of J. C. Goosie, sixty-four, sole owner and proprietor—sweeps away 12 percent after course expenses. Last year the total purse was about $1.2 million, compared with more than $54 million on the PGA Tour.

"Our operation is simple," Goosie told me over the telephone. (He doesn't show up at Space Coast events when he qualifies for tournaments on the Senior PGA Tour.) "We want ex–college players to come down here and spend about sixteen thousand dollars to seventeen thousand dollars—that's for everything, entry fees, living expenses, everything—and play for a year. If a guy's good, he's gonna make twelve or thirteen thousand dollars of that back. If he's very good, he may break even. So for fifteen to thirty cents on the dollar, next to nothing, he's gonna get experience he can't buy nowhere else."

J. C. Goosie invented the minitour concept twenty years ago, basically because he and his pals who couldn't get on the regular tour needed a place to play. The idea caught on. Over the years quite a few Space Coast alums have made names for themselves on the PGA, including stars like Paul Azinger and Craig Stadler. Recently, however, the best subtour talent has gravitated to the PGA Tour–sponsored Nike Tour (formerly the Ben Hogan Tour) and the four-year-old T. C. Jordan Tour. That leaves Goosie and a few other upstart minitours, like the Golden State Golf Tour, in California, defending the honor of single-A golf.

Conditions are what you'd expect: spiky greens, sprinkler systems that occasionally burst to life in the middle of a player's backswing, passing motorists yelling "Fore!" as a joke and no sign of a gallery anywhere. The absence of fans has advantages: Players feel free to relieve themselves in the woods whenever they like and to indulge in the same colorful expletives that golfers everywhere enjoy. The day-to-day manager of the Space Coast Tour is a former pro and real estate agent named Bobby Simpson, who has an odd way of holding his head, like a turtle peeking out of its shell. The starter is an affable Cajun nicknamed Crow, who spends the balance of his week at the dog track. And the rules officials include retired old pros who disperse around the course in golf carts and can often be spotted snoozing.

Such is the sweet narcotic bliss of golf, however, that nobody seems to mind.

I followed Jones around the back nine at DeBary, and it took me a while to identify his value-added as a golfer. His drives, though accurate, were not particularly long, and his swing, though serviceable, was brusque and pared down, pistonlike—not at all the elegant, modern Fred Couples ideal. He did appear perfectly comfortable standing over the ball, which is not always the case with golfers on the Space Coast Tour, many of whom bounce up and down neurotically and back way from the shot so often you begin to wonder if they might be afraid of hurting the ball.

After a few more holes, however, I began to understand that Jones's distinction is not his ball-striking ability so much as his raw animal hunger to score birdies. He works the course like a perpetual-motion machine, darting after his balls with the ferocity of a terrier, swinging extra clubs to groove the right feel, pacing like a CEO in a doctor's office whenever he has to wait, sizing up putts from every angle of the compass. On the eleventh hole he missed a seven-foot birdie putt and stayed on the green for several minutes afterward, inspecting the turf around the hole with the disgust of a surgeon trying to comprehend a botched operation.

Jones's attitude stood in marked contrast to that of his playing companion for the day, D. W. Smith, forty-two, a courtly Mississippian wearing a straw fedora. Smith, a very fine golfer himself (during one seventeen-round stretch last summer, he shot 90 under par), lolled about in the cart between shots chatting with other golfers like a pastor at a church social. "Look at D.W.," Jones said derisively, nodding as Smith nonchalantly got up to arch his back like a cat enjoying the sun. "If *I* was two over, I'd be eyeballing down the fairway to see how I could get me a birdie."

During a brief delay on the fourteenth tee, Jones took me aside to apologize for a minor display of temper—he had tossed a club—on the previous hole. "I expect a little more out of myself is all," he said. "When you're playing this bad, it just gets under your skin, that's all. You gotta get after yourself, gotta get a little bit mad." The day before, he said, he had shot 67 in a hurricane to win the one-thousand-dollar first prize at a tournament in Lady Lake.

With that he stepped up to his ball, mumbled something like "Come on, now, just gimmie a chance" and sizzled a 3-iron straight down the center of the fairway. "Whoo-ee, Jethro," Smith cooed in appreciation. Jones acknowledged the compliment with a tight-lipped smile and stood aside, practicing his hip turn as the others hit.

"Personality-wise," I jotted in my notebook, "this guy's a natural for the PGA Tour."

I had hoped to talk with Jones more extensively after the round. But before I could collar him, an entertaining golfer named Billy Glisson asked me for a ride to his car. I had met Glisson a few days earlier. He claims to be the World's Leading All-Time Minitour Winner, and he probably is, though many would consider that a dubious honor.

"I come down here for one thing and one thing only, and that's to win," he told me in his hurry-up South Carolina accent as we barreled down a derelict stretch of highway. He was dragging on a Viceroy and blowing smoke out the window. "Coming in second don't cut it. That's why I've won ninety-one-plus minitour events. I reckon it's like Nicklaus."

Glisson, forty-six, is a friendly, lackadaisical mess of a man. He has a broad, blunt nose, longish, dirty blond hair that curlicues out the back of his golf cap and such a monster belly that he never even tries to tuck his shirttail in. He tends to wear the same pair of baggy gray shorts day after day and leaves a butt trail of Viceroys around the course which Hansel and Gretel would envy. I estimate he smokes three packs per round. Glisson also engages in the disturbing habit of popping his ball in his mouth between holes despite all the insecticides around.

If the Space Coast Tour attracted media attention the way the PGA Tour does, Glisson's personal history would be the stuff of legend. During the early years he supported his golf habit by working as the night manager of an Orlando brothel that operated out of a beauty salon. He got so good at golf, however, that by the early eighties he was supposedly winning more than fifty thousand dollars a year on the minitours. In 1981 he made it to the big tour and did pretty well. "Got on TV four or five times," he bragged matter-of-factly. Unfortunately, he soon suffered a nearly fatal stroke—"Too much drinking and carrying on, I reckon"—and so, after a couple of years' recovery, it was back to the minors.

Glisson lasted long enough on tour to make a mark, however. He is remembered, among other reasons, for confusing the courtesy-car volunteers with his frequent requests to pick up more than one "Mrs. Glisson" at the airport. At one tournament, the real Mrs. Glisson spotted her husband strolling the fairway holding hands with a Mrs. Glisson not herself and stole his Corvette out of spite, leaving only his street shoes in the parking space.

Despite a too-quick backswing and constant exasperation at slow play, Glisson still wins his share of minitour events. That's why the 79 he had shot that morning was such a thorn. "Couldn't make a putt," he grumbled as we drove. "When you play golf for a living, you gotta have total concentration. All I could think about was my damn car."

His car, a black 1983 Eldorado with an I'D RATHER BE GOLFING bumper sticker in the rear window, had broken down that morning on an I-40 exit ramp. He had had to hitch a ride, by chance with Gene the Machine, to make it to the tournament on time. We found the car, apparently repaired, tilting half-in, half-out of a muddy ditch beside the weather-beaten combination garage and sign shop where he had left it. The proprietor charged Glisson only thirty-five dollars "Hot damn," Glisson said, beaming like he'd just holed out a pitching wedge from a hundred yards. "I thought they'd take me to the cleaners."

Even so, he had to borrow twenty dollars to make it back to the friend's apartment where he stays, sleeping on the couch, while competing in Orlando. And a few days later the Eldorado broke again. This time the repairs cost eight hundred dollars.

Glisson has a new wife and two children back in South Carolina. I asked him why he still plays tournament golf. "It just gets in the blood, I reckon," he replied, "and you can't get it out."

The next day, back at DeBary Plantation, Gene the Machine failed to win the tournament. He cranked out what for him was another disappointing round of even par to finish three shots off the pace. The winner, in a sudden-death playoff, was Doug Weaver, another former tour pro like Glisson but unlike Glisson in nearly every other possible respect. I realized this immediately when I offered to buy him a drink at the clubhouse bar to celebrate his exciting victory, and he enthusiastically accepted by ordering milk.

Weaver, thirty-three, is a solidly built redhead with a deep southern voice and a lightly pocked face. I thought he was joking about the milk, of course, but he wasn't. He ordered a tall glass of it, took one sip, then dashed off to a telephone to tell his wife the good news of their forty-three-hundred-dollar payday. "God must be teaching us to be very dependent on Him," Weaver said when he returned, "because every time we get almost broke, I win a tournament."

Two years earlier, he said, the family had been in a similar pickle. Their bank account was practically zero, his wife was pregnant, his swing was incoherent, and he had just shot 81–82 in a pro-am tournament at Pebble Beach. After the tournament, he and his wife, Patricia, walked down to the beach below the course and prayed. "Dear God," they beseeched, "if we're going to play golf in 1991, You're going to have to put the money in our hands because we're too embarrassed to ask anyone for it ourselves anymore." Sure enough, a few days later Weaver received an offer from a potential sponsor—one of his partners in the disastrous Pebble Beach pro-am, no less—of thirty thousand dollars over the next two years. He was back in business.

I asked Weaver what keeps him golfing when the financial abyss yawns. "I realize I could go back to South Carolina and get a good job," he replied. "But the Bible says a young man without vision shall perish. That doesn't mean really perish, but he just won't have a good life." He paused to take his last gulp of milk. "This is the dream God has laid on our hearts."

The shocking thing about the pro-golf scene in Orlando is the sheer number of men, like Weaver and Glisson and all the cadets, who manage to arrange their lives to play golf every day "for a living." Because in addition to Goosie's operation, two other, even lesser minitours operate in the area: the Tommy Armour Tour and the North Florida PGA Winter Tour. Together the three tours qualify Orlando, without a doubt, as the Bush-League Professional Golf Capital of the Universe.

I called on the Tommy Armour Tour one Saturday during its one-day tournament at the Overoaks Country Club. First-place prize money was one thousand dollars, and the second-place check (which went to Gene the Machine for shooting 67 again) was six hundred dollars. When I arrived, the players who had already finished were standing around in a grove of live oak trees, the branches hung with Spanish moss, sipping beer or soft drinks and chatting amiably amongst themselves. It looked a lot like a big southern picnic or family reunion. "No offense," a competitor recently arrived from New Jersey told me, "but this is the lamest tour I've ever played in."

The man who owns the Tommy Armour Tour is a perplexed-looking forty-nine-year-old named Terry Fine. Fine plays in his own tournaments as a way of tuning up for the Senior Tour. The day I visited, he shot an 81. "The biggest complaint the players have down here in Florida," he said, "is the blatant stealing out of the purse that takes place on some of the other tours." By "other tours" he was clearly alluding to Goosie's, though Fine later said he did not mean to suggest by "stealing" that Goosie was doing anything illegal—merely that he was keeping too high a percentage of the pot for himself.

No love is lost between Fine and Goosie. For Goosie, the Tommy Armour Tour is "kind of a sore thumb." He claims not to mind the competition—"good, honest competition we can handle"—as much as the way Fine "slipped around behind my back, giving my players his cards, that sort of thing," when Fine was getting his tour off the ground three years ago.

As for Fine, he likes to portray himself as the golfers' true friend. He prides himself on keeping a higher percentage of the players' money in the pot, after expenses and profits, than does Goosie. But since his major sponsor, the Tommy Armour Golf Company, contributes less to his tour than the Spalding Company does to the Space Coast Tour, the players still get a better return with Goosie. To compensate, Fine was working on a deal to offer all Tommy Armour Tour members in good standing a 10 percent discount at Wolf Camera outlets across the South. "One thing we're trying to do at the Tommy Armour Tour is add a little dignity," he said. Earlier, the tour had been known as the Hooters Tour, after a restaurant chain that features busty waitresses in tight T-shirts and hot pants. So dignity-wise, that's progress right there.

I wandered over to the clubhouse porch, where a number of competitors were loitering after their round. They constituted the usual assortment of oddballs one finds in bush-league golf: a bartender and occasional dancer at a Chippendales-like club, a frightened-looking kid from South Africa who appeared to be no older than twelve, a forty-one-year-old tenured Delta pilot who competes regularly by virtue of his eighteen off days per month and a surly, ponytailed, practice-range pro who was griping about how much Fred Couples earned for switching to Parallax clubs (supposedly four million dollars) and showing off his own abnormally long driver. This club's head weighed about ten pounds and was made of Kryptonite or plutonium or something and if manipulated correctly could propel the ball, he said, 339 yards. He let me try it on the range. It was like swinging a maypole with several small children attached. My best attempt almost reached the 100-yard marker.

As I was preparing to leave, a twenty-four-year-old golfer named Joe Shahady took me aside to suggest privately that I might want to mention in the article how much he enjoys eating PowerBars. PowerBars, according to some information Terry Fine made available, provide delicious, nutritious, *sustained* energy to help golfers maintain the focus required for hitting straight drives and making crucial putts. I forgot to mention earlier that the PowerBar company is an official sponsor of the Tommy Armour Tour. Any player quoted in the press singing the praises of PowerBars gets a five-hundred-dollar bonus.

I finally had a chance to sit down and talk with Gene the Machine after the first round of the next Space Coast tournament, a two-day affair at the Kissimmee Bay Country Club. He had just shot a 66 but couldn't resist complaining about a couple of knee-knocker putts he missed. "I just couldn't get anything started on the front nine," he grumbled.

Off the course Jones is not nearly as daunting as he is when stalking a golf ball. He has a mild, fidgety manner and a hang-dog vulnerability. During the interview, whenever a subject arose that he didn't feel comfortable with, such as the past, he flitted off to something more benign, usually golf. "I used to be down on myself because I didn't have any money and all, but the insight I had was that the more failures you go through, the higher you can achieve," he said. "You can work hard in golf and make it."

Reportedly, Jones was a superstar in high school in Orlando. He won the Florida PGA Junior title and the U.S. Olympic Junior championship before turning pro at eighteen. Then something happened, all the details of which I could not discover. A car wreck was part of it; for five years he wore a neck brace. Apparently, too, he didn't get along with people; he was introverted and, as he puts it, "too hardcore" about golf. For a long time he drifted. He sold pots and pans in Forth Worth, cleaned swimming pools in Orlando and mowed the grass at a country club in South Carolina. "I had went as low as I could go," Jones says, "but I won't say I was going crazy, because I still always believed that I could play."

His rescuer was Malcolm McDonald, on Orlando-area surgeon and friend of the family. Dr. Mac, as Jones calls him, remembered what a fine player Jones had been as a youth and convinced him four years ago to move back from South Carolina. To make that financially possible, McDonald bought Jones and his wife a trailer and a few acres of land outside Orlando and encouraged him to reconcile with his dad, a teaching pro.

The turning point for Jones, golfwise, seemed to come last year when he qualified in a preliminary round to compete in the Greensboro Open, a PGA Tour event. "At Greensboro, you'd hear ten thousand people giving you the clap, and it was really motivating," Jones said. "I'm not gonna say I belong out there on the tour, but that experience made me think I might."

In 1992, by the time we were talking, Jones had already won seventeen tournaments on the minitour scene. "It scares me how well I'm doing," he said. "Right now I'd be afraid to take a week off."

Then he excused himself to go home and practice for the next day's final round. He was tied for the lead.

To get to Kissimmee Bay from DeBary Plantation, you motor down the interstate past the fantasy factory at Universal Studios and the counterfeit reality of Walt Disney World. Then you turn left into a nightmare strip of bogus American roadside attractions. You pass Gatorland, Pirate's Island, Medieval Times and Fun 'n Wheels. By the time you reach the county jail, where you turn right, Long John Silver's seems like a high-class seafood shoppe.

I mention this because it occurred to me as I drove to Kissimmee that it's no coincidence that the Bush-League Professional Golf Capital of the Universe should be in a city like Orlando, which is wholly predicated on the suspension of disbelief. Because that's what golf is all about, too. For ostensibly mature adult men to persuade themselves that the possibility of slicing a dimpled ball into some completely artificial, blue-dyed lagoon is a risk with as dire and pulse-quickening consequences as being eaten by a bear or ambushed by the Viet Cong demands not only the suspension of disbelief but also the collusion of an entire social ecosystem. That the players are engaged in *professional* golf (albeit third-rate professional golf) only adds to the gravitas and urgency of the adventure. The delusion grows that these rounds really matter, that the players' very careers hang in the balance on each and every shot. This, I concluded, could be the ultimate source of professional golf's dark and addictive thrill and possibly the key to understanding why men of the bush league so willingly sacrifice all the nice things that their wives would like them to buy with the money they don't earn, such as new drapes for the living room and higher-quality knickknacks.

That was my thinking, anyway.

For the final round of the Kissimmee Bay tournament, Jones was paired in the next to last foursome with three cadets named Scott Pleis, Bo Fennell and Chris Hehmann. Hehmann was a rookie who had apparently never before been so high on the leader board for a final round.

Diluting the potential tension of the round was the observational presence, in a golf cart, of Steve Pleis, Scott's brother, and Brad McClendon, a brawny, crew-cut, good old boy from Louisiana. Steve Pleis and McClendon, having gone out in the first group of the day, had already finished their rounds. They had zipped around the course in near record time—"They played like they were in some kind of hurry to take a shit," a rules official told me—and now had a bad case of the giggles, especially when it came to Hehmann.

"He's playing out of his ying-yang," McClendon chortled at 11 when Hehmann mis-hit an approach shot but then chipped in from fifty feet for a birdie. On 14, when Hehmann left a forty-foot putt almost fifteen feet short, Steve said, "There's a lot of chicken left on that bone," and he and McClendon sat stifling their laughter like Sunday schoolers in a church pew. Eventually Hehmann self-destructed.

Jones, of course, was having none of it. He continued to play nearly flawless golf, hitting most greens in regulation and rolling his lag putts to within inches for tap-in pars. If Jones even noticed Pleis and McClendon trailing the group, he didn't show it. The Machine was focused, readying himself for what he had told me the day before was his primary focus and favorite part of a tournament: the final three holes. Coming off the fifteenth green, Jones said he figured two birdies out of three would give him a chance to win. "We'll see what we can do," he said.

He got one birdie at the par-3 sixteenth, draining a forty-footer. On 17, a 416-yard par 4, he parked his approach shot five feet from the pin, and I had no doubt the Machine would hammer home the putt. But he didn't. The ball gave the hole a smell but then lipped out. On 18, all Jones could muster was a routine par.

His 69 tied him for fourth. "One of these days," he said tersely and walked off the course.

In the clubhouse bar afterwards, a couple of dozen players were waiting around to pick up their prize checks. Roger Rowland, a towheaded cadet from nearby Ocala, was hunched over his beer at the bar and shaking his head from side to side. He had just won the tournament with twin 66s. "Man, I'll tell you," he was muttering, "you plain gotta play some golf to win one of these things."

Billy Glisson was there, chain-smoking Viceroys and throwing back Seven and 7s as he regaled the Pleis brothers with tales from the good old days. "There was a lot more going on in those chairs than just blow-dries, I guarantee" was one line I overheard, presumably in reference to the beauty parlor/brothel where he used to work. For some reason he was carrying a jumbo driver and waggling it, Bob Hope–style, as he delivered his shtick. The Pleis brothers seemed only mildly amused.

To my surprise Gene Jones walked in and took a stool at the bar. I had the impression that drinking with the boys was not something he did very often.

"Hey, Machine," someone called out. "There's a rumor going around that you're making so much money you don't even cash your checks."

The barroom grew quiet to hear his response. "That's right," Jones said and took a long sip of beer. "I just go home every night and stare at 'em."

The line got a laugh, and that seemed to relax him. When a relative old-timer sauntered by and said, "Hey, Gene, what happened out there? I'm not used to seeing your name that far down the list," Jones smiled and seemed to relish the implicit compliment.

I took the stool next to Jones and offered to buy him a beer, but he bought me one instead. I asked him about his round. "Golf's a tough business," he replied with a shrug. "It's all about making the short ones."

He got out a pencil and calculated on a cocktail napkin that the missed five-footer on 17 had cost him eight hundred dollars. "But I still had a two-thousand-dollar week. I'll be getting fourteen hundred dollars from Goosie and another six hundred fifty dollars from the Spalding bonus pool. That's pretty good money for a country boy." Then he began pulling jewelry out of a pouch that he carries around in his golf bag: a gold Rolex, a gold pinky ring with a gaudy dollar sign on its face and a key ring hung with a tiny gold golf club and a spike wrench.

Finally, the tour manager, Bobby Simpson, began circulating with the checks: large, yellow Space Coast bank drafts signed by J. C. Goosie himself. Jones folded his neatly into quarters and tucked it in his wallet beside two sus-piciously similar-looking pieces of paper. "What are those?" I asked.

He took them out and showed me: uncashed Space Coast checks for three thousand dollars and one thousand dollars. "I guess I am getting a little behind," Jones admitted sheepishly. But as he returned the checks to his wallet, he held my glance for a moment, and I could see how powerfully proud he was of winning checks that large. He was proud of all that he had accomplished with his life in the last few years. Maybe he does take the checks home and stare at them, I thought.

The instant Jones left the bar, a journeyman pro named Dan Oschmann said: "The son of a bitch. I wish he'd get the hell out of here and let the rest of us make some money." He meant it as a joke, but he was serious, too.

In the PGA Tour Qualifying Tournament, which began two weeks later, Jones obliged. He was one of only forty-three players out of nearly nine hundred entrants—including a large proportion of the Space Coast irregu-lars—to win a coveted tour card for 1993.

I talked to the Machine by telephone afterwards. "I'm looking to earn a million dollars," he said. As of late April, however, Jones had made the cut in just two tournaments, earning a total of $4,340.

A Good Walk Spoiled

BY MARK KRAM

Several years ago, a friend gave me a T-shirt for my birthday that announced my willingness to GOLF FOR FOOD. Of course, given my game, I'd starve to death before the turn. Still, I wondered how far someone really might go to feed his golfing jones. When I read Mark Kram's penetrating *Philadelphia Daily News* profile of former golfing golden boy Ricky Meissner I had my answer. And then swallowed hard.

Dateline: Liberty, Mo.

For a guy who spent the better part of his 55 years out on golf courses, a place like the Clay County Detention Center can feel horribly confining. With the exception of an hour in the exercise yard, Ricky Meissner spends his days in the big communal area adjacent to his cell, where the inmates are allowed to play cards, watch TV and use the telephone all day. In a modern facility in suburban Kansas City that houses 180 prisoners, Meissner pores through the law books he picks off the library cart in search of a legal loophole in his case. Far away from his anticipated career as a pro golfer and the promise he once had, he drifts off to sleep at night and occasionally revisits those days in his dreams, only to wake up with a shudder as he blows yet another gimmie putt.

One could say that the tangled-up life of Ricky Meissner has been a series of tee shots into the rough. Once a top amateur golfer in the Washington area with what appeared to be a successful career ahead of him, Meissner became a figure of some notoriety in the late 1970s when he began robbing banks to support himself on the fringes of the PGA Tour. In a wild spree that ended just a day shy of a year, Meissner held up 19 banks in 11 states before authorities captured him in June 1978. Although Meissner did not earn a single cent on the tour legitimately, he guesses that he grabbed just under $400,000 in stolen cash. He pleaded guilty to two of the bank jobs in December of that year and was sentenced to 25 years in prison. He served five years. Quietly, he dropped out of sight when he was released in 1983, and would have become just an object of dimly remembered curiosity were it not for a recent development: Ricky Meissner is once again back in the rough.

A jury in Kansas City, Mo., convicted Meissner in February of robbing a suburban golf retailer. Charged with stealing more than $100,000 in expensive golf clubs, which police say he unloaded through an unidentified fence in Florida, Meissner was sentenced as an enhanced offender to 50 years in prison on May 4. He will not be eligible for parole until 2037. Suspected but cleared in a series of other golf-store heists across the South and Midwest through the 1990s, Meissner swears he did not do the Kansas City job either, that he was tricked into certain incriminating statements by a detective in the robbery unit. While he did not testify on his own behalf in court, he says he has proof that he was elsewhere when the Kansas City robbery was committed, that he became the target of this and other investigations because of the bank holdups he once committed. He is appealing the Kansas City conviction.

A sports writer once called Ricky Meissner "the golden boy of golf." Why he fell so far short of the promise he held is hard to say. He was obsessed by the sport in a way that other champions are, but there always seemed to be two Ricky Meissners: one who was always fooling with his grip, the other who could never fully get one. Even when it was clear enough to others he would be better off running a golf course or becoming a club pro somewhere, he could not bring himself to concede that he would never fulfill his potential. To prove to everyone (and himself) that he was just as talented as the top players on the circuit, he convinced himself that he would do whatever it took to succeed—even if it included walking into a bank and cleaning out the cash drawers. What happened in the end was the thrill he once derived from golf was eclipsed by a thrill of a far riskier sort.

"My life?" said Meissner, seated on a stool behind a Plexiglas partition with a phone to his ear. "Well, I never set out to harm anyone, but I would say this: I am not exactly what you would call a perfect citizen. Somewhere along the line I just crossed the line, you know? How else can I say it?"

*   *   *

It would be hard to find anyone who had a greater passion for golf than Ricky Meissner. Initially, when he was a teenager in Olney, Md., the sport allowed him to forge an identity, a realm of endeavor in which he could even up the score with guys he perceived to be his social betters. It was only in his 20s and 30s that he saw that the sport could be a conduit to the finer things in life: lavish country clubs, big cars and plenty of cash. Although he would not become the golfer that he set out to be, golf remained for him a place of enduring fantasy. He said recently that he was so hooked on it that he had planned to try his hand on the Senior PGA Tour.

"I loved it," Meissner said. "I knew I could play. I just had a feel for it. I loved the surroundings—the wide-open spaces, the big pines, the greens." He grinned, and with a chuckle added, "You know I love it if I was able to talk the guys in here into watching a tournament on TV the other day."

Golf held Ricky Meissner under its spell from the day he stepped on a course at the Argyle Country Club in Silver Spring, Md. The son of a by-the-book D.C. detective, Dick Meissner, Ricky became acquainted with the game at age 11, when the pro at the club where his dad played hired him to pick up balls on the driving range during the summer. When he began hitting a few himself, he was told by the pro that he had a natural swing. By the end of that summer, he had entered and won his first tournament. He went on to become the Maryland Junior Amateur Champion and win other regional championships, including one in which actor Robert Mitchum presented him with a trophy. By the age of 16 in 1962, Pepsi-Cola, in conjunction with the Jaycees, had chosen to send him across the United States to participate in tournaments. A friend who knew Meissner from those days observed: "Ricky had ability. He did. He had a big swing off the tee but no short game."

When you get right down to it, there is no better way to say it: In life—as in golf—Ricky Meissner just lacked the overall game to succeed. Undisciplined, he appeared to acquaintances back then to be his own worst enemy. A four-sport athlete but just an average student at The Bullis School, an all-boys prep school then located in Silver Spring, Ricky became a problem for his parents, who invariably found themselves in the position of having to step in and bail him out of jams. Meissner declined to blame either of his parents for what happened to him years later, saying: "No one else was to blame but me." (Neither of his parents would agree to be interviewed for this story. Dick Meissner died on March 28 without knowing that his son had been convicted again.)

The golden boy at 18: Physically—at 6-4, 185 pounds or so—he looked like a young Tom Weiskopf, appealing enough in appearance and personality that he always had dates in high school (including a few with actress-to-be Goldie Hawn). Certain when he graduated from Bullis that he had a lucrative career ahead of him on the PGA Tour, Meissner left the Washington area and headed to Florida, where he attended a junior college and honed his game at a country club managed by his grandmother. It was during this time that he met and married his first wife, Claire, with whom he would later have two sons. (None would agree to be interviewed for this story.)

What he planned to do was head out on the tour in the summer of 1965. It did not happen. Instead—in what today could only be called a whim—Ricky and an old school friend decided to sign up for the Marines. They would go in on the buddy system. But when his "buddy" failed his physical due to high blood pressure, Ricky found himself on a plane to Vietnam as a baker. He ended up in Da Nang and suddenly found himself surrounded by the horrors of war; a double-decker bus packed with civilians exploded before his very eyes. To help bring some sanity back to his surroundings, Ricky remembers that he once got out the golf clubs that his parents had shipped to him and began chipping balls in an area adjacent to the base.

"Get the hell out of there," someone shouted at him from afar. "Quick!"

"Why?" Meissner replied.

"Minefield!" the guy shouted back.

A change had come over Meissner when he returned from Vietnam in December 1966. Like other veterans, he came back feeling that "people looked down on me," that "the war was for nothing." Moreover, he suddenly found that he was not the same golfer somehow, that he no longer possessed the edge he once had. He said his killer instinct had abandoned him. Unable to qualify for his PGA Tour card in three qualifying schools from 1967 to '70, he supported himself through a series of odd jobs and sharpened his game enough on the local circuit to qualify for the U.S. Open in 1970 at Hazeltine (Chaska, Minn.) and in 1974 at Winged Foot (Mamaroneck, N.Y.). While he missed the cuts both of those years, he stuck with the sport and in 1977 circumvented qualifying school by joining the PGA apprentice program, which made graduates eligible to play qualifying rounds each week as "rabbits" in order to gain entrance to an event. When a problem arose with the sponsorship he had lined up, Meissner remembered that he asked for a loan from the Veterans Administration to get himself started.

"Is there any kind of program I can qualify for?" Meissner asked one of the clerks at VA. "Like some sort of small-business loan? I could use $15,000."

"For what?" asked the clerk.

"To go on the PGA Tour," Meissner explained.

"To do what?" asked the clerk, eyes wide.

"Golf," Meissner said. "I figure $15,000 should get me going." The clerk just laughed.

★   ★   ★

Ricky Meissner always preferred to rob banks when it was raining. The way he had it figured, it would not arouse any suspicion among bystanders if they saw someone running from a bank in bad weather. With a hat lowered over his eyes and his jacket drawn to the chin, he would look just like any other harried depositor as he ducked into his car and drove off. And if someone did spot him, it was always hard to jot down the license plate through the hazy veil of a downpour. By the time the police converged on the scene, Meissner was out on the highway and headed off to yet another stop on the tour.

It was that easy.

Until he began robbing banks in June 1977 to finance his golf career, Meissner was just like any other "rabbit" on the PGA Tour: good enough to dream. He was one member of a pool of 160 or so who would compete Mondays for just a handful of spots in the tournament field in a given week. By this point divorced from Claire, Meissner would travel between tour stops in a borrowed van on borrowed funds. Generally, he would cook his dinners on a portable hibachi and bed down in the back of the van at night. While he remembers that there were always groupies who followed the tour, Meissner found life on the road to be a lonely existence. On those occasions when he treated himself to accommodations at a motel (usually twice a week), he used to stay up at night and practice his putting in the room. He remembers thinking: "All I need are a couple of breaks."

But the reality in early 1977 was that he was running out of cash. Unable to qualify at the Jackie Gleason Inverrary Classic (Lauderhill, Fla.), the Florida Citrus Open (Orlando) and so on, Meissner led the Tallahassee Open in April in the early going but finished well out of the money. Unsure how he would be able to stay out on the tour, Meissner said he was driving back from a trip to upstate New York when he stopped off at a bank in Delaware to change a $100 bill. Suddenly, he found himself gazing at the cash drawer: The crisp piles of $20s and $50s seemed to call out to him. Vividly, he remembers that it dawned on him that he had found the solution to his problem. Getting back into his van, he drove back to his home in suburban Maryland; two weeks later he walked into the Equitable Savings and Loan in Silver Spring with a .32-caliber automatic under his sweater. He walked out 30 seconds later with $2,600.

"I began robbing banks in order to play on the tour," Meissner said. "I told myself I would do this one, and that would be it. But I was wrong. One led to two, and that led to others.

"Once I would fail to qualify on Monday, I would drive around town, look for a bank to hit—hit it—then drive on to wherever I had to play the following week."

An uneasiness fell over him whenever he was planning to rob a bank. He became sick with diarrhea for days leading up to it. While he would always leave a robbery with a sense of elation, especially when he spread out his take on the bed and counted it, he would grow increasingly tense during the preparation stages. Careful to choose only small branch banks with never more than one teller on duty, he would change the license plates on his car and allow his beard to cover his face in a heavy shadow. On the day of a robbery, he would carefully dye his hair black and affix a false mustache to his upper lip. It was odd: Whenever he inhaled a whiff of the glue he used to seal that final piece of his disguise in place, a heightened feeling of readiness overcame Meissner. He observed, "The glue seemed to put me in the mood."

The year sped by in a blur. Unable to get his career going on the tour, he found that he was actually playing worse each week, that the secret life he was leading had eclipsed whatever abilities he possessed. He held up banks in Maryland, Virginia, Ohio, Delaware, New York, Illinois, Florida, Arizona, New Mexico, California and Texas. Suddenly, he was no longer driving a van but a Cadillac, and he began staying in the better hotels. It appeared to his peers that he had landed a sugar daddy to sponsor him. Meissner even began helping some of them financially and began to fancy himself as a latter-day Robin Hood. In a scene that could have come out of the film "Bonnie and Clyde," Meissner remembers he once stopped alongside a road in Florida to help an elderly couple from Georgia whose car had broken down.

"They were driving this old Chevy station wagon and were on their way to Disney World," he said. "They were just so upset. They said their trip had been ruined. I drove them to a dealership, and there was this $8,400 silver station wagon on the showroom floor. I bought it for them. I handed them another $1,600 and told them to have a good time at Disney World."

What Ricky Meissner told himself was that stealing from banks was just a form of personal revenge. Banks were federally insured, and he figured the government owed him for the years it had stolen from him in Vietnam. Of course, it was utterly selfish of him and altogether screwy logic: Others had come back from the war far worse off than Ricky Meissner. But he convinced himself that he was just taking out "a sort of loan" without doing the required paperwork. Because he took only what was in the cash drawer (he never went into the vault for fear of being locked in), the jobs he engineered were relatively small; the largest was $37,000. And he was always careful never to carry a loaded weapon, a fact that a teller at an Ohio bank found less than reassuring when he told her his intentions.

"Oh, God," the woman cried hysterically. "Please. Oh, no."

"Lady," Meissner said calmly. "No one is going to get hurt here. Calm down."

The woman sobbed, "Oh, please . . ."

"Look, this gun is not even loaded," Meissner said. He even opened it up and showed her. "See? Now relax."

"Oh, God," the woman said.

Meissner walked out of the bank.

"She was just so upset that I decided, the heck with it," he said. "I never wanted to harm anyone."

What Ricky Meissner likes to say today is that he allowed himself to get sloppy in order to be caught. Married again by June 1978 to a woman he had met on the tour—Cherie would divorce him when she learned what he had been doing when he was supposed to be "out golfing"—Meissner came back to the Washington area and set up housekeeping. He says he had $25,000 in a safe-deposit box. When those funds were soon depleted, he "spontaneously" decided to rob the Maryland National Bank in Bethesda, Md., on June 7, 1978. It was his 19th bank, and his final one. Someone set off the alarm, someone else shouted "Robber!" and someone else jotted down his license plate, which he had carelessly not changed. The FBI was waiting for him when he got home.

"I was sort of relieved," Meissner said. "You know? It had been a long year, and now it was finally over."

*　　*　　*

Detective Todd Butler, of the Kansas City Police Department, has spent countless hours seated across from criminals in the interview room at downtown headquarters during his 15 years with the robbery unit. But when Ricky Meissner sat down across from him back in 1997, Butler could not remember when he had encountered a suspect as utterly intriguing. He was a series of shedding layers: On one hand, highly intelligent, articulate and altogether cunning; on the other, arrogant, egotistical and far too foolishly drawn in by the ploys of an experienced interrogator. Butler wondered to himself what Meissner could have accomplished in life if he had not become a professional criminal.

"It was really an amazing life he led," said Butler, his arms folded on the table in one of the interview rooms. "You could write a book on where he has been and what he has done. I used to wonder who could play him if they ever did a film, then it dawned on me: Sean Connery! The criminal no one could catch!"

How Ricky Meissner ended up in Kansas City and back in jail began with his release from prison on his 1979 bank robbery conviction. Set free after serving five years of relatively soft time at Danbury (Conn.) and Allenwood (Pa.), during which a prison psychiatrist diagnosed him as suffering from "post-traumatic stress syndrome" due to his exposure to combat, Meissner settled down back in the Washington area with his third wife, Theresa, a woman he had known since childhood and who began corresponding with him when he was locked up. She became spouse No. 3 in 1984. Using a contact he had developed in prison, Meissner landed a well-paying job as a salesman for a local garbage removal company. But a part of him could not let go of golf. With his 50th birthday just a few years off—the age at which players become eligible to participate on the Senior Tour—he and Theresa sold their house in Maryland and built a place in Florida on a golf course in a gated community called Plantation Bay in Ormond Beach, just north of Daytona Beach.

No one could figure out how Meissner could afford to live in Plantation Bay. Although the former Theresa Meissner would not speak on the record for this story (she has since readopted her maiden name and said that she wants "no publicity from Ricky"), it was speculated that he still had funds from the bank robberies years ago. "Untrue," said Meissner, who told people he was a golf instructor. Lt. Warnell Williams, of the Flagler County Sheriff Department, said everyone wondered how Meissner could live so lavishly. Aware that Meissner had a prior bank-robbery conviction, he developed Meissner as a suspect in a series of burglaries at Plantation Bay. Williams was so certain that Meissner was the culprit that he began following him around the course in a golf cart. He arrested Meissner in 1994 for purchasing stolen clubs from the dressing room of the Sawgrass Country Club in Jacksonville the year before. Meissner pleaded no contest to a charge of grand theft and was sentenced to five years of probation. Observed Meissner, who contended that he was innocent of the charge, "They threatened me with five years in jail, but said I could get off with probation if I copped to it."

But that was just the beginning of the problems that Meissner would soon face. Unable to get himself started on the Senior Tour in any significant way (he came up short in his few efforts to qualify), Meissner found himself charged in the robbery of a golf shop in Ennis, Texas, in October 1995. Police said he stole $20,000 in expensive golf clubs, and added that the crime bore a striking resemblance to unsolved cases in Florida (1991), Georgia and Louisiana (1993), Alabama and Indiana (1994), and Florida again (1995). Police say the suspect in each of these cases was always polite, that he used a gun and that he bound the clerks in the back room before cleaning the store out of top-of-the-line clubs. But Meissner was never charged or even questioned in these cases. Eventually, the Ennis charges were dropped, and in June 1996 he was cleared of stealing $20,000 worth of clubs from a golf store in Arlington, Texas, when he boldly came back into the store to face his accusers.

"Am I the man who robbed you?" Meissner asked the two clerks who had identified him as the robber from a photograph.

They both said no.

"They were adamant that he was not the guy," Arlington police detective Danny Nutt said. "I have to hand it to him. He had guts to go back in there."

Charges were filed and later dropped against Meissner in an August 1997 robbery of $40,000 worth of clubs in St. Louis; Meissner had a hotel receipt that showed he was in Indiana on the evening the theft occurred. But it was in St. Louis that he became acquainted with Butler, who had come over from Kansas City to investigate the robbery that June of $100,000 in clubs. Butler told Meissner that a photograph placed him at the scene of the Kansas City robbery. Butler freely admitted that he then "tricked" Meissner. He told him that he believed the robbery was an "inside job" by the two clerks, that Meissner had not been involved in the holdup.

"But you have to explain why they were able to identify you," Butler told him. "I would hate to see you go away on an armed-robbery conviction when you are just essentially a con artist. Justify your presence there for me."

Meissner walked into the trap. "He told me he had been at the store, that he had shoplifted some clubs and had a confrontation with one of the clerks at the door," said Butler, who believed that Meissner in one year compiled "$900,000 in golf clubs" from the robberies in which he is a suspect and sold them through a fence in Florida. "What Meissner did was admit that he was in the store. He later slipped up and told us information that only the robber would have known. We had him."

The detective told the two clerks at the Golf Discount Store that he had a feeling that Meissner would come back into the store. Sure enough, that is exactly what he did. Butler said Meissner walked back into the store and purchased a set of golf grips so that he could show the receipt in court, so he could tell the jury: "See, I went back in there and no one recognized me." But the two clerks did recognize him. When he came in and looked up at them with a grin on his face, they immediately called 911. The police converged and arrested him for attempting to intimidate witnesses. When Butler interviewed him back at headquarters, he said that Meissner called his wife and explained why he had gone back in the store. " 'Well,' " Butler said he told her, " 'it worked in Texas.' "

Larry S. Buccero, the assistant prosecuting attorney for Clay County in Missouri, observed: "Was he stupid to admit to being in the store? Yeah, it was real stupid. He would have been better off if he had continued to deny it."

Said Meissner, "Very true."

Evidence Meissner says would have cleared him was not presented in court because he would been forced to take the stand himself, in which case the jury would have become acquainted with the secret life that Ricky Meissner was leading before his divorce from his third wife in 1999. The jury would have heard that Meissner had hooked up with an exotic dancer in Florida and had lavished her with cash and gifts in order to secure her companionship. She told Butler in her statement to him that Meissner had paid for her "boob job" and that it was common for him to leave cash for her tacked up on a telephone pole behind a Chevron station off I-95. While the dancer told Butler that Meissner had given her $70,000 all told, Meissner said it was "nowhere near that; $7,000 maybe." Either way, it would not have played well before the jury, who did not find the evidence that was presented on his behalf to be especially convincing. Theresa L. Baker, a friend from Florida, and her two daughters, Karin, 13, and Kelly, 11, testified that they had dinner with Meissner, the dancer and another woman in Alabama on the evening the Kansas City robbery occurred.

"The jury just did not buy it for a second," said Buccero. "I spoke with the jurors afterward and they said it was clear to them that he had committed the crime. Yes, the detective tricked him, but they said detectives are supposed to do that in order to solve a crime."

Added Buccero: "He is basically a professional thief who ought to be locked up."

★　　★　　★

The erstwhile "golden boy of golf" sat behind the Plexiglas partition with a folder full of papers at his side. Unlike the tanned, well-groomed ex-athlete who showed up at prison two years ago, Meissner has aged somewhat since he has been incarcerated. Circles and lines have formed a pattern at the edges of his eyes. Carefully, he opened up the folder he had before him and found the items he was looking for: One was a hotel receipt that he says proves that he had checked in at a Florida hotel on the day of the Kansas City robbery; the second was a sheet that showed the calls that had gone out from his cellphone that same day; the final was a paper that showed he did not waive his rights to talk to police in St. Louis the day he was interviewed by Butler.

"I feel I have been wrongly convicted," said Meissner, who has since been cleared in golf-store robberies in North Carolina and Florida. "I only went along with what Butler said because I believed him when he said he thought it had been an inside job. He double-crossed me. Is that ethical?"

While his fellow inmates do crossword puzzles or gaze at the TV, Meissner spends his days thinking: Where did I go wrong? How did I end up in here? Nights, he escapes in his sleep to better days—the days before he crossed the line. Vividly, he can see himself as he once was: young, talented, the whole world before him.

Ricky Meissner . . . good enough to dream. But he always wakes up with a start, steeped in the shadowy stillness of his cell and overcome by disorientation. Urgently—if only for a split second—he will wonder to himself, "Where am I? Where am I?" Finally, it will dawn on him.

"Oh, yeah. Hell. I am still in hell."

The Rivercliff Golf Killings
or *Why Professor Waddems Never Broke a Hundred*

BY DON MARQUIS

A cockroach and a cat falling in love? In the hands of a less agile stylist than Don Marquis (1878–1937), the high concept never would have had a chance, but he turned it into the classic series of Archy and Mehitabel books. When the former columnist for the *New York Sun* and *New York Tribune* turned his satiric eye to golf—as he did in this 1921 story—he'd naturally find, in its very nature, an inherent excuse for getting away with murder.

I am telling this story to the public just as I told it in the grand jury room; the district attorney having given me a carbon copy of my sworn testimony.

The Case of Doc Green

QUESTION: Professor Waddems, when did you first notice that Dr. Green seemed to harbor animosity towards you?

ANSWER: It was when we got to the second hole.

QUESTION: Professor, you may go ahead and tell the jury about it in your own words.

ANSWER: Yes, sir. The situation was this: My third shot lay in the sand in the shallow bunker—an easy pitch with a niblick to within a foot or two of the pin, for anyone who understands the theory of niblick play as well as I do. I had the hole in five, practically.

"Professor," said Doc Green, with whom I was playing—

QUESTION: This was Dr. James T. Green, the eminent surgeon, was it not?

ANSWER: Yes, sir. Dr. Green, with whom I was playing, remarked, "You are all wrong about Freud. Psychoanalysis is the greatest discovery of the age."

"Nonsense! Nonsense! Nonsense!" I replied. "Don't be a fool, Doc! I'll show you where Freud is all wrong, in a minute."

And I lifted the ball with an explosion shot to a spot eighteen inches from the pin, and holed out with an easy putt.

"Five," I said and marked it on my card.

"You mean eight," said Doc Green.

"Three into the bunker, four onto the green, and one putt—five," I said.

"You took four strokes in the bunker, Professor," he said. "Every time you said 'Nonsense' you made a swipe at the ball with your niblick."

"Great Godfrey," I said, "you don't mean to say you are going to count those gestures I made to illustrate my argument as *golf strokes?* Just mere gestures! And you know very well I have never delivered a lecture in twenty-five years without gestures like that!"

"You moved your ball an inch or two with your club at every gesture," he said.

QUESTION: Had you really done so, Professor? Remember, you are on oath.

ANSWER: I do not remember. In any case, the point is immaterial. They were merely gestures.

QUESTION: Did you take an eight, or insist on a five?

ANSWER: I took an eight. I gave in. Gentlemen; I am a good-natured person. Too good-natured. Calm and philosophical; unruffled and patient. My philosophy never leaves me. I took an eight.

(Sensation in the grand jury room.)

QUESTION: Will you tell something of your past life, Professor Waddems—who you are and what your lifework has been, and how you acquired the calmness you speak of?

ANSWER: For nearly twenty-five years I lectured on philosophy and psychology in various universities. Since I retired and took up golf it has been my habit to look at all the events and tendencies in the world's news from the standpoint of the philosopher.

QUESTION: Has this helped you in your golf?

ANSWER: Yes, sir. My philosophical and logical training and my specialization in psychology, combined with my natural calmness and patience, have made me the great golfer that I really am.

QUESTION: Have you ever received a square deal, Professor, throughout any eighteen holes of golf?

ANSWER: No, sir. Not once! Not once during the five years since I took the game up at the Rivercliff Country Club.

QUESTION: Have you ever broken a hundred, Professor Waddems?

ANSWER: No, sir. I would have, again and again, except that my opponents, and other persons playing matches on the course, and the very forces of nature themselves are always against me at critical moments. Even the bullfrogs at the three water holes treat me impertinently.

QUESTION: Bullfrogs? You said the bullfrogs, Professor?

ANSWER: Yes, sir. They have been trained by the caddies to treat me impertinently.

QUESTION: What sort of treatment have you received in the locker room?

ANSWER: The worst possible. In the case under consideration, I may say that I took an eight on the second hole, instead of insisting on a five, because I knew the sort of thing Dr. Green would say in the locker room after the match—I knew the scene he would make, and what the comments of my so-called friends would be. Whenever I do get down to a hundred an attempt is made to discredit me in the locker room.

QUESTION: Well, you took an eight on the second hole. What happened at the third hole?

ANSWER: Well, sir, I teed up for my drive, and just as I did so, Doc Green made a slighting remark about the League of Nations. "I think it is a good thing we kept out of it," he said.

QUESTION: What were your reactions?

ANSWER: A person of intelligence could only have one kind of reaction, sir. The remark was silly, narrow-minded, provincial, boneheaded, crass and ignorant. It was all the more criminal because Dr. Green knew quite well what I think of the League of Nations. The League of Nations was my idea. I thought about it even before the late President Wilson did, and talked about it and wrote about it and lectured about it in the university.

QUESTION: So that you consider Dr. Green's motives in mentioning it when you were about to drive—

ANSWER: The worst possible, sir. They could only come from a black heart at such a time.

QUESTION: Did you lose your temper, Professor?

ANSWER: No, sir! No, sir! No, sir! I *never* lose my temper! Not on any provocation. I said to myself, Be calm! Be philosophical! He's trying to get me excited! Remember what he'll say in the locker room afterwards! Be calm! Show him, show him, show him! Show him he can't get my goat.

QUESTION: Then you drove?

ANSWER: I addressed the ball the second time, sir. And I was about to drive when he said, with a sneer, "You must excuse me, Professor. I forgot that you invented the League of Nations."

QUESTION: Did you become violent, then, Professor?

ANSWER: No, sir! No, sir! I never become violent! I never—

QUESTION: Can you moderate your voice somewhat, Professor?

ANSWER: Yes, sir. I was explaining that I never become violent. I had every right to become violent. Any person less calm and philosophical would have become violent. Doc Green to criticize the League of Nations! The ass! Absurd! Preposterous! Silly! Abhorrent! Criminal! What the world wants is peace! Philosophic calm! The fool! Couldn't he understand that!

QUESTION: Aren't you departing, Professor, from the events of the 29th of last September at the Rivercliff golf course? What did you do next?

ANSWER: I drove.

QUESTION: Successfully?

ANSWER: It was a good drive, but the wind caught it, and it went out of bounds.

QUESTION: What did Dr. Green do then?

ANSWER: He grinned. A crass bonehead capable of sneering at the progress of the human race would sneer at a time like that.

QUESTION: But you kept your temper?

ANSWER: All my years of training as a philosopher came to my aid.

QUESTION: Go on, Professor.

ANSWER: I took my midiron from my bag and looked at it.

QUESTION: Well, go on, Professor. What did you think when you looked at it?

ANSWER: I do not remember, sir.

QUESTION: Come, come, Professor! You are under oath, you know. Did you think what a dent it would make in his skull?

ANSWER: Yes, sir. I remember now. I remember wondering if it would not do his brain good to be shaken up a little.

QUESTION: Did you strike him, then?

ANSWER: No, sir. I knew what they'd say in the locker room. They'd say that I lost temper over a mere game. They would not understand that I had been jarring up his brain for his own good, in the hope of making him understand about the League of Nations. They'd say I was irritated. I know the things people always say.

QUESTION: Was there no other motive for not hitting him?

ANSWER: I don't remember.

QUESTION: Professor Waddems, again I call your attention to the fact that you are under oath. What was your other motive?

ANSWER: Oh yes, now I recall it. I reflected that if I hit him they might make me add another stroke to my score. People are always getting up the flimsiest excuses to make me add another stroke. And then accusing me of impatience if I do not acquiesce in their unfairness. I am never impatient or irritable!

QUESTION: Did you ever break a club on the course, Professor?

ANSWER: I don't remember.

QUESTION: Did you not break a mashie on the Rivercliff course last week, Professor Waddems? Reflect before you answer.

ANSWER: I either gave it away or broke it, I don't remember which.

QUESTION: Come, come, don't you remember that you broke it against a tree?

ANSWER: Oh, I think I know what you mean. But it was not through temper or irritation.

QUESTION: Tell the jury about it.

ANSWER: Well, gentlemen, I had a mashie that had a loose head on it, and I don't know how it got into my bag. My ball lay behind a sapling, and I tried to play it out from behind the tree and missed it entirely. And then I noticed I had this old mashie, which should have been gotten rid of long ago. The club had never been any good. The blade was laid back at the wrong angle. I decided that the time had come to get rid of it once and for all. So I hit it a little tap against the tree, and the head fell off. I threw the pieces over into the bushes.

QUESTION: Did you swear, Professor?

ANSWER: I don't remember. But the injustice of this incident was that my opponent insisted on counting it as a stroke and adding it to my score—my judicial, deliberate destruction of this old mashie. I never get a square deal.

QUESTION: Return to Dr. James T. Green, Professor. You are now at the third hole, and the wind has just carried your ball out of bounds.

ANSWER: Well, I didn't hit him when he sneered. I carried the ball within bounds.

Shooting three," I said calmly. I topped the ball. Gentlemen, I have seen Walter Hagen top the ball the same way.

"Too bad, Professor," said Doc Green. He said it hypocritically. I knew it was hypocrisy. He was secretly gratified that I had topped the ball. He knew I knew it.

QUESTION: What were your emotions at this further insult, Professor?

ANSWER: I pitied him. I thought how inferior he was to me intellectually, and I pitied him. I addressed the ball again. "I pity him," I murmured. "Pity, pity, pity, pity, pity!"

He overheard me. "Your pity has cost you five more strokes," he said.

"I was merely gesticulating," I said.

QUESTION: Did the ball move? Remember, you are under oath, and you have waived immunity.

ANSWER: If the ball moved, it was because a strong breeze had sprung up.

QUESTION: Go on.

ANSWER: I laid the ball upon the green and again holed out with one putt. "I'm taking a five," I said, marking it on my card.

"I'm giving you a ten," he said, marking it on his card. "Five gesticulations on account of your pity."

QUESTION: Describe your reactions to this terrible injustice, Professor. Was there a red mist before your eyes? Did you turn giddy and wake up to find him lying lifeless at your feet? Just what happened?

ANSWER: Nothing, sir.

(Sensation in the grand jury room)

QUESTION: Think again, Professor. Nothing?

ANSWER: I merely reflected that, in spite of his standing scientifically, Dr. James T. Green was a moron and utterly devoid of morality and that I should take this into account. I did not lose my temper.

QUESTION: Did you snatch the card from his hands?

ANSWER: I took it, sir. I did not snatch it.

QUESTION: And then did you cram it down his throat?

ANSWER: I suggested that he eat it, sir, as it contained a falsehood in black and white, and Dr. Green complied with my request.

QUESTION: Did you lay hands upon him, Professor? Remember, now, we are still talking about the third hole.

ANSWER: I think I did steady him a little by holding him about the neck and throat while he masticated and swallowed the card.

QUESTION: And then what?

ANSWER: Well, gentlemen, after that there is very little more to tell until we reached the sixteenth hole. Dr. Green for some time made no further attempt to treat me unjustly and played in silence, acquiescing in the scores I had marked on my card. We were even as to holes, and it was a certainty that I was about to break a hundred. But I knew what was beneath this silence on Doc Green's part, and I did not trust it.

QUESTION: What do you mean? That you knew what he was thinking, although he did not speak?

ANSWER: Yes, sir. I knew just what kind of remarks he would have made if he had made any remarks.

QUESTION: Were these remarks which he suppressed derogatory remarks?

ANSWER: Yes, sir. Almost unbelievably so. They were deliberately intended to destroy my poise.

QUESTION: Did they do so, Professor?

ANSWER: I don't think so.

QUESTION: Go on, Professor.

ANSWER: At the sixteenth tee, as I drove off, this form of insult reached its climax. He accentuated his silence with a peculiar look, just as my club head was about to meet the ball. I knew what he meant. He knew that I knew it, and that I knew. I sliced into a bunker. He stood and watched me, as I stepped into the sand with my niblick—watched me with that look upon his face. I made three strokes at the ball and, as will sometimes happen even to the best of players, did not move it a foot. The fourth stroke drove it out of sight into the sand. The sixth stroke brought it to light again. Gentlemen, I did not lose my temper. I never do. But I admit that I did increase my tempo. I struck rapidly three more times at the ball. And all the time Doc Green was regarding me with that look, to which he now added a smile. Still I kept my temper, and he might be alive today if he had not spoken.

QUESTION (by the foreman of the jury): What did the man say at this trying time?

ANSWER: I know that you will not believe it is within the human heart to make the black remark that he made. And I hesitate to repeat it. But I have sworn to tell everything. What he said was, "Well, Professor, the club puts these bunkers here, and I suppose they have got to be used."

QUESTION (by the foreman of the jury): Was there something especially trying in the way he said it?

ANSWER: There was. He said it with an affectation of joviality.

QUESTION: You mean as if he thought he were making a joke, Professor?

ANSWER: Yes, sir.

QUESTION: What were your emotions at this point?

ANSWER: Well, sir, it came to me suddenly that I owed a duty to society; and for the sake of civilization I struck him with the niblick. It was an effort to reform him, gentlemen.

QUESTION: Why did you cover him with sand afterwards?

ANSWER: Well, I knew that if the crowd around the locker room discovered that I had hit him, they would insist on counting it as another stroke. And that is exactly what happened when the body was discovered—once again I was prevented from breaking a hundred.

THE DISTRICT ATTORNEY: Gentlemen of the jury, you have heard Professor Waddems' frank and open testimony in the case of Dr. James T. Green. My own recommendation is that he be not only released, but complimented, as far as this count is returned. If ever a homicide was justifiable, this one was. And I suggest that you report no indictment against the Professor, without leaving your seats. Many of you will wish to get in at least nine holes before dinner.

Titanic Thompson

JOHN LARDNER

Like father, like son. The youngest of Ring Lardner's four children, John Lardner (1912–1960), wrote prose that could fill you with laughter; he also found himself drawn to some of the more colorful and shady inhabitants—Titanic Thompson, for one—of the sporting scene. A weekly columnist for both *Newsweek* and *Look,* he contributed frequently to such magazines as *Sport, True,* and the *Saturday Evening Post,* and both his World War II dispatches and musings on television were featured regularly in *The New Yorker.* In the early '50s, *Newsweek* published a collection of his sports columns under the deliciously politically incorrect title, *Strong Cigars and Lovely Women.* Originally penned for *True* in 1951, "Titanic Thompson" was reissued 10 years later in the posthumous collection *The World of John Lardner.*

One day not long ago, a St. Louis hotel detective tipped off a cop friend of his that there was a fellow in a room on the eighth floor who packed a gun. They decided to do a little further research. They went into the room without knocking, and it didn't take long to find the gun. It was pointing at them. The man who held it was tall, dark, thin, well dressed and fiftyish.

"Take it easy," he said. Then, observing the cop's uniform, he set down the gun, a small Army model, on a table, and smiled pleasantly. "I thought it might be a stick-up," he said. "I have to be careful."

Down at the station house, where the man was taken to explain why he was armed and why he drew his hardware so quickly, they got a polite and possibly a truthful answer. He happened to have $3,930 on him. He was ex-pecting to claim a race horse with it. When he carried cash, he liked to feel protected. He had a license for the gun. His name was Alvin C. Thomas. At this point, the police lost interest in the details of the story and merely sat looking at the speaker with the frank curiosity of zoo-goers looking at a duck-billed platypus—for Alvin C. Thomas, as they knew and as he readily confirmed, is also Titanic Thompson. All the cops in the house took a good, long stare. They then released him, and he went on his way.

On a small scale, Titanic Thompson is an American legend. I say a small scale, because an overpowering majority of the public has never heard of him. That is the way Titanic likes it. He is a professional gambler. He has some-times been called the gamblers' gambler. He does not resent his fame among fellow hustlers as a "man with a million propositions," as a master of percent-age, but he likes to have it kept within the lodge. In the years of his early man-hood, no one knew of him except gamblers, a few rich suckers, a few golf pros, and, by rumor, the police of New York City, the Middle West, and California, his favorite bases of operation. The cops had heard that he clipped people at everything, from golf to throwing quarters at a crack in the floor. But the peo-ple he clipped were mostly members of his own profession. Those outside it, honest suckers, did not complain. Suckers seldom do. Besides, they believed—and often they were right—that they had been beaten by pure skill.

One night in 1928, the most celebrated card game in American crimi-nal history took place. As a result of it, Arnold Rothstein, a so-called under-world king, was murdered. And then it turned out that someone named Titanic Thompson had sat in on the game, and might know something about the killing.

That was the end, for a while, of Titanic's obscurity. Members of the Grassy Sprain Country Club, near New York City, blurted out a story that had been on their minds for a month. One day, some time between the Rothstein killing and Titanic's arrest as a material witness, Leo P. Flynn, a big-time fight manager and matchmaker who once handled Jack Dempsey, had brought a stranger out to the club. Leo was known there as a sport and a pretty fair golfer. This time, though, he didn't want to play golf himself. He wanted to match the stranger, whom he called Titanic, against the club professional, George McLean.

A side bet of $2,500 was arranged, with Flynn backing Thompson and several members pooling their funds in support of the local pride. That day, McLean won. He won with ease—the stranger, though he hit some good shots, did not seem to be in George's class. Besides, he was left-handed, and top-notch left-handed golfers are almost as rare as left-handed catchers. The McLean faction listened to Flynn's talk of a return match. McLean listened to the stranger's mild appeal for a ten-stroke handicap.

"I'm not in your league," said the unknown, running his hand through his floppy dark hair, "but I think I can do better than I did today. Give me a real edge in strokes, and we'll bet real dough."

The handicap, after some needling back and forth, was fixed at eight strokes. The real dough, supplied mostly by Mr. Flynn and another golfing sport, a Mr. Duffy, was $13,000, and the members covered every dime of it in behalf of their pro. Mr. Duffy, it happened, was Big Bill Duffy, a jolly henchman of Owney Madden, the racketeer. The members did not know this, but it would probably have made no difference if they had. They did not see how you could fix a golf match, and they did not see how an amateur could beat a good pro. It may not have occurred to them that for $13,000 Titanic was not, strictly speaking, an amateur.

The stranger shot much better, or luckier, golf this time than he had in the first match, but at the end of sixteen holes he had used up his eight-stroke advantage. The match was dead even, and McLean prepared to close in. On the short seventeenth, his tee shot stopped six feet from the pin. Titanic studied the distance and dropped one four feet closer. Perhaps that shot unnerved McLean. At any rate, he missed his putt. The stranger sank his. Titanic stood one up. He halved the last hole in par, and Mr. Flynn and Mr. Duffy picked up the $13,000—of which they gaily gave Mr. Thompson his share—and called for drinks for the house. The members went home to brood on the fact that a golf match can indeed be fixed—"fixed upward," as gamblers say—if the fixer is a talented athlete who knows how to hide the symptoms until the price is right.

On the day the news broke of Titanic's arrest in the Rothstein case, Grassy Sprain started the legend rolling. It has been gathering strength ever since. Generally speaking, New York newspaper readers forgot Thompson soon after the trial of George A. McManus for Rothstein's murder (Titanic was a state witness who gave the state no help at all). To most of the rest of the world, he was then, and still is, unknown. But in the small circle in which his name is famous, Titanic Thompson stories have been collected, pooled, and warmed over slow fires for nearly a quarter of a century, till now they amount to a kind of saga—the sharpshooter's Adventures of Robin Hood.

Rothstein's death reminded Broadway story-swappers of what might on other levels be called the Adventure of the White Horses. The horse-playing set to which Titanic and Rothstein belonged had formed the habit of spotting white horses from the train that took them to the Belmont or Jamaica track. One morning, some twenty of these smoking-car handicappers made up a pool, of $50 each, on the number of white horses that would be counted on the trip that day. Rothstein's estimate was surprisingly high; Titanic studied the tycoon thoughtfully before he made his own guess, just one horse above Rothstein's. There was an outburst of white horsemeat along the Long Island Rail Road tracks that day—a batch of fifteen animals at one crossing, a batch of twelve at another. The first batch had been planted by Titanic, the second by Rothstein.

"That will teach you not to be close with your money," said Titanic to Rothstein, as he pocketed the pool. "For thirty bucks, you could have had a whole livery stable."

Bear in mind that if Titanic had taken from the rich to give to the poor, as Robin Hood and Jesse James are said to have done, the legend-makers of the gambling world would want no part of him. He would be the wrong kind of hero. But Mr. Thompson has always taken very frankly to give to himself, or to split with the people who stake him. He has seldom made a bet he wasn't sure of winning. He always carries a gimmick—sometimes his hidden athletic skill, sometimes his trained knowledge of percentage, and occasionally a little something extra.

Here are some of the tales they tell:

1. Titanic once bet a peanut vendor $10 he could throw a peanut across Times Square in New York. He took a peanut from the vendor's stack, palmed a loaded one in its place, and pitched the phony goober up against the marquee of the Hotel Astor, across the street.

2. Billy Duffy once backed Titanic in a bet against a powerful amateur golfer, noted for his long drives. Titanic offered to let his opponent make three drives on each hole and play the best drive of the three. It sounded like a big margin to spot a strong hitter, and the party of the second part snapped the bet up. Playing his best drive, he piled up a big lead on the first nine holes. By that time, his arms were so tired from three full swings a hole that he could hardly knock the ball off the tee. Titanic breezed home in the last nine.

3. Titanic once bet $10,000 that Nick (the Greek) Dandolos, another high operator, would not sink a 25-foot putt. Kissed by the goddess Athena, the Greek holed the ball. Thompson, however, was not one to let $10,000 of his money rest long in someone else's jeans. He bet Nick double or nothing that

he could hit a silver dollar with a gun eight times out of eight, from ten feet away. After the ceremony, the Greek gave back the ten grand and kept what was left of the dollar for a souvenir.

4. Titanic's mathematics were as sound as Pascal's. In fact, they were based on the reasoning of that great seventeenth-century Frenchman. He once bet a fellow gambler that two of the first thirty persons they met and spoke to would prove to have the same birthday. Strong in the thought that he had 365 days running for him, the second hustler was pleased to accept. Suspecting, not unnaturally, a frame-up, he was careful to approach total strangers and chance passers-by, who could not be known to Titanic. He lost the bet on the twenty-eighth question, when a duplicate birthday turned up.

"To tell you the truth," said Titanic afterward, "on each of the last five guys we spoke to, the odds were better than even money in my favor. I'll explain the mathematics to you some time."

Your correspondent will also be glad to explain the mathematics some time, to any reader. He does not quite understand them, but he knows what they are. Titanic's reasoning on the birthday proposition was founded on the fact that the chance against him at first was 364/365th, which, when multiplied by the succeeding chances—363/365th, 362/365th, and so forth—came fairly soon to represent 1/2, or one chance in two, or even money.

5. Tony Penna, the golf professional, tells of a bet by Titanic that he could throw a pumpkin over a three-story house. The pumpkin, when he produced it, was the size of an orange—but still a pumpkin. Going perhaps into the realm of pure myth, Penna adds that Titanic once bet he could throw a baseball over the Empire State Building. He won it (says Penna) by taking an elevator to the top platform and throwing from there.

6. Titanic once bet a dice impresario named Nutts Nitti that he could find a hairpin in each block of a stretch of twenty consecutive New York City blocks. He won. The hairpins had been planted in advance.

7. Titanic once bet he could throw a quarter at a potato, from fifteen feet away, and make it stick in the potato at least once in ten tries. Encountering resistance from his opponent, he agreed to settle for seven tries, and scored on the fourth one.

8. Titanic was motoring into Omaha, his temporary base, with a friend one day. As they passed a signpost on the road, Titanic, without looking at it, offered

to bet that they would reach the city limits within ten minutes. The signpost made it ten miles to town. The friend, a noticing sort of man, took the bet. He lost. Titanic had moved the signpost five miles closer that morning.

9. There is a standard prop in Titanic's repertory—a two-headed quarter, which he uses with more than standard speed, skill, and acting talent. His opening line, after dinner, is "Let's toss for the check." His next line, while the coin is in the air, is "You cry." If his opponent cries tails, Titanic lets the quarter fall—heads. If the other fellow cries heads, Titanic swings his hand nonchalantly, catches the coin, puts it back in his pocket, and speaks to this effect: "Oh, to hell with gambling for ham and eggs. Let's go Dutch."

10. Titanic is credited with being the man who introduced Rothstein to the art of betting on automobile license plates, at Rothstein's expense. He bet Rothstein, as they stood on a Broadway corner, that the first New Jersey plate to come along would make a better poker hand than the first New York plate. Thirty seconds later, from his parking spot around the corner (there were parking spots in those days), a colleague of Titanic's drove into view in a New Jersey car. His plate number carried three threes.

11. In a Hot Springs, Arkansas, stud-poker game, a player named Burke became justly incensed one evening because he could not win.

"That deck is ice cold, and so is the other one," he bawled. "I ain't had a pair in an hour."

"You ought to know," said Titanic soothingly, "that the odds are against getting a pair in any five-card hand. Now, if you dealt yourself six cards—"

"With these cards," yelled Burke, "I couldn't pair myself if I dealt all night!"—and the way was paved for a Thompson proposition. Titanic offered to let Burke deal himself ten cold hands of six cards each. Before each hand, he offered to bet that there would be a pair in it. They say that the agony of Burke, as he paired himself in eight of the ten hands and thus lost $300 by the sweat of his own fingers, was something to see. Titanic had known that the addition of a sixth card changes the odds on catching a pair from 13 to 10 against to nearly 2 to 1 in favor. And to bet even money on a 2-to-1 favorite, he would walk quite a distance and stay quite a while.

12. In his early days, Titanic, going through a storeroom in the basement of a sporting club in Ohio on his way to the men's room, spotted a rat and nimbly tipped a barrel over the animal. Later, in the course of the dice game upstairs,

he raised the subject of the prevalence of rats in Ohio sporting clubs and made a bet that he could find and shoot one any time. The bet was taken. Titanic returned to the cellar, shot the dead rat, and brought it back to the table with him.

13. Titanic, shooting right-handed, lost a close golf match to an amateur who played in the 90s. Next day, he bet the winner double their first bet that he could beat him playing left-handed. Left-handed, his natural style, Titanic shot an 80. The victim continued to shoot in the 90s.

14. Titanic once bet he could drive a golf ball 500 yards. The bet was popular on all sides, and the interested parties followed Titanic out to the golf course of his choice, on Long Island. He picked a tee on a hill overlooking a lake. It was wintertime. His drive hit the ice and, it seemed to his opponents, never did stop rolling. It went half a mile, if it went a yard.

Titanic, as the district attorney found out in the Rothstein case, does not talk much. All that anyone knows about his origins and early life comes from stray remarks, spaced far apart, that he has let fall to other gamblers on the golf course or at the card table. This writer has seen him only once. It was in the "private" or "upstairs" crap game at the old Chicago Club in Saratoga. Joe Madden, the literary barkeep, pointed him out to me from the sidelines. I saw a slender fellow about six feet tall, his dark hair cut long, wearing a neat gabardine suit and two fair-sized diamond rings. When Titanic left the game a little later, Madden said, "He's going down to the drugstore to get a load of ice cream. That's his dish."

"That's his dish for breakfast," corrected one of the gamblers at the table. "But he don't eat breakfast till he gets up for the races, maybe two o'clock in the afternoon."

A discussion of Titanic's habits ensued. It reminded me of a session of fight men on Jacobs Beach or in the press room at the Garden, discussing some figure of legend like Stanley Ketchel. I asked where the name Titanic had come from. The answer was one I'd heard before, the only one I've ever heard. It may or may not be true.

In a poker game in New York on Thompson's first tour of the East, one player said to another, "What's that guy's name?"

"It ought to be Titanic," said the second player. "He sinks everybody."

The logic here was a little unsound—if I remember the S.S. *Titanic* story, "Iceberg" would have been the right name. But gamblers are seldom good on names. Thompson, for instance, is an easy garbling of Titanic's real name, Thomas. There seems to be no doubt, judging by police files, that he was born Alvin Clarence Thomas, in the state of Arkansas, about 1893. He still talks with a slight Southwestern accent. As a boy, he once said, he acquired the throwing skill that served him handsomely later by killing quail with rocks. He was a good horseshoe pitcher and an expert shot.

Athletic talent is a rare thing in a professional gambler, but what surprised the golf pros of the Pacific Coast and the Southwest, who knew him in his early days and accepted him as an athlete to begin with, was his lightning speed of mind at gambling. He would make twelve to fifteen bets on a single hole, keeping track of them in his head while others took time to make notes. He would lose one bet and make another on the next shot that would bring his stake back doubled. Penna and others noticed that his bets during the match often were bigger than his bet on the match as a whole.

"Yeah, that's right," said Titanic, when someone spoke of this. "I like to bet 'em when they're out there on the course with me. Especially on the greens. Why? Figure it out for yourself."

It was not hard to figure. When a golfer is out there on the course, any new bet he makes is probably made with his own money, without the help of a backer. When he bets with his own money, he gets nervous. Especially on the greens.

In Titanic's youth, they say, he was impatient with mental slowness of any kind, but it could not have been long before he came to recognize that quality, in the people around him, as so much bread and jam for him. Among the money golfers who knew him at one time and another were Penna, Dick Metz, Len Dodson and Ben Hogan. He always told them, as he often told the cops when they picked him up on the curious charge of shooting golf too well, that he was "a former pro." It may have been so, but the chances are that he was a former caddy who, on discovering his own skill at the game, almost immediately became a professional gambler rather than a professional golfer. It was a nice economic choice. The best professional golfers in the country, even in these days of rich prizes, do well to earn $30,000 in a year from tournaments. Titanic has sometimes made $50,000 in a few weeks of well-timed chipping and putting at golf resorts.

"I've been broke," he told a Coast newspaperman once, "but never for more than six hours at a time. When I tap out, somebody I once helped loans me a stake, and I'm back in action again."

Titanic Thompson broke into the Rothstein game, as a young man, because he was good company and a good player—though the state of New

York tried to prove, a little later, that trained fingers had something to do with it. The fateful game that led to Rothstein's death and to Titanic's first appearance in print took place on the night of September 7–8, 1928. It was held at the apartment of Jimmy Meehan, a regular member of the circle, on the West Side of New York. Rothstein, because he was rumored to have a finger in every branch of organized crime in the city, was the best-known player in the game, but all the others were noted figures in the gambling, bookmaking, and horse-playing worlds. They included Martin "Red" Bowe, Nigger Nate Raymond, Sam and Meyer Boston, Abe Silverman, George A. McManus, and Titanic Thompson. The game was stud poker, but as it went along it took on a pattern familiar in that group—it became a "high-card" game, with the biggest money being bet on the size of the first-up card in the stud hand.

There were rumors along Broadway in the following week that Rothstein had lost a packet. There were also rumors that the winners had not been paid in full. It took a gunshot, however, to make the story public property. On November 4, 1928, someone put a revolver slug into Rothstein's body in Room 349 of the Park Central Hotel. Rothstein staggered from the room and died just outside it. The killer pushed aside a screen and threw the gun into the street below. The New York newspapers went to town. It became the biggest crime story since the murder of Herman Rosenthal by Whitey Lewis, Dago Frank, Lefty Louie, and Gyp the Blood.

The overcoat of George McManus, a smiling gambler, brother of a police lieutenant, had been found in Room 349. Soon afterward McManus was indicted for murder, along with three gunmen who never did show up for trial. On November 26, the D.A., Joab H. Banton, arrested Jimmy Meehan, Red Bowe, Sidney Stajer (Rothstein's secretary), Nigger Nate Raymond, and Titanic as material witnesses. All of them but Bowe were held in $100,000 bail. For some reason it was Titanic, then and later, who caught the public's fancy—maybe because he was said to be a Westerner, a lone wolf, a romantic and single-duke gambler of the old school.

It turned out that Titanic had a wife, Mrs. Alice Thomas, who had been living with him at the Mayflower Hotel. A few days after his arrest, she paid him a tearful visit at the West Side prison on Fifty-fourth Street. Titanic then sent for the D.A.'s men, made "important disclosures" (the paper said), and was released in $10,000 bail. What kind of minstrel show he gave to win his freedom is not known. Unofficially it was reported that he had admitted to being in Room 349 just before the murder, leaving when he saw that there might be trouble. Whatever he said, it was plain that the D.A. thought he had laid hold of a fine, friendly witness. The D.A. was very wrong.

When the McManus murder case came to trial, in November 1929, Titanic was running a night club and gambling spot in Milwaukee. He was also running a fever in a Milwaukee hospital. So important was his evidence considered by the prosecution that the trial was delayed for a week. Titanic, in Milwaukee, showed for the first time that he was in no mood to blow whistles.

"I don't know what they want me as a witness for," he told reporters, whom he received in scarlet pajamas in the hospital. "I wasn't with Rothstein on the night of the murder and hadn't seen him or McManus for two months previously. We played cards at that time, and McManus lost a lot of money. That's all I know about the case."

When he did get to New York to testify, the courtroom was packed. Titanic sat in the rear of the room, twisting his fingers nervously, till he was called. The crowd buzzed as he took the stand. McManus, in the dock, sat up and smiled at Titanic. Titanic nodded to McManus. Ferdinand Pecora, later a famous judge, then an assistant D.A. and a strong trial lawyer, moved in on Titanic confidently. It had been established that McManus had lost $51,000 to Rothstein in the celebrated high-card game while Rothstein was losing about $219,000 to some of the others. Pecora's pitch was obvious. He implied that Rothstein, possibly with Titanic's help, had fleeced McManus of the fifty-one grand. Titanic would have no part of this hypothesis. After identifying himself by saying that he gambled on everything from golf to horse races, and referring to McManus as "a square and honest guy," he began to spar Pecora to a standstill.

"Was the game on the level?" asked the prosecutor.

"It couldn't be any other way on high cards," said Titanic with a deeply scornful gesture. "A man who never dealt in his life was peddling the papers. We had to show him how to shuffle."

To "peddle the papers" is to deal. The crowd was delighted with this local color.

"Now, think," said Pecora angrily, after a while. "Wasn't this game crooked?"

"Anyone ought to know," said Titanic, still scornful, "that that's impossible."

"Couldn't a clever dealer give the high card to any man he chose?"

"Certainly not," said Titanic. "It ain't being done."

On other questions, his memory failed.

"You see," he told Pecora patiently, "I just don't remember things. If I bet on a horse today and won ten grand, I probably would not be able to recall the horse's name tomorrow."

While the public gasped at this specious statement, the defense took over for cross-examination. At once, Titanic's memory improved, and his attitude got friendlier. He said that McManus had shown no ill will after the game.

"He's a swell loser," said Titanic tenderly. "Win or lose, he always smiles."

In short, he probably gave the state less change for its money than any state's witness in recent memory. And it's a matter of record that George A. McManus was acquitted of the murder of Arnold Rothstein.

It's a matter of record, too, that Titanic was annoyed by his notoriety during the trial. For several months afterward, he complained that he could no longer get a "good" game of golf, by which he meant a game with gravy on the side. He may have misstated the case a little. Recently I asked Oswald Jacoby, the card wizard, about a story in the newspapers that said that John R. Crawford, an ex-G.I. and a spectacular newcomer to card-playing circles, resented the publicity he got in a big Canasta game for charity because no one wanted to play cards with him any more.

"Don't you believe it," said Mr. Jacoby. "People always want to play with a man with a big reputation. The more money they have, the more they like it."

Be that as it may, Titanic, in Tulsa soon after the trial, was bothered by the galleries that followed him—but he did find one man who wanted to play golf with him just to be able to say he'd done it. Titanic fixed up "a little proposition" for him and won $2,000. There must have been other men with the same ambition, or else Ti's celebrity began to fade, for we cross his trail again in Little Rock, Arkansas, soon afterward, playing golf for $2,000 and $3,000 a round.

True, even a roving gambler likes to stop and run a "store" now and then, but since the time of his first fame, Titanic has found it more comfortable to keep on the move. He and a large restaurant operator and racketeer, whom we will call Tony Rizzo, were moving by train not long ago from California to Tony's base at Hot Springs.

"Tony," said Titanic, "do you ever regret being illiterate?"

"Whaddya mean?" said Tony, hurt. "I ain't so dumb."

"I'm going to teach you to spell two ten-letter words," said Titanic. "The words are 'rhinoceros' and 'anthropoid.' If you can still spell them when we get off the train, I'll pick up the checks for this trip. But take a tip from me—keep spelling them or you'll forget them."

For the rest of the trip, Rizzo kept spelling out, in order, the letters r-h-i-n-o-c-e-r-o-s and a-n-t-h-r-o-p-o-i-d. He still knew them at the Hot Springs station. Titanic paid off.

The gambler set the second stage of the proposition for Tony's restaurant. He first brought an unknown partner, a respectable-looking fellow as shills go, into the act. He rehearsed the shill in the spelling of ten ten-letter words, including "rhinoceros" and "anthropoid." The next night he sat down in Rizzo's restaurant, as usual, with Owney Madden and other lovable tourists. Rizzo himself, as usual, was sitting at a table by himself, wolfing his pizza in solitary grandeur.

"Do you know," said Titanic confidentially, "that that Rizzo just pretends to be ignorant? He puts on a dumb front for business. The guy has got diplomas from two colleges."

This speech aroused great skepticism at Titanic's table, which in turn aroused bets. Titanic covered a thousand dollars' worth, his argument being that Tony could spell any ten-letter word, any one at all, that Mr. Madden and the boys chose to mention. As Titanic expected, a pause followed, while the boys tried to think of a ten-letter word to give Tony. They were somewhat embarrassed. At this point, Titanic's partner hove into view, and Titanic hailed him.

"Excuse me, sir," he said, "but you look as though you might be able to help us. May I ask your business? A lawyer? Fine. Would you mind writing down ten ten-letter words on a piece of paper here, for these gentlemen to choose from?"

The stranger obliged. Looking around, he wrote down the word "restaurant," which appeared on Tony's window. He wrote down several others he found on the bill of fare, such as "cacciatore." In and among the rest he inserted the words "rhinoceros" and "anthropoid." He turned the paper over to the boys, who immediately set to work making scratches in the morning line, to protect their bets. They scratched "restaurant"—Tony saw it on the window all day, he might know it. They scratched "cacciatore." "He's Eyetalian," said Mr. Madden, "and he might know all that kind of stuff." This left them, in the end, with "rhinoceros" and "anthropoid." At random, they scratched "rhinoceros." They summoned Mr. Rizzo and desired him to spell the word "anthropoid."

"Sure," said Tony, taking a deep breath. "R-h-i-n-o-c-e-r-o-s."

Titanic paid off the $1,000. The bet belongs to his legend partly because he lost it and partly because he won the money back, with galloping dominoes, the same night. As I said before, he is prosperous just now. A fellow gambler who ran across him in Evansville, Indiana—you are apt to find him anywhere—says that Titanic's pajamas and dressing gowns, always brilliant, are more brilliant than ever. His supply of jewels, rings, and stickpins is at high tide. A man like Ti, my informant explains, buys jewels whenever he is in the money, to sell or hock when times are hard.

The Titanic legend would not be so solidly honored in the gambling world, it would not be complete, if the quiet Mr. Thompson had never used the gun he always carries, in defense of the money he takes from the rich to give to himself. The police of Little Rock, years ago, found a letter in Titanic's room which demanded "2 thousand cash or you will be sorry." The police of St. Louis, more recently, found him ready to draw at the sound of a door being opened.

And in Tyler, Texas, a few years back, it was proved clearly that in matters involving Titanic Thompson and his money there is very little kidding. Titanic had had a good day on the golf course. His caddy noticed it. The caddy was sixteen years old, but he had grown-up ideas. At a late hour the same evening, a shot was fired in Tyler, and the police arrived to find the caddy with a bullet in him, while Titanic stood in attendance.

"I shot him," said the gambler. "It was self-defense. He tried to stick me up for my roll."

The young man died next day. A mask and an unfired gun were found on his person, and the plea of self-defense was allowed. Titanic moved along, with a stronger toehold on history than ever.

Big Divorces and Small Divots

BY GARY MCCORD

Gary McCord once kicked me. I am forever grateful. So is the excuse the golf gods gave me for a swing.

It was 1966, and a magazine no longer in existence had dispatched me to weigh in on the high-profile golf school—the Kostis/McCord Learning Center—that McCord runs in Scottsdale with his network broadcasting cohort Peter Kostis. About a half hour into the first morning's instruction, McCord stepped up to me as I addressed a ball with my six-iron. He looked down at my foot, aimed, as it always was, geometrically perpendicular to where I wanted the ball to go. Thwack! With his own left foot, he kicked and shoved mine into the proper position. Amazingly, my next shot flew precisely where it was supposed to go.

Given his trademark mustache and the breezy wit he exhibits as an analyst for CBS—remember that quip about bikini waxing the greens at Augusta?—it's easy to think of McCord as the reigning clown prince of golf, and leave it there. That would be a mistake. He is certainly one of the game's true characters, but he's too big a personality to be reduced. A survivor of more than two decades on the PGA Tour, and now a multi-winner on the senior tour, he's turned into one of golf's smartest and most affable communicators. Quite remarkably, McCord's personality loses nothing when he moves it into print. His *Golf for Dummies* is a cheerfully adept instructional with a brilliant tip that involves a potato chip. The wild golf outing that follows, from his collection-cum-memoir, *Just a Range Ball in a Box of Titleists,* may actually be an instructional device in disguise. It'll have you so bent over laughing, you might as well tee up a ball while you're down there and give it a whack.

I have paraded around this golfing world with a ticket to divine sanctuary, my PGA Tour card. It has accessed me to venues of exquisite beauty. Towering palm trees of the Hawaiian Islands, the emerald green landscape of Ireland, the rugged terrain and noble beauty of Australia. All have eclipsed my brow as I have been searching the fairways of life.

The sheer grandeur and pageantry of this game has nestled within my soul. It levels the spirit and hides the anticipation of death. Golf is life's motivational speech.

As I glance back, beyond the alamedas of the world's greatest golf courses, I discover a place of awakening. The womb of enlightenment. The place in which all of life's dark treaties were negotiated to simple thought and careless action. That place where refuge and lifelong association are housed.

Your persona has been formed by social, environmental, and spiritual awakenings. You don't cast those manuscripts of life upon the wind and let them settle into some corner of this cockeyed world. You form those social skills early. Man is socially mutable, and I came from the land of the idiots.

I have no recollection of abuse from my childhood. I was a good child from good parents. I did as they told me and stayed away from trouble in the difficult time of the sixties. Sports was my social catalyst. I was antiseptically clean and nurtured in a sterile corral.

As I started the Tour in 1974 and moved from Riverside, California, to Escondido, California, past and present collided. I came from Victoria Country Club in Riverside, a posh club that had roots back to 1908. The membership was as old as the furniture. I learned much about my golf game there, but socially I was a runt. Then came San Luis Rey Downs Golf and Country Club, a public facility that could have been called an asylum.

Order had now changed to disorder. In the long run of things, here is how it will be played out. Solar energy, the product of a hot sun turning in cold space, will eventually burn out. Molecular chaos will prevail, and we'll all be left sitting in a lukewarm cosmic bath watching our dicks fall off. Except at San Luis Rey, where Fairway Louie will be asking our bookie, Unemployed Lloyd, what's the price on the game this week and can he play on house money until he sells his double-wide to pay off last week's losses? San Luis Rey is such a mutation that cataclysmic events will not persuade the place to die. Charles Darwin never met Fairway Louie and the boys.

I was introduced to "Head Pro" in January of 1974. There had been an awful fire that had destroyed the pro shop and all of the saleable inventory. What a shame, all that spectacular stuff the public hadn't bought for the last three and a half years was now dark polyester fire remnants. Luckily, the fire insurance had been paid, the week prior.

Head Pro told me of the time-consuming efforts that were now in place to "remodel" the old shop so it would look like new. They had already brought in the double-wide mobile home and had anchored it and placed potted daisies around the periphery to appease the women's twilight league.

The golf course, twenty-six-room lodge, and thoroughbred racing facility had been recently sold to Millie Vessels, who had just lost her husband, Frank, to an unfortunate shooting death. Millie Vessels came into town in her white Lincoln Continental limousine, with a wad of insurance money, a fondness for drink, and questions about her husband's death.

The golf course is a pretty good layout. There is a nursery of grasses in the fairways, poa-annua greens that you need help from the Psychic Friends Network to read, plus various dead trees that the native wildlife (illegal aliens) burn to keep warm at night. The golf course wanders around a floodplain that is constantly moist from California floods. The stream carries the overflow and is always harassing the fairways. Mud golf is always fun in the winter. Encroaching never lessens the fun at the "Downs" because there is always a wager in the air. Silt or no silt.

I grew so fond of this place that I became a resident of the place after my divorce. I had little left in the way of real property after my marriage. A 1974 Mercedes-Benz, some old Munsingwear golf shirts, a table clock given to me by an uncle who is doing time for forgery, and three sets of golf clubs. Just enough to start a new life amongst the derelicts. There was an old train caboose the club had fixed up and put on the golf course as a snack shop. It was six hundred square feet and had a nice porch on which I could entertain my guests. There was a john adjacent to the caboose and plenty of green grass. I moved in, and like my life, I was bringing up the rear in my new abode.

The cast of characters that made up this denizen of derelicts were my friends. They made fun of my bad play on the Tour and defended my right to exist when I was home. They were my cradle of insanity.

There was my junior college and college mentor, Fairway Louie. He taught me more about life than Phil Donahue. We had two bookies at the Downs; one was Willie "Brain Damage" Rains, who had a tattoo on each cheek of his ass with the letter "W" inscribed. When he mooned you, it spelled "WOW." Think about it. He was clever, too; sometimes he would moon you upside down and it would spell "MOM." Willie wasn't the best of bookies, but he was honest. A tribute rare among that species.

Our other bookie was Unemployed Lloyd, who never had a job, but always had his beeper on. Unemployed and Brain Damage were always fighting over spreads and neither had any money. A tribute rare among that species.

There was The Kitchen. He was the size of a Hugo and cost more to run. He had a three handicap, but on the kitchen table he was tour material. I saw him eat forty-three Twinkies at one sitting on a bet with some local gamesters. The Kitchen weighed 428 pounds, all fat.

There were two Vietnam veterans: Mad Max and Lock & Load. Mad Max, for fun, delivered pizzas in Cambodia during his tenure in Vietnam. He was a great wheelman and existed on one and a half hours of sleep. No matter how early you got to the Downs, Mad Max was there before you, staring at his coffee, complaining about his insurance business.

Lock & Load still has a passion for guns. He subscribes to those survivalist magazines and has more guns than a Third World country. He had me over to his "arsenal," to what he called his home, and showed me the new grenade launcher he had just bought. The guy has some wiring missing. He was always neatly attired in his camouflage fatigues and his Hawaiian golf shirt. He had some combat boots fitted with spikes. He wasn't meant to play golf.

The two horse trainers who frequented the golf course from the adjoining racetrack facilities were Muzzy and Packy. They were trainers for the thoroughbred horses of the rich and famous and they loved to play golf. They got into more trouble than Dennis Rodman trying to put on his wedding dress.

Always in the lounge was 20/20. He was legally blind, but loved to play gin and drive golf carts. 20/20 was supposedly blinded by a Gypsy curse, although we could never verify it.

You could also find The Breathalyzer. He had so many DWIs he wasn't allowed to drive. As the judge said, "Until Satan drives you to Hell." He had so many Breathalyzer tests he had "Listerine" embroidered on his golf bag as his official sponsor.

On the golf course you could find Master Sergeant Fenemore "Roots" Washington. He served at nearby Camp Pendleton for twenty-three years and then took over the green superintendent's job at the base's golf course. He retired when most of the base was shut down and came to work at San Luis Rey. He was a strict disciplinarian and could grow grass on aluminum. Roots was in charge of fifteen illegal aliens who worked on the golf course. His biggest concern was keeping the INS out of the maintenance barn and losing his workers to their homeland, Mexico.

The foreman of this maintenance crew was a Honduran National we named Chez-Juan. He was a slight man of dubious gender. Chez-Juan would arrive at work wearing glorious white Purcell sneakers and short socks equally as white. He would have on freshly pressed Byblos walking shorts that were cuffed. On his torso would be a Jockey tank top that was aflame with pastel colors. His neck would be highlighted by a gleaming scarf and his head would be bare except for black curly hair that was always maintained with a razor cut. He had some medallions hanging vaguely down his cleavage and a tattoo on his right forearm that said, "Vamanos." He was a darling. He also could operate every bit of machinery that Roots had with care and precision.

The indoor people were equally as divergently adrift. The starter in the double-wide was a bald hairdresser named Colonel Klink. The head professional was an unassuming former muffler installer at Sears Automotive who had taken the job on two different occasions. The manager of the club, Joe, worked at night managing the local topless bar.

The bartender, Paul, or as we call him, Quick Pour, had his two ex-wives working for him as waitresses. It's a festive night in the lounge where all have gathered and Quick Pour is screwing up drink orders. The two ex's are reminding him of his past failures, but we can't hear the interaction because the country-and-western band, Los Gringos, is over the legal decibel limit. All is well on this Friday night at the Downs.

It would be very difficult to pick just one circumstance that has caught my attention during the twenty-three years I have been hanging around the Downs. They all blend into chaos. I do remember one particular Friday that should have warranted a guest appearance on *Geraldo*.

It was a beautiful July morning during the summer of '83. The early-morning fog had just ascended and the smell of freshly mown grass was biting the air. It was Friday. Friday the thirteenth. This was a special day at San Luis Rey Downs. It was the day of the tournament we called the "Ex-Wives Conflict." We got the idea when Quick Pour hired his two ex-wives to work in his bar. The format was simple—you played golf with your ex-wife in a nine-hole worst-ball tournament. You both teed off and played the worst shot until the ball had been holed. It was the format from hell, but our spouses had put us through worse. There were sixteen people signed up to play. Four foursomes of dysfunctional relationships trying to act civil in a hostile environment. I love this game.

I had arrived early at the golf course to meet Fairway Louie and the rest of the guys. It was 6:15 and we were to join Packy and Muzzy at the thoroughbred training facility. It was the day the horses were going swimming. There was a large pool in which injured thoroughbreds would swim and rehabilitate their injuries. It was also the chance to bet on who would win the thoroughbred freestyle. Packy and Muzzy would release the big ponies and we would be at the other end of the pool wildly exhorting our chosen thoroughbred to victory. This is not normal behavior.

We all wandered over to the dining room at the golf course for our daily consumption of lukewarm animal fat and powdered eggs. The talk at the table was centered around Packy and Muzzy's Colorado deer-hunting trip from which they had recently returned. The boys didn't have much luck with their hunting, but they were all equipped for the parade through the deer check at Wolcott, Colorado. As they were coming down the mountain on the last day of hunting season, there was a long line of off-road vehicles with various carcasses strapped to their fronts. Fish and Game officers were combing the vehicles as they approached the checkpoint and making sure the hunters had not bagged more than the legal limit.

As Packy and Muzzy approached, there was a look of astonishment on the faces of the Fish and Game boys. Muzzy was "buck" naked lying on the hood of the rented Jeep Grand Cherokee. He was roped on with his head hanging over the front end of the Jeep. There was blood poured all over his body. Driving the car was Packy, with a full deer's outfit on, complete with hooves. The deer, Packy, stopped the car and wanted to know where a good taxidermist was for his prize human. The officers waved them through and immediately closed the checkpoint.

There were fourteen of us at our regular breakfast table next to the window overlooking the toxic creek. Beatrice was our waitress. She was a grandmotherly woman of generous weight. She moved faster than she should be able to, but our food was never served on time. Beatrice had a hard life. She'd migrated from Des Moines, Iowa, where her farm had been foreclosed and then her husband hanged himself in the barn with her apron. Beatrice never wore an apron again. She remarried a substitute teacher and moved next to the seventh fairway in a leased condo. Their life sucked, but she was our favorite waitress. We tipped her accordingly.

The owner had just arrived, Millie Vessels. She sat in her customary place in the corner where she could watch what went on. It must be 9:30 A.M. She was prompt to a fault. We heard from Beatrice that there was another terrible fight between Millie and her son, Scoop, last night at dinner. Scoop ran the Downs, but is ever in conflict with his mother.

"What kind of fight this time?" asked Mad Max. He was on his seventh cup of coffee since awaking at 3:15 this beautiful morning.

"After they got their entrée, both had the special, rack of Spam au jus. They started this terrible fight about who invented Spam. Millie was in a

paroxysm of rage. She claimed a guy named Roy invented Spam. Scoop dis-
agreed. She flung her mashed potatoes at him with an over-the-top motion
and hit Scoop in the chest. He retaliated with a slice of Spam, hitting her in the
middle of her beehive hairdo. It stuck. Words and food were flying. She
stormed out of the dining room, but not before she fired everyone in the restaurant, including Scoop."

"How come you're still working this morning?" asked Fairway Louie.

"She did the same thing last week, but forgot about it the next day."
Scoop walked in and sat down with his mother. They exchanged high fives.

Head Pro came in and asked what the pairings should be for the day.
This was a delicate matter. Most of these adversarial marriages had ended in a
serenade of slander. The ex-wives actually looked forward to each Friday the
thirteenth as an excuse to inflict more mental duress on my buddies. The boys,
on the other hand, thought maybe they could get a romp in the rack from
their ex's. The plots gained in complexity.

We decided Mad Max's ex-wife, Tanya, should not be in the same group
as The Breathalyzer's ex-wife, Noreen, because they were dating the same guy,
Miguel. He was a waiter at the Sizzler in Bonsall. The Kitchen was bringing his
ex-wife, Linda, who most of us could use as a shade tree. She tipped the scales at
just under 350 pounds. We couldn't put both of them in the same golf cart. They
wouldn't fit. We had to have Steve "Swizzle Stick" Shelman ride along. He was
the night bartender at the Indian bingo parlor in Bonsall. He weighed about the
same as Don Knotts, and his ex-wife, "the Twirl," looked like a piece of loose
wire standing vertically. They would make a "fitting" foursome.

We had a late withdrawal and were short two antagonists. Joe, the club
manager, was walking by and heard of our dilemma. "If you want, I can grab
one of the girls from The Baby Doll House and bring her as my ex. She'll
probably end up as my former anyway!" We all thought that was a good idea,
and besides, Dawn had huge snap-ons she paraded with no discretion. What a
tournament.

After two and a half hours of changing lineups, we all agreed on the
pairings of the four foursomes. It was one hour to critical mass and the ladies
were starting to arrive. They arrived in their ex's former cars. The guys would
sneak out and take a look at their former real property. Most of them were
misty-eyed as they walked back into the double-wide to pay their greens fees.
That was one of the rules, each participant had to pay for himself. We had already paid enough.

I would stand by the register and watch Head Pro ring up the fees. You
could tell if one of the guys thought he might get a romp in the rack—he

would pay for hers. I, of course, would spread the news. The guilty were met with cries of "scum-sucking traitor dogs" by the male participants. This was male social bonding.

There was a list of five rules that had nothing to do with the play of the tournament. They were more legal in nature.

1. No guns or sharp instruments were allowed in the golf cart.
2. Women could not allude to the size of your dick during the course of your golf swing. Any other time was appropriate.
3. You may never talk about the "real" reason for your divorce. Either party.
4. Current "boyfriends" or "girlfriends" were not allowed on the premises.
5. There was a standing eight count for any fighting between couples.

The $22 tournament fee included nine holes of golf with cart. One drink, and a festive dinner, Cold Duck, and a quiet evening at the Mike Tyson Combat Dance shortly after conclusion of play. Two hole-in-one prizes were donated by the club. If a woman made a hole in one on the sixth- or eighth-hole par-3s, she would receive a two-day cruise on Club Med to Cabo San Lucas with a Chippendale dancer of her choice. That is why we had such a large turnout, by the former spouses, for the Ex-Wives Conflict golf tournament.

If a man made a hole in one on the sixth or eighth hole, he would be allowed to get back any piece of real property that he lost in the divorce, except the former house. The women agreed to this because of the Chippendale deal, and because the last time their former husbands had made a hole in one was when the Dead Sea was just sick.

There was a prize for the "farthest" away on the par-3s. For the ladies, it was a $20 gift certificate for costume jewelry at Wal-Mart.

For the men, two free "lap dances" at The Baby Doll House entertainment club. There was a lot of mis-clubbing going on due to the nature of the prize.

The tournament began without incident, unless you count the kidney punch that The Breathalyzer's ex, Noreen, threw at him when he asked her, "Is that your cleavage or a scar from your open-heart surgery?" It was ruled a clean punch.

The cocktail cart was huffing and puffing around the front side, trying to keep all participants focused. Nadine, the cocktail cart queen, was a dropout from the local university. She had a constant frown and a world-class body. The ex-wives blamed her for most of the divorces.

Worst-ball format with your ex-wife can take a lot out of you. It is insufferable in duration and endless in pity. Scores of seventeen and twenty-one were posted on the first hole for worst-ball, and they were the lowest scores. The afternoon raged on with the speed of a marauding glacier. Tempers and four-irons were flaring. Most of the ex-couples now remembered why their marriages were dissolved.

All in all, it was a pretty peaceful day. Mad Max said he lost control of his cart, as it narrowly missed his ex, Tanya, and careened into the lake on nine. After rescuing their bags from the sunken cart, Mad Max was heard to say, "If it only had rack-and-pinion steering, I could have had her!" The rest of the day went without incident.

After a brief cocktail party, where we exceeded our one-drink limit, we all sat down for the entrée. I noticed a commotion at one of the tables and then everybody in the room was starting to giggle. The Breathalyzer said, "Look at this menu." I picked up mine and started to peruse.

Under appetizers, it read:

Cream on a Cracker—Just about anything and cream cheese is wonderful. $5.50

Faggie Funghi—These slippery little marinated mushrooms are great to roll around on your tongue. You might say they're a limbering-up exercise for the main course. $6.25.

Under soups, it read:

Bitchyssoise—Basically, this is a bitched-up cucumber soup. It has, however, enormous soothing properties. When I'm in one of my bitchy moods, this pulls my fangs back in. $3.50

Under salads, it read:

Chicken in the brown—Certain to get your cock crowing. $4.50

Under entrées, it read:

Beat your Meatloaf—A truly sensual way to dispose of two pounds of ground round. $10.50

The Seaman's Rod—Set sail for an adventure in eating where men are gay in swashing their bucks, and buckling their swashes. The taste of this dish will have you coming about in no time. $12.95

What kind of menu was this! San Francisco takeout? As the dining room was laughing hysterically, I noticed two derelicts engaging in light conversation at the bar. It was Packy and Muzzy, the poignant pranksters. They had a stack of menus in front of them and were showing the forgery to Quick Pour, the bartender. Seems that the boys got bored over at the paddocks one day and were reading this gay recipe book they had acquired from Chez-Juan.

They decided to steal a menu from the dining room and have it forged and replaced with sixty new menus of the "light cuisine."

The Cold Duck was served and most of us were getting cold tongue from our ex-wives. The band, Los Gringos, was playing up a storm and the Mike Tyson Combat Dance had begun. There was plenty of slow dancing and long embraces as the whiskey dulled our senses. Tears of misgivings were walking slowly down the cheeks of former spouses. There was back alimony in the air.

Finally, well into the night, Head Pro announced the losers of the Ex-Wives Conflict Worst Ball Golf Tournament, Mad Max and his lovely ex, Tanya. As is customary, Los Gringos played Frank Sinatra's "My Way," as the former couple had to read, word for word, their final divorce decree. It brought tears to the eyes of the audience, as everyone got maudlin. We combat-danced the night away and finally all of us made our way out the doors into the shimmering night. As we stood together, ex-spouses united by golf, and looked at the dead palm tree silhouette against the San Diego full moon, we could only surmise it must have been Muzzy and Packy who had let the air out of all the former wives' car tires. What a tournament!

Care to Join Our Little Old Game?

BY EDWIN "BUD" SHRAKE

As versatile as a utility wedge, Bud Shrake has shouldered a bagful of job descriptions—sportswriter, sports columnist, journalist, novelist, biographer, screenwriter, collaborator—that would likely have weighed down a less nimble writer. A staffer at *Sports Illustrated* from 1964 to 1979—"Care to Join Our Little Old Game?" appeared toward the end of his tenure—he has a permanent place on most serious golfers' bookshelves as cowriter of the best-selling volume published to date on the game, *Harvey Penick's Little Red Book.* The Penick-Shrake collaboration extended to four more golf best-sellers, *And If You Play Golf, You're My Friend, For All Who Love the Game, The Game of a Lifetime,* and the best-of collection, *The Wisdom of Harvey Penick.*

Shrake's latest novel, *Billy Boy,* is golf-themed, featuring the exploits of a 16-year-old caddie at Colonial Country Club, his drunken rodeo cowboy father, and Ben Hogan; off the course, his Texas-based novels include *But Not for Love, The Blessed McGill,* and *The Borderland.* In 1976, he and long-time golf buddy Dan Jenkins sharpened their wits and jointly bit into *Limo,* a comic treasure set in the world of network television; frighteningly, it's more timely today than when first published.

Using money as the measure of size, they played the biggest golf tournament in the world in Las Vegas last week. You could take the purses from a dozen Greater Open Classics and still be barely within range of the amount of cash that 58 guys teed up for in the third Professional Gamblers Invitational at the Sahara Nevada Country Club.

The players bet each other more than $2 million during the three-day tournament. Nobody is quite sure who the winner was. A bookmaker from St. Louis came out well over $100,000 ahead, but he didn't win all his matches. The only one who did was Don Keller, who owns some drive-in cafés around Dallas. Keller is built like a monster squash and carries in his mouth a cigar that looks like an exhaust pipe. He couldn't break 90 if he had the only pencil on the course. But the way the PGI is handicapped, it is heart and luck that count, and Keller bounced his grounders onto enough greens to win the trophy—if there was one. "I think we ought to give Keller a pistol and a ski mask so he doesn't have to come all the way out here to rob people," said Jack Binion, who organized the tournament, made the matches and in his own wagers got "drown-ded," as the gamblers say.

Several of the country's king poker players were in the tournament. In fact Doyle Brunson, who won the World Series of Poker the last two years at Binion's Horseshoe Casino in downtown Las Vegas, not only inspired Jack Binion to start the PGI, but he also was one of its attractions to the other players.

Since early May, when he picked up $340,000 at the poker tournament, Brunson has lost enough money playing golf to pay the electric bill for a medium-sized nation. Nobody is supposed to have as much cash money as Doyle is said to have lost on the golf course in the last 2 1/2 months. Brunson is a very high player who has the reputation of never flinching from a bet on the golf course or at the poker table. He has won millions at poker in games with the other king players and all challengers in Las Vegas, which is where you have to win at poker to be a king player.

But Brunson is what he calls "a bona fide golf 'dengerarate.' " He is preparing a book, which he will publish himself, with the title *How to Win $1,000,000 Playing Poker.* "I may do a sequel called *How to Lose $1,000,000 Playing Golf,*" Doyle said the night before the PGI began. He was eating watermelon in the Sombrero Room at Binion's Horseshoe. The next morning he was to play Butch Holmes, a commodities broker from Houston. The match had been rated even by Jack Binion, whose decision in such matters for the PGI is supreme. Doyle thought he ought to get a stroke.

The entry fee to play in the PGI was $1,900. That was broken into three $600 Nassaus on the three days of the tournament, plus $100 for carts and greens fees. Binion thinks of the $600 Nassaus as just a way to say hello to the person you are matched with. If you're not willing to go for a lot more action than that, you will not be invited to return.

"Action don't mean the same to Doyle as it does to most people," says Pug Pearson, himself a former winner of the poker world series. "I asked Doyle one day if he was going out to sweat some players, and he said, 'Naw, there wasn't enough action.' Doyle had $70,000 bet on the deal."

So when Brunson is losing at golf, there is blood in the water. Some of the sharks who came to Las Vegas for the PGI will stay and play golf with Doyle the rest of the summer. The only reason the gamblers quit playing golf in the fall in Las Vegas is that betting on football requires much time for study.

"My goodness, they go crazy over football," says Louise Brunson, Doyle's wife. Louise is a pretty woman with a quick smile. Like the wives of several other king poker players, Louise is very active in Christian work. She sends Bibles to Taiwan and cassettes of Christian testimony to folks in prison. Before they got married, Doyle promised Louise he would give up gambling. Then Doyle was operated on for a melanoma and given four months to live, at the outside. Louise was working as a pharmacist. She was five months pregnant and prayed Doyle would live long enough to see the baby. Doyle got up and started raising every bet, and the cancer went away.

"The doctors at M. D. Anderson Institute said it was a miracle," Louise says. "Everybody thought Doyle was as good as dead. One day when he came home between hospitals to make out his will, more than 200 people showed up at the house to tell Doyle goodbye. But the Lord lifted Doyle out of that bed. I know the Lord has got some kind of plan for Doyle.

"On holidays like Thanksgiving or Christmas I always cook a big, huge meal because I know Doyle will bring home a bunch of his friends who have no place to go. Last year I was in the kitchen fixing a turkey and country ham with redeye gravy, and Doyle and his friends were in the den watching the football game on TV. I heard Doyle say he had $60,000 bet on the game. Can you imagine that? All I could think of was how many hours I would have had to work in that drugstore to clear $60,000. Doyle lost the bet. His friends lost, too. They were kind of sullen at dinner. That's about the only way I can ever tell if Doyle is winning or losing."

There is no such thing as an obscure golf pro coloring his hair and changing his name and arriving in Las Vegas—or in Fort Worth, or Mobile, or other towns where the king gamblers play golf—to lift Doyle Brunson's bankroll. You check them out. Too much is at stake to let a thief in the game. A couple of weeks ago, Doyle was driving his golf cart down a fairway and reading the bets he had written on a paper place mat from a coffee shop. Doyle added up the numbers and felt an ice machine go off in his chest. It turned out he had bet $276,000 on that particular round of golf. "That is enough money to make you think about what you are doing," Doyle says. "You're not just playing for numbers on a big scoreboard. This is real money out of your pocket if you lose. I'd like to see Jack Nicklaus, sometime, with a six-foot putt that if he misses he's got to go in the clubhouse and peel off $50,000."

"We don't bar golf hustlers from our PGI tournament," Jack Binion says. "Most of the guys in our tournament *are* golf hustlers, on some scale. But I try to handicap them so if they play their regular game, they've got an even match. Guys I don't know so well, I make some phone calls. Golf handicaps have always been a swindle. Suppose you play to an eight at Olympic in Seattle. That might be a three here. Who knows? But if you know the guys, you'll know Doyle Brunson and Butch Holmes will both shoot 78 to 81 on this course, day in and day out, and they ought to be an even match."

Binion got the idea for the PGI while playing golf in Fort Worth with Doyle, Pug Pearson, Sailor Roberts and other friends who have since persuaded Jack to retire from the game for a while. Binion's last game of golf cost him $11,000. But he thought high-playing golfers around the country should learn about each other. There are guys who shoot 105 but are willing to bet $6,000 per hole if the match is fair. The rules of the PGI allow players who shoot 100 or so to tee up the ball anywhere they please, including sand traps. The 90-shooters can roll the ball around to improve a lie. The 80-shooters are supposed to play it as it is. Stamping down the line of a putt is permitted. You can tote as many clubs as you wish. Doyle Brunson carries four putters. Also, you can use grease.

Johnny Moss, the famous poker player and golf gambler who is now in his early 70s and runs the poker room at the Dunes, recalls using grease from time to time in big games with Titanic Thompson. Brunson says he first learned about grease 12 years ago from a jeweler in Arlington, Texas. Pearson says he learned about it from Doyle. Mostly they use grease in Texas and in Las Vegas. Many a sucker has seen grease used in Florida or California or New York without realizing it.

Any sort of grease will do, although Vaseline is the most popular. What you do is smear grease on the club face before a shot. The grease cuts the spin off the ball. The ball is thus inclined neither to hook nor to slice, and it flies farther. At the PGI you might hear a player wondering whether to hit a dry three-iron or a wet five-iron. Of course the use of grease is against USGA rules. "But you've got to use grease if the other guys are using it," says Dolph Arnold, who is Butch Holmes' partner in the commodities business and something of a king poker player in Houston, which is close to big league.

"Some people say the grease is psychological," says Jack Strauss, a gambler of note. "Well, the people who say that must not have tried it. Grease puts 10 to 20 extra yards on a shot. If you happen to be playing somewhere grease is not familiar, they'll look at you funny if they catch you doing it. I told some people one time I was putting on the grease to keep my clubs from rusting. It hadn't rained there in two years."

The players at the PGI were king gamblers, bookmakers, ranchers, pizza-chain owners, restaurateurs, car dealers, accountants, brokers and what-not. They shared the love of gambling. Some were better at it than others. They all knew where their choking price was. If prodded, most of them would admit to a suspicion of superiority over the ordinary golf pro. The feeling is that the pros don't play for enough real money to be able to tell how much heart they've got.

One day last week Jack Strauss made a side bet of $600 to $100 that he would beat Red Whitehead of Dallas on at least one hole. Red can play about twice as good as Jack. "I've never paid off on that bet in my life and I've given it to better players than Red," Jack said. He then birdied the first hole, where he'd made a nine the day before, and beat Red's par.

On the opening afternoon of the PGI, Bobby Baldwin from Tulsa hit his drive at the 18th in high grass behind a tree near a fence. Whatever other bets he may have had, Baldwin was losing $9,000 to Brunson and he had pressed. In the opinion of Jack Binion, Baldwin is already a king poker player and is on his way to becoming the premier poker player. Brunson is the premier poker player right now in no-limit games. Baldwin is thin, has curly hair and wears glasses. Brunson calls him Owl.

"How come you call him Owl?" asked Amarillo Slim Preston on the 18th tee. Slim was riding around the course in a cart checking his bets. On one match Slim said he was betting a Cadillac a hole. A $9,500 Cadillac, he said. "Don't he look like an owl to you?" Brunson said. "Naw, an owl is a wise old bird," said Slim.

"I thought I was wise until I got into this can," Baldwin said.

The 18th is a par 5. Doyle was at the front edge of the green in two. Baldwin threshed his ball out from under the tree. He was now in the fairway 190 yards from the green in two. If he lost the hole, he would be out $18,000 to Brunson. The day was lemon-colored. It was 117°, a record for the date in Las Vegas. The carts of the bet sweaters were drawn up around the green, which is guarded by sand traps and water. Baldwin does not have the training to deal with that situation in golf. He pulled out a four-iron and hit the ball five feet from the pin and saved his money with a birdie putt.

"Some guys can roar like a forest fire back in their hometown," Amarillo Slim said, "but out here with real big money up, so much dog comes out in 'em that they could catch every possum in Louisiana. Those would be the guys that grew up scraping and hustling and playing for every cent they had every day."

Slim doesn't play golf. But last year at the PGI he won $5,000 in a footrace with a football player. They raced from Jack Binion's tee shot to the green. Slim also won a bet from Leon Crump, who, Slim says, is the best good golfer in the world for money. Crump bet he could drive a golf ball over the top of the Hilton Hotel. He hit the eighth floor.

Brunson had some bad news in his match on the second day of last week's PGI that made Baldwin's birdie disappear from mind. Sam Simms from Nashville was five under par on the back nine. Simms was matched against Brunson, and the betting had been heavy.

"You might as well go back to Nashville, because that five under par of yours ain't getting you no more action here," Doyle said.

"The only time I'm out of action is when I'm out of money," Simms said. "It's music to a gambler's ears, the sound of suckers crying. Good thing this ain't 50 years ago. I know what you'd have done to me then."

"Damn right," Brunson said.

Golf with the Boss

BY DAN JENKINS

About the only thing that I can add to the nonpareil legend of Dan Jenkins is that his daughter Sally, who has blossomed into a best-selling writer herself, began her career as an intern at the next desk when I was a columnist at the late *Los Angeles Herald Examiner.* I want to make it clear that I mean *intern* in the *old* pre-Clintonian sense of the word, which I made sure to remind Dan of when the subject came up in conversation. There *are* standards.

And Dan Jenkins is certainly one of them.

He's been such a force of nature for so long on the sports beat that it's hard to imagine that football and golf—his favorite playing fields—really existed before he injected his particular pith into covering them. From his work in *Sports Illustrated* and *Golf Digest* to his collections of golf musings—*Dogged Victims of Inexorable Fate* and *Fairways and Greens*—to his raucous novels, including *Semi-Tough, Baja Oklahoma, Rude Behavior,* and the dead-solid perfect golf classic *Dead Solid Perfect,* Jenkins's prose has been memorably rife with rich language and bawdy wryness. In "Golf with the Boss," written for *Golf Digest* in 1990 and collected in *Fairways and Greens*—he does his dead-solid Jenkins best to honor the office then occupied by his playing partner . . . and still have a good old time.

It became clear to me one day that Mr. George Bush of 1600 Pennsylvania Avenue, Washington, D.C., is the best thing that's happened to golf since Teddy Roosevelt ran up San Juan Hill with a mashie niblick in his fist; since Dwight Eisenhower whistled a spoon onto Omaha Beach, a tough par 4 over water; in fact, since Gerald Ford ate the all-weather grip on a putter, believing it to be a tamale.

Why is President Bush the best thing that's happened to golf lately? I'll tell you why.

One, he is the only President of the United States who has ever known my name. Two, he is the only President of the United States who ever confessed to reading my stuff. Three, he is the only President of the United States who ever invited me to play golf with him.

I should explain right here that the President and I became friends because he has immaculate taste in literature. On the bookshelves of his private office at Camp David, you will find the usual heavy stuff, such as *Semi-Panama Its Ownself* by Manuel Noriega, and *Dead Solid Broke* by Mikhail Gorbachev, but you will also find my complete works: *Farewell to Pars, The Old Man and the 7-Wood, Tender Is the Tee Shot, Moby Grooves,* and *The Score Also Rises.*

This is how we got to know one another. President Bush follows sports with a keen interest when he's not helping shove Communism into an unplayable lie. He enjoys watching sports on TV, talking sports, and reading about sports.

Thus, me being a sports guy, my wife and I found ourselves receiving invitations to a White House lawn party.

That day on the White House lawn, while a Navy combo in dress blues was playing good country music, while Millie, First Dog, was brought out to frolic, while horseshoes were pitched, and while a lot of deficit-worriers were hitting the food line, I had a few occasions to chat with the President on a variety of subjects, one of which was golf.

"How good a golfer are you, Mr. President?"

I had always thought that if I ever met a President of the United States, I would address him as "Mr. President" rather than "Yo, babe," the greeting often used by athletes who visit the White House.

That afternoon, the President said he had once been a tolerable golfer, years ago when he lived in Midland, Texas, but that he wasn't too hot anymore, although he loved to "hack" at the game when he could find the time.

I said, "In your job, I guess it's better if you don't have a real low handicap."

He laughed. Not convulsively, but enough that I didn't get kicked out of the joint.

A little later on, the President said, "My problem with golf is I have to deal with a humiliation factor."

There were ways around that, I said. White tees only, roll it over everywhere, mulligans were free.

"Can't take a mulligan," he said. "Too much pride."

I said, "Mr. President, let me tell you something. I've been around the game a long time. Par doesn't give a damn about pride. I've seen par wring pride's neck."

We discussed the possibility of a golf game somewhere down the road.

A few weeks later, I received a self-typed note from him saying he had been working on his game a little and he was finally seeing the light at the end of the short-game tunnel. The short game had always been his biggest problem where golf was concerned. He mentioned he would arrange a game for us someday soon, if I was available.

"Have graphite shafts, will travel," I thought to myself.

President Bush, incidentally, is an inspiration to anybody who yearns to give up ice-cream sundaes. He's sixty-six but can pass for twenty years younger, a vigorous, athletic, flat-bellied man who not only likes golf, he likes baseball, football, plays tennis, dabbles in wallyball, pitches horseshoes with the best. He works out on cycles, Stairmasters, treadmills. Three times a week he jogs two miles, averaging about nine minutes a mile. He wishes his schedulers could find more time for him to go bonefishing and quail hunting.

You could take comfort that he's an inspiration in another way. Here is a man who has served his country in more different jobs than perhaps anybody in history—decorated Navy pilot of a torpedo plane in World War II, U.S. congressman, UN ambassador, ambassador to China, CIA director, Vice President, and now as the Boss. Try that on for a résumé.

I missed the first opportunity to play golf with him. He called me at home in Ponte Vedra Beach, Florida, to ask if I could come up to Washington, D.C., and complete a foursome with a couple of Democrats in the Senate. Two guys who were important to him in trying to get things done for the country, I assumed. He didn't name them. I had to beg off because I had just been released from the hospital after suffering what my wife said was a heart attack but what I knew was a fake heart attack brought on by the fast bent greens at Marsh Landing and the bunkers at Sawgrass, my home courses in Ponte Vedra. The President wished me a speedy recovery and said we would reschedule, but of course a good bit of time passed as such trifling things as summits and some guy in Iraq and the economy kept intruding on his golf.

Along in here, I received another self-typed note from him in which he acknowledged that the economy was batting about .187—his words—but he was hopeful of getting something done to improve it, and in which he observed that the guy in Iraq was a "bad dude," and something might have to be done about him, too, but eventually we *would* play golf.

Then one day I got another phone call, one that caused some merriment among friends. It came to the pressroom at Medinah in Chicago when Hale Irwin and Mike Donald were on the last few holes of their playoff for the U.S. Open.

I had been out on the course on the front nine of the playoff, but now I was watching it on TV in the press lounge with a couple of old comrades, Jim Murray of the Los Angeles *Times* and Blackie Sherrod of the Dallas *Morning News.* Somebody came up and told me I had a long-distance call at the front desk.

"Now?" I said incredulously. "In the middle of this?"

"Radio guy," Murray said.

"Yeah, probably," I said. "Some nitwit wants to know what I think of Cameroon going into the Southeastern Conference."

I refused to budge, except to go get coffee. But two minutes later, a Medinah press volunteer rushed up and said, "You may want to take the call. It's from the White House!"

Murray and Sherrod glanced at each other, and Blackie said, "He knew to look for you indoors."

I power-walked to the phone at the front desk.

"Dan, where did they find you?" a voice said.

"I'm in the pressroom at Medinah, Mr. President. I'm at the U.S. Open."

"Well, of course you are," said the President. "I'm watching it. Listen, I won't keep you, but I flew over this course the other day. It looks pretty interesting. Can you come up next Friday? We'll play eighteen, go to a minor-league baseball game, and spend the night at Camp David."

Want to talk about an offer you can't refuse?

Five days later I discovered myself milling around in the Oval Office with the Boss and the other two invitees who would complete our foursome: Walter Payton, the retired Chicago Bears running back who has settled into immortaldom, and Congressman Marty Russo, a severely low-handicap Democrat from Illinois.

The Oval Office looks like a neat place to go to work every day. Paintings, Western sculptures, windows on two sides through which you can see where Ike's putting green used to be, and some trees Andrew Jackson planted. The door stood open to the outer office, and there was laughter out there—a happy staff. The President showed us some objets d'art, gathered everybody around for a photograph, and said. "Let's go to lunch."

I knew we wouldn't be eating at a McDonald's, but I hadn't expected to go up to the dining room of the private residence of the White House. We walked down a hall, got on an elevator, and stepped off near the Lincoln Bedroom. The President then led us on a tour of the residence pointing out things of interest, with great pride and enjoyment. I was reminded of some American history I hadn't retained from Paschal High and Texas Christian University in Fort Worth.

We lunched on a light pasta, green salad, homemade peach ice cream. We made Gorbachev talk, S&L bailout talk, try-to-fix-the-economy talk, and golf talk.

Just after lunch, a pleasant-looking gentleman stepped off the private elevator, as if he had access to the President whenever he chose. I was delighted to learn that he does. It was General Brent Scowcroft, the National Security Adviser. He was accompanied by two other gentlemen.

"Excuse me, I better go talk to these guys," the President said. They all went into the living room and sat down.

I wandered back into the Lincoln bedroom and out onto the balcony to smoke and gazed out at the Washington Monument in the distance and down at Marine One, the dark green chopper sitting on the White House lawn. I watched my golf bag being loaded.

The President's confab with the National Security Adviser only lasted a few minutes.

"No big deal?" I uttered inquisitively as were going down on the private elevator.

"No big deal," he said, smiling.

I couldn't help thinking back to a morning when I was on the set of the *Today* show with Tom Brokaw, who was then the host. Tom had been kind enough to have me on the show to plug a book that badly needed plugging. But during a commercial break, Brokaw took a call from a phone by his side.

Stunned, he turned to me and said, "Anwar Sadat's been shot."

So much for the book plug.

What's the point? Only that most writers are selfish, cynical, desperate swine who always expect the worst. I was relieved that the guy in Iraq, or another loon in another part of the world, hadn't done something that would cancel the golf game.

Down on the ground floor now, we were heading toward the door leading out to the chopper when the President said, "Wait a second. Let's go have some fun."

He walked past two guards and around a tall screen where a White House tour was in progress. Hordes of tourists were crammed into a corridor and up a staircase. Shocked and overwhelmed to see the President his ownself, when it was the last thing they had expected, they burst into whoops and applause.

He went over to shake hands, do high fives, exchange pleasantries. Returning to our group, he said, "Heck it's *their* house and *their* President. They deserve to see the guy."

I must tell you that Marine One is a nice way to travel. Forward in the cushiony, comfortable, remarkably quiet chopper were the President, the congressman, myself, Walter Payton, and Walter's nine-year-old son, Jarrett, who would have some tales to tell when he went back to school. Seated behind us were a handful of staff and Secret Service personnel, the earpiece and talk-box brigade.

There was no decor on Marine One except for the Presidential seal on the door to the flight deck and a small painting of the Boss's house in Maine. Out the window I think I might have noticed some other choppers flying escort.

We landed somewhere in the Maryland hills and got into a limo with the President. Then in a fifteen-vehicle motorcade that included a SWAT van, we rode through the countryside. When a President goes to play golf, it involves a bit more than donning the old cleats.

For security reasons, the Holly Hills Country Club in Ijamsville, Maryland (the *j* is silent), had not been given much warning about "Guess who's coming to play golf today?" But word had quickly circulated to about two hundred members and friends, and when we got there they had already been frisked and told their dos and don'ts by the Secret Service.

The President shook a lot of hands and autographed a lot of golf caps and we all suited up in the locker room and hit a few practice balls and took a few putts. From Marlin Fitzwater, the White House press secretary, I had been informed that the pool of press photographers and writers would only be allowed to show up on the first tee, the ninth green, the tenth tee, and the eighteenth green. Otherwise we would have the course to ourselves.

Along with having your own jet, your own helicopter and your own song, I marked this as being one of the great perks of being President. No creepers and crawlers to play through on a golf course.

The owner of the Holly Hills Country Club, a lady named Ann Grimm, was on hand to greet us and answer some of my questions.

The club was fourteen years old. She had owned it for the past three, but was in the process of taking it equity. It had an upper-middle-class membership. The course had been designed by an architect named Robert Russell, who was said to be a "local fellow." The layout was generally ranked among the ten best in the Mid-Atlantic PGA section.

"You're being discovered," I said.

"Isn't it wonderful?" she replied.

"Where am I?" I asked.

(Travel note: If I had been driving, I was a little under an hour from D.C. Take 270 west to 75 north to 144 and look for the Holly Hills Country Club sign, or the red-brick, two-story clubhouse.)

In the golf shop, the President swapped his Texas Rangers baseball cap for a Holly Hills cap, to go along with his red golf shirt, khaki slacks, and brown DryJoys.

On the first tee, the President slipped on an old white glove that was turning to rust. It looked like it had been worn by a tree planter a decade earlier.

"Hey, whoa," I said, getting a new Hogan glove out of my bag and handing it to him. "Don't embarrass me."

"I never turn down a free glove," he said.

Glancing at the old one again, I said, "I guess you don't get many offers."

The Holly Hills course plays to 6,800 yards from the blues, par 72, but looking out on all the deep valleys and swollen hills to confront us, I suggested we play from the whites, a journey of about 6,500 yards. Nobody protested.

I also put the hit-till-you're-happy rule into effect for the cameras on the first tee. The President didn't actually approve of this until his first drive was a grounder, then he liked the idea.

He has a good swing. He's a natural left-hander who plays right-handed—like Ben Hogan, I told him. He doesn't take it all the way back to horizontal but he follows through nicely, and when he catches it on the screws, it goes. His mulligan was a beauty. People applauded.

In the lusty tradition of most sportswriters, I sky-hooked one about 215 yards. Walter Payton swung a little better than the usual ex–running back. With a long-iron, he smacked a towering slice that must have carried 300 yards. If he had hit the ball with one of his bulging forearms, it might have carried 500 yards. Marty Russo, the congressman, only had to take one stylish, powerful swing for me to see why he had been the congressional golf champion ten times.

Anyhow, we were away.

In our entourage of golf carts were Secret Service guys, a medical doctor, a White House photographer, an aide or two, and a fellow carrying a black briefcase, who would often be seen strolling along, by himself in the rough. A convivial Secret Service agent named Lou would never be more than a few feet from the President at all times. I gathered it would be Lou's job to hurl his body in front of the President in case I shanked a 5-iron.

Throughout the round I would take a club out of the bag and start to line up a shot, but would be distracted by the sight of a golf cart on a distant hilltop. Up there, two men would be peering through huge pairs of binoculars at—I don't know—Pennsylvania or something.

I looked through the binoculars once. I won't say they're powerful, but if I had been facing a window of the White House, seventy miles away, I could have read Abe's signature on the Emancipation Proclamation in the Lincoln Bedroom.

On the first three holes, the President encountered some trouble with his pitching and chipping, mainly because he was rushing his swing. He plays fast, I am happy to report, and likes to play fast, and doesn't understand why anybody would play slowly.

He could do mankind a wonderful service, I suggested, if he signed into law the death penalty for slow-playing golfers.

"I've never had a golf lesson," he confided.

"That's a natural swing—really?"

"Yep. For better or worse."

It was for the better. And it got him his first par on the 500-yard fourth hole, an up-and-over par 5 with a dogleg to the right. Good drive, good fairway wood, good pitch, two putts.

"Way to go, Boss," said the congressman, as the President holed a five-foot second putt for his par.

It was after the president had made a par that I felt at ease in nodding toward the man with the briefcase, and saying, "Is that what I think it is?"

"Yeah, the situation phone," he said.

I stared at the briefcase off and on for the rest of the day. The phone never rang. Knowing there's a situation phone around doesn't make golf any easier, if I may say so.

As a longtime captive of the game, I am a collector of memorable stretches of golf holes. Things like Amen Corner at the Augusta National, the eleventh, twelfth, and thirteenth. Eight, nine, and ten at Pebble Beach—Abalone Corner. The sixteenth, seventeenth, and eighteenth at TPC—Deane's Bad Dream, or whatever you want to call it.

To this list I would almost be tempted to add the sixth, seventh, and eighth at Holly Hills. Rugged, scenic, beguiling.

More or less ignorant of the dangers on these holes, I'm sure we got through them better than we would if we ever played them again.

The sixth, a 480-yard par 4, sharp dogleg left, might be the toughest hole in Western civilization. You have two choices off the tee box. Drive it straight and go out-of-bounds over a little fence, or hit a soaring hook up and over the tall trees and pray that the ball stays out of the forest. If you take a lesser club than a driver off the tee to stay in the narrow fairway, you can't get home.

Me and the Boss and Walter Payton ricocheted our way to bogeys at the sixth, and Marty Russo parred it only because he happened to sink a downhill, 20-foot putt over the slick bent-grass green.

The President hit his best shot of the day at the seventh. He nailed a 3-iron that cleared the water and bunkers and left him an 18-foot birdie putt. As destiny would have it, I hit one of my best shots of the day here, a 7-wood that stopped three feet behind the flag.

"You dog!" said the President. "What did you hit?"

"The trusty 7-wood," I said.

"A 7-wood? What's that?"

I said, "Some people say it's a 3-iron/4-iron, but I say it's the secret to a happy life."

As if to inspect the legality of it, the President fondled my wooden, custom-made 7-wood, or 7-Silly, as it is known in some circles.

The ninth hole is a par 5 that goes back uphill to the clubhouse, where the cameras would be waiting. For the cameras, I half-bladed a 9-iron third shot and then three-putted for a disgusting bogey on what was an easy hole, but it was an eventful hole for the congressman. He rolled in a 25-footer for a birdie and had a momentary out-of-body experience.

Shouting and hopping around, he yelled, "Can you *believe* it? This is the greatest minute of my life! I'm with the *President* and *I birdie* the hole for CNN!"

Calmly, I said, "Marty, do you really want your constituents to know how well you play golf?"

Incidentally, if it's a fact that a man reveals his true character on a golf course, I can only attest that the President was easier to be around than any captain of industry I've ever been paired with in a pro-am. He seemed also to take himself far less seriously than any CEO of any plastics company I've ever encountered. He was the friendliest and most relaxed person in every room, and on every fairway.

He frequently walked to the green from 100 yards in, and bummed rides on everybody's golf cart. Thanks to my incessant questioning between shots, he spoke of many things other than golf—of food, of travel, of other sports, of Gorbachev's sense of humor. "He told me a lot of jokes when we weren't working," the President said. "And he asks more questions than you do—what does that car cost, what does a house like that cost?"

We all did ourselves proud for the cameras at the tenth tee. It was a downhill par 4 with plenty of room, and we could jump at our drivers. I thought I had seriously hurt my tee ball until the President made a good pass and fired it past me.

Down the steep hill, we found his ball five yards ahead of mine in the fairway. I didn't see how this had been possible, him with the funny Yonex and a Titleist and me with my secret weapons, a Mizuno and an Ultra.

"You killed that one, Boss," the congressman said. "I clock it at two-eighty."

"I don't know how," the President said.

"You made a good swing," I explained.

"Well, it comes and goes." He shrugged. "If I can just get rid of the humiliation factor . . ."

The President made three pars on the back side and would have made two others if he hadn't three-putted. He played better as the day wore on.

The twelfth hole, a 145-yard par 3, is worth recalling. Here, the President, from about 130 yards away, hit a crisp 9-iron onto the green only 12 feet from the cup. He missed the birdie putt, which I attributed to his use of the long putter. This hole was also where a cluster of club members sneaked onto the course and were permitted to gallery the game and playfully holler at the participants. I assumed they had already been frisked by the Secret Service.

"How do you like the course, Mr. President?"

"Great!"

"How's your game?"

"Yeah."

Laughter.

Another laugh came when I hit a poor shot, a timid chip from the edge of the green that left me 10 feet short of the hole.

A wit in the gallery said, "Does your husband play golf too?"

Chuckling, the President said, "I hadn't heard that one."

By my scoring, the President shot a two-mulligan 86, "Sweetness" Payton shot a three-mulligan 85, I shot a three-mulligan 78, and Marty Russo shot a one-mulligan 68, four under par. A shocking display, I thought, for a public servant.

We showered and changed in the Holly Hills locker room and motorcaded to dinner at the Jug Bridge seafood restaurant in Frederick, Maryland, a tasty roadhouse the Secret Service had selected. After dinner, we motorcaded to Hagerstown, and to the elation of 3,500 people trooped into a Class AA baseball park to watch Hagerstown beat Harrisburg, 6–3. We sat just past the third-base line and the President waved and chatted with the faces of America, and admired the rich natural turf, and gazed at the old factory rising above the right-field wall, and smiled at the Moose Lodge sign out in center. "This is great," he said.

Americans tossed him baseballs to autograph and toss back. He made some good one-handed catches.

Close by, a fan got the Boss's attention, gave him a thumbs-up sign, and hollered, "I know what you're going through—I'm president of my city council back home!"

The President broke up laughing.

I sat there wondering when a President of the United States had ever been to a minor-league baseball game, or if one ever had. It pleased me that this was something the old Yale baseball captain had wanted to do.

On to Camp David, then, to spend the night. As resorts go, you take whatever you want in Palm Springs or Hawaii, and I'll take Camp David.

Run by the Navy, these lush and leafy 200 acres in the Catoctin Mountains of Maryland have been special to every President since Franklin D. Roosevelt chose the property back in 1942 as a place where the Commander in Chief could go to relax, revitalize himself, and get some work done away from the microscope of the press and the often ceremonial Oval Office.

FDR originally called the retreat Shangri-la. It was Ike who changed the name to Camp David, for his grandson. Consisting of a number of rustic but comfortably furnished cabins scattered among the trees, of heavily shaded pathways, and of every conceivable type of recreational facility, the grounds are at your complete disposal once you're inside the compound as the Boss's guest.

In my cabin, I could have picked up the phone and asked an officer serving under Commander Mike Berry to send over any one of 300 movies in the film library for my VCR, or I could have lit a fire and explored all of the available beverages, or I could have gone for a midnight ride on all the bicycles outside my cabin door—and apparently without getting shot.

Instead, I fell to sleep in a large cozy bed that, having a sense of history, I hoped had been slept in by such high handicappers as Khrushchev, Brezhnev, Gorbachev, Maggie Thatcher, or Menachem Begin.

I was up early the next morning to throw the switch on the coffee machine and read the Washington *Post* and the New York *Times* that had been delivered to my cabin door. As suggested by the President the night before, I strolled down to have breakfast at Laurel Lodge, which is also where his office is located.

I was foolishly standing around among the umbrellas and tables on the veranda of Laurel, wondering where the entrance was, when a voice through a sliding-glass door summoned me to come in. The President, in a windbreaker, golf shirt, khakis, and Top-Siders, was alone in his office, pecking away on a typewriter. He said he had been at work since six-thirty.

His rather modest workplace at Camp David had more interesting memorabilia than most offices. There was a large painting of the torpedo plane he flew in World War II, and a model of it on his desk. In a tiny wooden box, which he was pleased to open, was a leather-band wristwatch Gorbachev had given him. Framed on a wall was a cardboard target with "Bush" scrawled on it and Noriega's bullet holes riddled in it—a souvenir brought back to him by the Panama invasion troops.

I left him to his work and went to have breakfast, but, as instructed, I returned to his office.

"Good grub," I said. "A guy could eat well in this job."

He grinned, stood up, and said, "Come on."

We got in his golf cart and he took me on a tour of the whole retreat, dropping little tidbits of lore along the way. He pointed out the beautiful little chapel he'd had built—each occupant apparently did something to improve Camp David.

I guess I was surprised to discover that Camp David had not had a church before now, but I didn't comment on it.

Presently, he stopped the golf cart in front of one of the older cabins. The sign on it said "Holly."

He said, "You might want to go sit on that bench there on the front porch for a minute."

I didn't ask why, I just did it, long enough to light a cigarette. When I got back in the cart, he smiled at me with a certain amount of relish, and said; "That's where FDR and Churchill sat when they were planning the D-Day invasion."

"Jesus," I mumbled.

We cruised around a while longer and eventually he drove me down to a sedan parked at Aspen Cabin, the presidential residence, from where an

Army sergeant would transport me to Washington National, about an hour away.

How could I thank him for the whole outing, other than to say I would vote for him five or six times in '92?

I did tell him to try to keep taking it back slowly.

As the car pulled away, I looked across a gorgeous lawn and my eyes lingered on the well-manicured bent-grass green of Ike's par-3 hole, which sits very near Aspen Cabin.

The pin was up front today. A 7-wood might be too much club.

Goldfinger

BY IAN FLEMING

Ian Fleming (1908–1964) wore several hats through his remarkable life: spymaster, banker, journalist, novelist, dedicated golfer. At the time of his death, he was in line to become captain of Royal St. George's, one of the venerable club's on the British Open rotation. Indeed, Fleming suffered his fatal heart attack at a committee meeting in the clubhouse. He wrote the first of his 14 James Bond novels in 1953; six years later, he put 007's golfing skills to the test in *Goldfinger*. Fleming set the match at the fictional St. Mark's, an obvious St. George's stand-in. True to Bond's character, Fleming turned the stirring event into as much a contest of unshakable wits as one of skillful shot-making.

G ood afternoon, Blacking. All set?" The voice was casual, authoritative. "I see there's a car outside. Not somebody looking for a game, I suppose?"

"I'm not sure, sir. It's an old member come back to have a club made up. Would you like me to ask him, sir?"

"Who is it? What's his name?"

Bond smiled grimly. He pricked his ears. He wanted to catch every inflection.

"A Mr. Bond, sir."

There was a pause. "Bond?" The voice had not changed. It was politely interested. "Met a fellow called Bond the other day. What's his first name?"

"James, sir."

"Oh yes." Now the pause was longer. "Does he know I'm here?" Bond could sense Goldfinger's antennae probing the situation.

"He's in the workshop, sir. May have seen your car drive up." Bond thought: Alfred's never told a lie in his life. He's not going to start now.

"Might be an idea." Now Goldfinger's voice unbent. He wanted something from Alfred Blacking, some information. "What sort of a game does this chap play? What's his handicap?"

"Used to be quite useful when he was a boy, sir. Haven't seen his game since then."

"Hm."

Bond could feel the man weighing it all up. Bond smelled that the bait was going to be taken. He reached into his bag and pulled out his driver and started rubbing down the grip with a block of shellac. Might as well look busy. A board in the shop creaked. Bond honed away industriously, his back to the open door.

"I think we've met before." The voice from the doorway was low, neutral.

Bond looked quickly over his shoulder. "My God, you made me jump. Why—" recognition dawned—"It's Gold, Goldman . . . er—Goldfinger." He hoped he wasn't overplaying it. He said with a hint of dislike, or mistrust, "Where have you sprung from?"

"I told you I played down here. Remember?" Goldfinger was looking at him shrewdly. Now the eyes opened wide. The X-ray gaze pierced through to the back of Bond's skull.

"No."

"Did not Miss Masterton give you my message?"

"No. What was it?"

"I said I would be over here and that I would like a game of golf with you."

"Oh, well," Bond's voice was coldly polite, "we must do that some day."

"I was playing with the professional. I will play with you instead." Goldfinger was stating a fact.

There was no doubt that Goldfinger was hooked. Now Bond must play hard to get.

"Why not some other time? I've come to order a club. Anyway I'm not in practice. There probably isn't a caddie." Bond was being as rude as he could. Obviously the last thing he wanted to do was play with Goldfinger.

"I also haven't played for some time." (Bloody liar, thought Bond.) "Ordering a club will not take a moment." Goldfinger turned back into the shop. "Blacking, have you got a caddie for Mr. Bond?"

"Yes, sir."

"Then that is arranged."

Bond wearily thrust his driver back into his bag. "Well, all right then." He thought of a final way of putting Goldfinger off. He said roughly, "But I warn you I like playing for money. I can't be bothered to knock a ball round just for the fun of it." Bond felt pleased with the character he was building up for himself.

Was there a glint of triumph, quickly concealed, in Goldfinger's pale eyes? He said indifferently, "That suits me. Anything you like. Off handicap, of course. I think you said you're nine."

"Yes."

Goldfinger said carefully, "Where, may I ask?"

"Huntercombe." Bond was also nine at Sunningdale. Huntercombe was an easier course. Nine at Huntercombe wouldn't frighten Goldfinger.

"And I also am nine. Here. Up on the board. So it's a level game. Right?"

Bond shrugged. "You'll be too good for me."

"I doubt it. However," Goldfinger was offhand, "tell you what I'll do. That bit of money you removed from me in Miami. Remember? The big figure was ten. I like a gamble. It will be good for me to have to try. I will play you double or quits for that."

Bond said indifferently, "That's too much." Then, as if he thought better of it, thought he might win, he said—with just the right amount of craft mixed with reluctance—"Of course you can say that was 'found money'. I won't miss it if it goes again. Oh, well, all right. Easy come easy go. Level match. Ten thousand dollars it is."

Goldfinger turned away. He said, and there was a sudden sweetness in the flat voice, "That's all arranged then, Mr. Blacking. Many thanks. Put your fee down on my account. Very sorry we shall be missing our game. Now, let me pay the caddie fees."

Alfred Blacking came into the workroom and picked up Bond's clubs. He looked very directly at Bond. He said, "Remember what I told you, sir." One eye closed and opened again. "I mean about that flat swing of yours. It needs watching—all the time."

Bond smiled at him. Alfred had long ears. He might not have caught the figure, but he knew that somehow this was to be a key game. "Thanks, Alfred. I won't forget. Four Penfolds—with hearts on them. And a dozen tees. I won't be a minute."

Bond walked through the shop and out to his car. The bowler-hatted man was polishing the metal work of the Rolls with a cloth. Bond felt rather than saw him stop and watch Bond take out his zip bag and go into the clubhouse. The man had a square flat yellow face. One of the Koreans?

Bond paid his green fee to Hampton, the steward, and went into the changing room. It was just the same—the same tacky smell of old shoes and socks and last summer's sweat. Why was it a tradition of the most famous golf clubs that their standard of hygiene should be that of a Victorian private school? Bond changed his socks and put on the battered old pair of nailed Saxones. He took off the coat of his yellowing black and white hound's-tooth suit and pulled on a faded black windcheater. Cigarettes? Lighter? He was ready to go.

Bond walked slowly out, preparing his mind for the game. On purpose he had needled this man into a high, tough match so that Goldfinger's respect for him should be increased and Goldfinger's view of Bond—that he was the type of ruthless, hard adventurer who might be very useful to Goldfinger—would be confirmed. Bond had thought that perhaps a hundred-pound Nassau would be the form. But $10,000! There had probably never been such a high singles game in history—except in the finals of American Championships or in the big amateur Calcutta Sweeps where it was the backers rather than the players who had the money on. Goldfinger's private accounting must have taken a nasty dent. He wouldn't have liked that. He would be aching to get some of his money back. When Bond had talked about playing high, Goldfinger had seen his chance. So be it. But one thing was certain, for a hundred reasons Bond could not afford to lose.

He turned into the shop and picked up the balls and tees from Alfred Blacking.

"Hawker's got the clubs, sir."

Bond strolled out across the 500 yards of shaven seaside turf that led to the first tee. Goldfinger was practicing on the putting green. His caddie stood near by, rolling balls to him. Goldfinger putted in the new fashion—between his legs with a mallet putter. Bond felt encouraged. He didn't believe in the system. He knew it was no good practicing himself. His old hickory Calamity Jane had its good days and its bad. There was nothing to do about it. He knew also that the St. Marks practice green bore no resemblance, in speed or texture, to the greens on the course.

Bond caught up with the limping, insouciant figure of his caddie who was sauntering along chipping at an imaginary ball with Bond's blaster. "Afternoon, Hawker."

"Afternoon, sir." Hawker handed Bond the blaster and threw down three used balls. His keen sardonic poacher's face split in a wry grin of welcome. "How've you been keepin', sir? Played any golf in the last twenty years? Can you still put them on the roof of the starter's hut?" This referred to the day when Bond, trying to do just that before a match, had put two balls through the starter's window.

"Let's see." Bond took the blaster and hefted it in his hand, gauging the distance. The tap of the balls on the practice green had ceased. Bond addressed the ball, swung quickly, lifted his head and shanked the ball almost at right angles. He tried again. This time it was a dunch. A foot of turf flew up. The ball went ten yards. Bond turned to Hawker, who was looking his most sardonic. "It's all right, Hawker. Those were for show. Now then, one for you." He stepped up to the third ball, took his club back slowly and whipped the clubhead through. The ball soared 100 feet, paused elegantly, dropped eighty feet on to the thatched roof of the starter's hut and bounced down.

Bond handed back the club. Hawker's eyes were thoughtful, amused. He said nothing. He pulled out the driver and handed it to Bond. They walked together to the first tee, talking about Hawker's family.

Goldfinger joined them, relaxed, impassive. Bond greeted Goldfinger's caddie, an obsequious, talkative man called Foulks whom Bond had never liked. Bond glanced at Goldfinger's clubs. They were a brand-new set of American Ben Hogans with smart St. Marks leather covers for the woods. The bag was one of the stitched black leather holdalls favored by American pros. The clubs were in individual cardboard tubes for each extraction. It was a pretentious outfit, but the best.

"Toss for honor?" Goldfinger flicked a coin.

"Tails."

It was heads. Goldfinger took out his driver and unpeeled a new ball. He said "Dunlop 65. Number one. Always use the same ball. What's yours?"

"Penfold. Hearts."

Goldfinger looked keenly at Bond. "Strict rules of golf?"

"Naturally."

"Right." Goldfinger walked on to the tee and teed up. He took one or two careful, concentrated practice swings. It was a type of swing Bond knew well—the grooved, mechanical, repeating swing of someone who had studied the game with great care, read all the books and spent 5,000 pounds on the finest pro teachers. It would be a good, scoring swing which might not collapse under pressure. Bond envied it.

Goldfinger took up his stance, waggled gracefully, took his clubhead back in a wide slow arc and, with his eyes glued to the ball, broke his wrists correctly. He brought the clubhead mechanically, effortlessly, down and through the ball and into a rather artificial, copybook finish. The ball went straight and true about 200 yards down the fairway.

It was an excellent, uninspiring shot. Bond knew that Goldfinger would be capable of repeating the same swing with different clubs again and again round the eighteen holes.

Bond took his place, gave himself a lowish tee, addressed the ball with careful enmity and, with a flat, racket-player's swing in which there was just too much wrist for safety, lashed the ball away. It was a fine, attacking drive that landed past Goldfinger's ball and rolled on fifty yards. But it had had a shade of draw and ended on the edge of the left-hand rough.

They were two good drives. As Bond handed his clubs to Hawker and strolled off in the wake of the more impatient Goldfinger, he smelled the sweet smell of the beginning of a knock-down-and-drag-out game of golf on a beautiful day in May with the larks singing over the greatest seaside course in the world.

The first hole of the Royal St. Marks is 450 yards long—450 yards of undulating fairway with one central bunker to trap a mishit second shot and a chain of bunkers guarding three-quarters of the green to trap a well-hit one. You can slip through the unguarded quarter, but the fairway slopes to the right there and you are more likely to end up with a nasty first-chip-of-the-day out of the rough. Goldfinger was well placed to try for this opening. Bond watched him take what was probably a spoon, make his two practice swings and address the ball.

Many unlikely people play golf, including people who are blind, who have only one arm, or even no legs, and people often wear bizarre clothes to the game. Other golfers don't think them odd, for there are no rules of appearance or dress at golf. That is one of its minor pleasures. But Goldfinger had made an attempt to look smart at golf and that is the only way of dressing that is incongruous on a links. Everything matched in a blaze of rust-colored tweed from the buttoned "golfer's cap" centered on the huge, flaming red hair, to the brilliantly polished, almost orange shoes. The plus-four suit was too well cut and the plus-fours themselves had been pressed down the sides. The stockings were of a matching heather mixture and had green garter tabs. It was as if

Goldfinger had gone to his tailor and said, "Dress me for golf—you know, like they wear in Scotland." Social errors made no impression on Bond, and for the matter of that he rarely noticed them. With Goldfinger it was different. Everything about the man had grated on Bond's teeth from the first moment he had seen him. The assertive blatancy of his clothes was just part of the malevolent animal magnetism that had affected Bond from the beginning.

Goldfinger executed his mechanical, faultless swing. The ball flew true but just failed to make the slope and curled off to the right to finish pin high off the green in the short rough. Easy five. A good chip could turn it into a four, but it would have to be a good one.

Bond walked over to his ball. It was lying cocked up, just off the fairway. Bond took his number four-wood. Now for the "all air route"—a soaring shot that would carry the cross-bunkers and give him two putts for a four. Bond remembered the dictum of the pros: "It's never too early to start winning." He took it easy, determined not to press for the long but comfortable carry.

As soon as Bond had hit the shot he knew it wouldn't do. The difference between a good golf shot and a bad one is the same as the difference between a beautiful and a plain woman—a matter of millimeters. In this case, the clubface had gone through just that one millimeter too low under the ball. The arc of flight was high and soft—no legs. Why the hell hadn't he taken a spoon or a two-iron off that lie? The ball hit the lip of the far bunker and fell back. Now it was the blaster, and fighting for a half.

Bond never worried too long about his bad or stupid shots. He put them behind him and thought of the next. He came up with the bunker, took his blaster and measured the distance to the pin. Twenty yards. The ball was lying well back. Should he splash it out with a wide stance and an outside-in swing, or should he blast it and take plenty of sand? For safety's sake he would blast it out. Bond went down into the bunker. Head down and follow well through. The easiest shot in golf. Try and put it dead. The wish, halfway down his backswing, hurried the hands in front of the clubhead. The loft was killed and there was the ball rolling back off the face. Get it out, you bloody fool, and hole a long putt! Now Bond took too much sand. He was out, but barely on the green. Goldfinger bent to his chip and kept his head down until the ball was halfway to the hole. The ball stopped three inches from the pin. Without waiting to be given the putt, Goldfinger turned his back on Bond and walked off towards the second tee. Bond picked up his ball and took his driver from Hawker.

"What does he say his handicap is, sir?"

"Nine. It's a level match. Have to do better than that though. Ought to have taken my spoon for the second."

Hawker said encouragingly, "It's early days yet, sir."

Bond knew it wasn't. It was always too early to start losing.

Goldfinger had already teed up. Bond walked slowly behind him, followed by Hawker. Bond stood and leant on his driver. He said, "I thought you said we would be playing the strict rules of golf. But I'll give you that putt. That makes you one up."

Goldfinger nodded curtly. He went through his practice routine and hit his usual excellent, safe drive.

The second hole is a 370-yard dogleg to the left with deep cross-bunkers daring you to take the tiger's line. But there was a light helping breeze. For Goldfinger it would now be a five-iron for his second. Bond decided to try and make it easier for himself and only have a wedge for the green. He laid his ears back and hit the ball hard and straight for the bunkers. The breeze got under the slight draw and winged the ball on and over. The ball pitched and disappeared down into the gully just short of the green. A four. Chance of a three.

Goldfinger strode off without comment. Bond lengthened his stride and caught up. "How's the agoraphobia? Doesn't all this wide open space bother it?"

"No."

Goldfinger deviated to the right. He glanced at the distant, half-hidden flag, planning his second shot. He took his five-iron and hit a good, careful shot which took a bad kick short of the green and ran down into the thick grass to the left. Bond knew that territory. Goldfinger would be lucky to get down in two.

Bond walked up to his ball, took the wedge and flicked the ball on to the green with plenty of stop. The ball pulled up and lay a yard past the hole. Goldfinger executed a creditable pitch but missed the twelve-foot putt. Bond had two for the hole from a yard. He didn't wait to be given the hole but walked up and putted. The ball stopped an inch short. Goldfinger walked off the green. Bond knocked the ball in. All square.

The third is a blind 240 yards, all carry, a difficult three. Bond chose his brassie and hit a good one. It would be on or near the green. Goldfinger's routine drive was well hit but would probably not have enough steam to carry the last of the rough and trickle down into the saucer of the green. Sure enough, Goldfinger's ball was on top of the protecting mound of rough. He had a nasty, cuppy lie, with a tuft just behind the ball. Goldfinger stood and looked at the lie. He seemed to make up his mind. He stepped past his ball to take a club from the caddie. His left foot came down just behind the ball, flattening the tuft. Goldfinger could now take his putter. He did so and trickled the ball down the bank towards the hole. It stopped three feet short.

Bond frowned. The only remedy against a cheat at golf is not to play with him again. But that was no good in this match. Bond had no intention of playing with the man again. And it was no good starting a you–did–I–didn't argument unless he caught Goldfinger doing something even more outrageous. Bond would just have to try and beat him, cheating and all.

Now Bond's twenty-foot putt was no joke. There was no question of going for the hole. He would have to concentrate on laying it dead. As usual, when one plays to go dead, the ball stopped short—a good yard short. Bond took a lot of trouble about the putt and holed it, sweating. He knocked Goldfinger's ball away. He would go on giving Goldfinger missable putts until suddenly Bond would ask him to hole one. Then that one might look just a bit more difficult.

Still all square. The fourth is 460 yards. You drive over one of the tallest and deepest bunkers in the United Kingdom and then have a long second shot across an undulating hilly fairway to a plateau green guarded by a final steep slope which makes it easier to take three putts than two.

Bond picked up his usual fifty yards on the drive and Goldfinger hit two of his respectable shots to the gully below the green. Bond, determined to get up, took a brassie instead of a spoon and went over the green and almost up against the boundary fence. From there he was glad to get down in three for a half.

The fifth was again a long carry, followed by Bond's favorite second shot on the course—over bunkers and through a valley between high sand dunes to a distant, taunting flag. It is a testing hole for which the first essential is a well-placed drive. Bond stood on the tee, perched high up in the sand hills, and paused before the shot while he gazed at the glittering distant sea and at the faraway crescent of white cliffs beyond Pegwell Bay. Then he took up his stance and visualized the tennis court of turf that was his target. He took the club back as slowly as he knew how and started down for the last terrific acceleration before the clubhead met the ball. There was a dull clang on his right. It was too late to stop. Desperately Bond focused the ball and tried to keep his swing all in one piece. There came the ugly clonk of a mishit ball. Bond's head shot up. It was a lofted hook. Would it have the legs? Get on! Get on! The ball hit the top of a mountain of rough and bounced over. Would it reach the beginning of the fairway?

Bond turned towards Goldfinger and the caddies, his eyes fierce. Goldfinger was straightening up. He met Bond's eyes indifferently. "Sorry. Dropped my driver."

"Don't do it again," said Bond curtly. He stood down off the tee and handed his driver to Hawker. Hawker shook his head sympathetically. Bond took out a cigarette and lit it. Goldfinger hit his drive the dead straight regulation 200 yards.

They walked down the hill in a silence which Goldfinger unexpectedly broke. "What is the firm you work for?"

"Universal Export."

"And where do they hang out?"

"London. Regent's Park."

"What do they export?"

Bond woke up from his angry ruminations. Here, pay attention! This is work, not a game. All right, he put you off your drive, but you've got your cover to think about. Don't let him needle you into making mistakes about it. Build up your story. Bond said casually, "Oh everything from sewing machines to tanks."

"What's your specialty?"

Bond could feel Goldfinger's eyes on him. He said, "I look after the small arms side. Spend most of my time selling miscellaneous ironmongery to sheiks and rajahs—anyone the Foreign Office decides doesn't want the stuff to shoot at us with."

"Interesting work." Goldfinger's voice was flat, bored.

"Not very. I'm thinking of quitting. Came down here for a week's holiday to think it out. Not much future in England. Rather like the idea of Canada."

"Indeed?"

They were past the rough and Bond was relieved to find that his ball had got a forward kick off the hill on to the fairway. The fairway curved slightly to the left and Bond had even managed to pick up a few feet on Goldfinger. It was Goldfinger to play. Goldfinger took out his spoon. He wasn't going for the green but only to get over the bunkers and through the valley.

Bond waited for the usual safe shot. He looked at his own lie. Yes, he could take his brassie. There came the wooden thud of a mishit. Goldfinger's ball, hit off the heel, sped along the ground and into the stony wastes of Hell Bunker—the widest bunker and the only unkempt one, because of the pebbles, on the course.

For once Homer had nodded—or rather, lifted his head. Perhaps his mind had been half on what Bond had told him. Good show! But Goldfinger might still get down in three more. Bond took out his brassie. He couldn't afford to play safe. He addressed the ball, seeing in his mind's eye its eighty-eight-millimeter trajectory through the valley and then the two or three bounces that would take it on to the green. He laid off a bit to the right to allow for his draw. Now!

There came a soft clinking away to his right. Bond stood away from his ball. Goldfinger had his back to Bond. He was gazing out to sea, rapt in its contemplation, while his right hand played "unconsciously" with the money in his pocket.

Bond smiled grimly. He said, "Could you stop shifting bullion till after my shot?"

Goldfinger didn't turn round or answer. The noise stopped.

Bond turned back to his shot, desperately trying to clear his mind again. Now the brassie was too much of a risk. It needed too good a shot. He handed it to Hawker and took his spoon and banged the ball safely through the valley. It ran on well and stopped on the apron. A five, perhaps a four.

Goldfinger got well out of the bunker and put his chip dead. Bond putted too hard and missed the one back. Still all square.

The sixth, appropriately called "the Virgin," is a famous short hole in the world of golf. A narrow green, almost ringed with bunkers, it can need anything from an eight- to a two-iron according to the wind. Today, for Bond, it was a seven. He played a soaring shot, laid off to the right for the wind to bring it in. It ended twenty feet beyond the pin with a difficult putt over and down a shoulder. Should be a three. Goldfinger took his five and played it straight. The breeze took it and it rolled into the deep bunker on the left. Good news! That would be the hell of a difficult three.

They walked in silence to the green. Bond glanced into the bunker. Goldfinger's ball was in a deep heel mark. Bond walked over to his ball and listened to the larks. This was going to put him one up. He looked for Hawker to take his putter, but Hawker was the other side of the green, watching with intent concentration Goldfinger play his shot. Goldfinger got down into the bunker with his blaster. He jumped up to get a view of the hole and then settled himself for the shot. As his club went up Bond's heart lifted. He was going to try and flick it out—a hopeless technique from that buried lie. The only hope would have been to explode it. Down came the club, smoothly, without hurry. With hardly a handful of sand the ball curved up out of the deep bunker, bounced once and lay dead!

Bond swallowed. Blast his eyes! How the hell had Goldfinger managed that? Now, out of sour grapes, Bond must try for his two. He went for it, missed the hole by an inch and rolled a good yard past. Hell and damnation! Bond walked slowly up to the putt, knocking Goldfinger's ball away. Come on, you bloody fool! But the specter of the big swing—from an almost certain one up to a possible one down—made Bond wish the ball into the hole instead of tapping it in. The coaxed ball, lacking decision, slid past the lip. One down!

Now Bond was angry with himself. He, and he alone, had lost that hole. He had taken three putts from twenty feet. He really must pull himself together and get going.

At the seventh, 1500 yards, they both hit good drives and Goldfinger's immaculate second lay fifty yards short of the green. Bond took his brassie. Now for the equalizer! But he hit from the top, his clubhead came down too far ahead of the hands and the smothered ball shot into one of the right-hand bunkers. Not a good lie, but he must put it on the green. Bond took a dangerous seven and failed to get it out. Goldfinger got his five. Two down. They halved the short eighth in three. At the ninth, Bond, determined to turn only one down, again tried to do too much off a poor lie. Goldfinger got his four to Bond's five. Three down at the turn! Not too good. Bond asked Hawker for a new ball. Hawker unwrapped it slowly, waiting for Goldfinger to walk over the hillock to the next tee. Hawker said softly, "You saw what he did at the Virgin, sir?"

"Yes, damn him. It was an amazing shot."

Hawker was surprised. "Oh, you didn't see what he did in the bunker, sir?"

"No, what? I was too far away."

The other two were out of sight over the rise. Hawker silently walked down into one of the bunkers guarding the ninth green, kicked a hole with his toe and dropped the ball in the hole. He then stood just behind the half-buried ball with his feet close together. He looked up at Bond. "Remember he jumped up to look at the line to the hole, sir?"

"Yes."

"Just watch this, sir." Hawker looked towards the ninth pin and jumped, just as Goldfinger had done, as if to get the line. Then he looked up at Bond again and pointed to the ball at his feet. The heavy impact of the two feet just behind the ball had leveled the hole in which it had lain and squeezed the ball out so that it was now perfectly teed for an easy shot—for just the easy cut-up shot which had seemed utterly impossible from Goldfinger's lie at the Virgin.

Bond looked at his caddie for a moment in silence. Then he said, "Thanks, Hawker. Give me the bat and the ball. Somebody's going to be second in this match, and I'm damned if it's going to be me."

"Yes, sir," said Hawker stolidly. He limped off on the shortcut that would take him halfway down the tenth fairway.

Bond sauntered slowly over the rise and down to the tenth tee. He hardly looked at Goldfinger who was standing on the tee swishing his driver impatiently. Bond was clearing his mind of everything but cold, offensive resolve. For the first time since the first tee, he felt supremely confident. All he needed was a sign from heaven and his game would catch fire.

The tenth at the Royal St. Marks is the most dangerous hole on the course. The second shot, to the skiddy plateau green with cavernous bunkers to right and left and a steep hill beyond, has broken many hearts. Bond remembered that Philip Scrutton, out in four under fours in the Gold Bowl, had taken a fourteen at this hole, seven of them ping-pong shots from one bunker to another, to and fro across the green. Bond knew that Goldfinger would play his second to the apron, or short of it, and be glad to get a five. Bond must go for it and get his four.

Two good drives and, sure enough, Goldfinger well up on the apron with his second. A possible four. Bond took his seven, laid off plenty for the breeze and fired the ball off into the sky. At first he thought he had laid off too much, but then the ball began to float to the left. It pitched and stopped dead in the soft sand blown on to the green from the right-hand bunker. A nasty fifteen-foot putt. Bond would now be glad to get a half. Sure enough, Goldfinger putted up to within a yard. That, thought Bond as he squared up to his putt, he will have to hole. He hit his own putt fairly smartly to get it through the powdering of sand and was horrified to see it going like lightning across the skiddy green. God, he was going to have not a yard, but a two-yard putt back! But suddenly, as if drawn by a magnet, the ball swerved straight for the hole, hit the back of the tin, bounced up and fell into the cup with an audible rattle. The sigh from heaven! Bond went up to Hawker, winked at him and took his driver.

They left the caddies and walked down the slope and back to the next tee. Goldfinger said coldly, "That putt ought to have run off the green."

Bond said off-handedly, "Always give the hole a chance!" He teed up his ball and hit his best drive of the day down the breeze. Wedge and one putt? Goldfinger hit his regulation shot and they walked off again. Bond said, "By the way, what happened to that nice Miss Masterton?"

Goldfinger looked straight in front of him. "She left my employ."

Bond thought, good for her! He said, "Oh, I must get in touch with her again. Where did she go to?"

"I couldn't say." Goldfinger walked away from Bond towards his ball. Bond's drive was out of sight, over the ridge that bisected the fairway. It wouldn't be more than fifty yards from the pin. Bond thought he knew what would be in Goldfinger's mind, what is in most golfers' minds when they smell the first scent of a good lead melting away. Bond wouldn't be surprised to see that grooved swing quicken a trifle. It did. Goldfinger hooked into a bunker on the left of the green.

Now was the moment when it would be the end of the game if Bond made a mistake, let his man off the hook. He had a slightly downhill lie, otherwise an easy chip—but to the trickiest green on the course. Bond played it like a man. The ball ended six feet from the pin. Goldfinger played well out of his bunker, but missed the longish putt. Now Bond was only one down.

They halved the dogleg twelfth in inglorious fives and the longish thirteenth also in fives, Goldfinger having to hole a good putt to do so.

Now a tiny cleft of concentration had appeared on Goldfinger's massive, unlined forehead. He took a drink of water from the tap beside the fourteenth tee. Bond waited for him. He didn't want a sharp clang from that tin cup when it was out-of-bounds over the fence to the right and the drive into the breeze favoring a slice! Bond brought his left hand over to increase his draw and slowed down his swing. The drive, well to the left, was only just adequate, but at least it had stayed in bounds. Goldfinger, apparently unmoved by the out-of-bounds hazard, hit his standard shot. They both negotiated the transverse canal without damage and it was another half in five. Still one down and now only four to play.

The 460-yard fifteenth is perhaps the only hole where the long hitter may hope to gain one clear shot. Two smashing woods will just get you over the line of bunkers that lie right up against the green. Goldfinger had to play short of them with his second. He could hardly improve on a five and it was up to Bond to hit a really godlike second shot from a barely adequate drive.

The sun was on its way down and the shadows of the four men were beginning to lengthen. Bond had taken up his stance. It was a good lie. He had kept his driver. There was dead silence as he gave his two incisive waggles. This was going to be a vital stroke. Remember to pause at the top of the swing, come down slow and whip the clubhead through at the last second. Bond began to take the club back. Something moved at the corner of his right eye. From nowhere the shadow of Goldfinger's huge head approached the ball on the ground, engulfed it and moved on. Bond let his swing take itself to pieces in sections. Then he stood away from his ball and looked up. Goldfinger's feet were still moving. He was looking carefully up at the sky.

"Shades please, Goldfinger." Bond's voice was furiously controlled.

Goldfinger stopped and looked slowly at Bond. The eyebrows were raised a fraction in inquiry. He moved back and stood still, saying nothing.

Bond went back to his ball. Now then, relax! To hell with Goldfinger. Slam that ball on to the green. Just stand still and hit it. There was a moment when the world stood still, then . . . then somehow Bond did hit it—on a low trajectory that mounted gracefully to carry the distant surf of the bunkers. The ball hit the bank below the green, bounced high with the impact and rolled out of sight into the saucer around the pin.

Hawker came up and took the driver out of Bond's hand. They walked on together. Hawker said seriously, "That's one of the finest shots I've seen in thirty years." He lowered his voice. "I thought he'd fixed you then, sir."

"He damned nearly did, Hawker. It was Alfred Blacking that hit that ball, not me." Bond took out his cigarettes, gave one to Hawker and lit his own. He said quietly, "All square and three to play. We've got to watch those next three holes. Know what I mean?"

"Don't you worry, sir. I'll keep my eye on him."

They came up with the green. Goldfinger had pitched on and had a long putt for a four, but Bond's ball was only two inches away from the hole. Goldfinger picked up his ball and walked off the green. They halved the short sixteenth in good threes. Now there were the two long holes home. Fours would win them. Bond hit a fine drive down the center. Goldfinger pushed his far out to the right into deep rough. Bond walked along trying not to be too jubilant, trying not to count his chickens. A win for him at this hole and he would only need a half at the eighteenth for the match. He prayed that Goldfinger's ball would be unplayable or, better still, lost.

Hawker had gone on ahead. He had already laid down his bag and was busily—far too busily to Bond's way of thinking—searching for Goldfinger's ball when they came up.

It was bad stuff—jungle country, deep thick luxuriant grass whose roots still held last night's dew. Unless they were very lucky, they couldn't hope to find the ball. After a few minutes' search Goldfinger and his caddie drifted away still wider to where the rough thinned out into isolated tufts. That's good, thought Bond. That wasn't anything like the line. Suddenly he trod on something. Hell and damnation. Should he stamp it in? He shrugged his shoulders, bent down and gently uncovered the ball so as not to improve the lie. Yes it was a Dunlop 65. "Here you are," he called grudgingly. "Oh no, sorry. You play with a number one, don't you?"

"Yes," came back Goldfinger's voice impatiently.

"Well, this is a number seven." Bond picked it up and walked over to Goldfinger.

Goldfinger gave the ball a cursory glance. He said, "Not mine," and went on poking among the tufts with the head of his driver.

It was a good ball, unmarked and almost new. Bond put it in his pocket and went back to his search. He glanced at his watch. The statutory five minutes was almost up. Another half-minute and by God he was going to claim the hole. Strict rules of golf, Goldfinger had stipulated. All right my friend, you shall have them!

Goldfinger was casting back towards Bond, diligently prodding and shuffling through the grass.

Bond said, "Nearly time, I'm afraid."

Goldfinger grunted. He started to say something when there came a cry from his caddie, "Here you are, sir. Number one Dunlop."

Bond followed Goldfinger over to where the caddie stood on a small plateau of higher ground. He was pointing down. Bond bent and inspected the ball. Yes, an almost new Dunlop one and in an astonishingly good lie. It was miraculous—more than miraculous. Bond stared hard from Goldfinger to his caddie. "Must have had the hell of a lucky kick," he said mildly.

The caddie shrugged his shoulders. Goldfinger's eyes were calm, untroubled. "So it would seem." He turned to his caddie. "I think we can get a spoon to that one, Foulks."

Bond walked thoughtfully away and then turned to watch the shot. It was one of Goldfinger's best. It soared over a far shoulder of rough towards the green. Might just have caught the bunker on the right.

Bond walked on to where Hawker, a long blade of grass dangling from his wry lips, was standing on the fairway watching the shot finish. Bond smiled bitterly at him. He said in a controlled voice, "Is my good friend in the bunker, or is the bastard on the green?"

"Green, sir," said Hawker unemotionally.

Bond went up to his ball. Now things had got tough again. Once more he was fighting for a half after having a certain win in his pocket. He glanced towards the pin, gauging the distance. This was a tricky one. He said, "Five or six?"

"The six should do it, sir. Nice firm shot." Hawker handed him the club.

Now then, clear your mind. Keep it slow and deliberate. It's an easy shot. Just punch it so that it's got plenty of zip to get up the bank and on to the green. Stand still and head down. Click! The ball, hit with a slightly closed face, went off on just the medium trajectory Bond had wanted. It pitched below the bank. It was perfect! No, damn it. It had hit the bank with its second bounce, stopped dead, hesitated and then rolled back and down again. Hell's bells! Was it Hagen who had said, "You drive for show, but you putt for dough"? Getting dead from below that bank was one of the most difficult putts on the course. Bond reached for his cigarettes and lit one, already preparing his mind for the next crucial shot to save the hole—so long as that bastard Goldfinger didn't hole his from thirty feet!

Hawker walked along by his side. Bond said, "Miracle finding that ball."

"It wasn't his ball, sir." Hawker was stating a fact.

"What do you mean?" Bond's voice was tense.

"Money passed, sir. White, probably a fiver. Foulks must have dropped that ball down his trouser leg."

"Hawker!" Bond stopped in his tracks. He looked round. Goldfinger and his caddie were fifty yards away, walking slowly towards the green. Bond said fiercely, "Do you swear to that? How can you be sure?"

Hawker gave a half-ashamed, lopsided grin. But there was a crafty belligerence in his eye. "Because his ball was lying under my bag of clubs, sir." When he saw Bond's open-mouthed expression he added apologetically, "Sorry, sir. Had to do it after what he's been doing to you. Wouldn't have mentioned it, but I had to let you know he's fixed you again."

Bond had to laugh. He said admiringly, "Well, you *are* a card, Hawker. So you were going to win the match for me all on your own!" He added bitterly, "But, by God, that man's the flaming limit. I've got to get him. I've simply got to. Now let's think!" They walked slowly on.

Bond's left hand was in his trousers pocket, absent-mindedly fingering the ball he had picked up in the rough. Suddenly the message went to his brain. Got it! He came close to Hawker. He glanced across at the others. Goldfinger had stopped. His back was to Bond and he was taking the putter out of his bag. Bond nudged Hawker. "Here, take this." He slipped the ball into the gnarled hand. Bond said softly, urgently, "Be certain you take the flag. When you pick up the balls from the green, whichever way the hole has gone, give Goldfinger this one. Right?"

Hawker walked stolidly forward. His face was expressionless. "Got it, sir," he said in his normal voice. "Will you take the putter for this one?"

"Yes." Bond walked up to his ball. "Give me a line, would you?"

Hawker walked up on to the green. He stood sideways to the line of the putt and then stalked round to behind the flag and crouched. He got up. "Inch outside the right lip, sir. Firm putt. Flag, sir?"

"No. Leave it in, would you."

Hawker stood away. Goldfinger was standing by his ball on the right of the green. His caddie had stopped at the bottom of the slope. Bond bent to the putt. Come on, Calamity Jane! This one has got to go dead or I'll put you across my knee. Stand still. Clubhead straight back on the line and follow through towards the hole. Give it a chance. Now! The ball, hit firmly in the middle of the club, had run up the bank and was on its way to the hole. But too hard, dammit! Hit the stick! Obediently the ball curved in, rapped the stick hard and bounced back three inches—dead as a doornail!

Bond let out a deep sigh and picked up his discarded cigarette. He looked over at Goldfinger. Now then, you bastard. Sweat that one out. And by God if you hole it! But Goldfinger couldn't afford to try. He stopped two feet short. "All right, all right," said Bond generously. "All square and one to go." It was vital that Hawker should pick up the balls. If he had made Goldfinger hole the short putt it would have been Goldfinger who would have picked the ball out of the hole. Anyway, Bond didn't want Goldfinger to miss that putt. That wasn't part of the plan.

Hawker bent down and picked up the balls. He rolled one towards Bond and handed the other to Goldfinger. They walked off the green, Goldfinger leading as usual. Bond noticed Hawker's hand go to his pocket. Now, so long as Goldfinger didn't notice anything on the tee!

But, with all square and one to go, you don't scrutinize your ball. Your motions are more or less automatic. You are thinking of how to place your drive, of whether to go for the green with the second or play to the apron, of the strength of the wind—of the vital figure four that must somehow be achieved to win or at least to halve.

Considering that Bond could hardly wait for Goldfinger to follow him and hit, just once, that treacherous Dunlop number seven that looked so very like a number one, Bond's own drive down the 450-yard eighteenth was praiseworthy. If he wanted to, he could now reach the green—if he wanted to!

Now Goldfinger was on the tee. Now he had bent down. The ball was on the peg, its lying face turned up at him. But Goldfinger had straightened, had stood back, was taking his two deliberate practice swings. He stepped up to the ball, cautiously, deliberately. Stood over it, waggled, focusing the ball minutely. Surely he would see! Surely he would stop and bend down at the last minute to inspect the ball! Would the waggle never end? But now the club-head was going back, coming down, the left knee bent correctly in towards the ball, the left arm straight as a ramrod. Crack! The ball sailed off, a beautiful drive, as good as Goldfinger had hit, straight down the fairway.

Bond's heart sang. Got you, you bastard! Got you! Blithely Bond stepped down from the tee and strolled off down the fairway planning the next steps which could now be as eccentric, as fiendish as he wished. Goldfinger was beaten already—hoist with his own petard! Now to roast him, slowly, exquisitely.

Bond had no compunction. Goldfinger had cheated him twice and got away with it. But for his cheats at the Virgin and the seventeenth, not to mention his improved lie at the third and the various times he had tried to put Bond off, Goldfinger would have been beaten by now. If it needed one cheat by Bond to rectify the score sheet that was only poetic justice. And besides, there was more to this than a game of golf. It was Bond's duty to win. By his reading of Goldfinger he *had* to win. If he was beaten, the score between the two men would have been equalized. If he won the match, as he now had, he would be two up on Goldfinger—an intolerable state of affairs, Bond guessed, to a man who saw himself as all powerful. This man Bond, Goldfinger would say to himself, *has* something. He has qualities I can use. He is a tough adventurer with plenty of tricks up his sleeve. This is the sort of man I need for—for what? Bond didn't know. Perhaps there would be nothing for him. Perhaps his reading of Goldfinger was wrong, but there was certainly no other way of creeping up on the man.

Goldfinger cautiously took out his spoon for the longish second over cross-bunkers to the narrow entrance to the green. He made one more practice swing than usual and then hit exactly the right, controlled shot up to the apron. A certain five, probably a four. Much good would it do him!

Bond, after a great show of taking pains, brought his hands down well ahead of the club and smothered his number three-iron so that the topped ball barely scrambled over the cross-bunkers. He then wedged the ball on to the green twenty feet past the pin. He was where he wanted to be—enough of a threat to make Goldfinger savor the sweet smell of victory, enough to make Goldfinger really sweat to get his four.

And now Goldfinger really was sweating. There was a savage grin of concentration and greed as he bent to the long putt up the bank and down to the hole. Not too hard, not too soft. Bond could read every anxious thought that would be running through the man's mind. Goldfinger straightened up again, walked deliberately across the green to behind the flag to verify his line.

He walked slowly back beside his line, brushing away—carefully, with the back of his hand—a wisp or two of grass, a speck of top-dressing. He bent again and made one or two practice swings and then stood to the putt, the veins standing out on his temples, the cleft of concentration deep between his eyes.

Goldfinger hit the putt and followed through on the line. It was a beautiful putt that stopped six inches past the pin. Now Goldfinger would be sure that unless Bond sank his difficult twenty-footer, the match was his!

Bond went through a long rigmarole of sizing up his putt. He took his time, letting the suspense gather like a thunder cloud round the long shadows on the livid, fateful green.

"Flag out, please. I'm going to sink this one." Bond charged the words with a deadly certitude, while debating whether to miss the hole to the right or the left or leave it short. He bent to the putt and missed the hole well on the right.

"Missed it, by God!" Bond put bitterness and rage into his voice. He walked over to the hole and picked up the two balls, keeping them in full view.

Goldfinger came up. His face was glistening with triumph. "Well, thanks for the game. Seems I was just too good for you after all."

"You're a good nine handicap," said Bond with just sufficient sourness. He glanced at the balls in his hand to pick out Goldfinger's and hand it to him. He gave a start of surprise. "Hullo!" He looked sharply at Goldfinger. "You play a number one Dunlop, don't you?"

"Yes, of course." A sixth sense of disaster wiped the triumph off Goldfinger's face. "What is it? What's the matter?"

"Well," said Bond apologetically. " 'Fraid you've been playing with the wrong ball. Here's my Penfold Hearts and this is a number seven Dunlop." He handed both balls to Goldfinger. Goldfinger tore them off his palm and examined them feverishly.

Slowly the color flooded over Goldfinger's face. He stood, his mouth working, looking from the balls to Bond and back to the balls.

Bond said softly, "Too bad we were playing to the rules. Afraid that means you lose the hole. And, of course, the match." Bond's eyes observed Goldfinger impassively.

"But, but . . ."

This was what Bond had been looking forward to—the cup dashed from the lips. He stood and waited, saying nothing.

Rage suddenly burst Goldfinger's usually relaxed face like a bomb. "It was a Dunlop seven you found in the rough. It was your caddie that gave me this ball. On the seventeenth green. He gave me the wrong ball on purpose, the damned che—"

"Here, steady on," said Bond mildly. "You'll get a slander action on your hands if you aren't careful. Hawker, did you give Mr. Goldfinger the wrong ball by mistake or anything?"

"No, sir." Hawker's face was stolid. He said indifferently, "If you want my opinion, sir, the mistake may have been made at the seventeenth when the gentleman found his ball pretty far off the line we'd all marked it on. A seven looks very much like a one. I'd say that's what happened, sir. It would have been a miracle for the gentleman's ball to have ended up as wide as where it was found."

"Tommyrot!" Goldfinger gave a snort of disgust. He turned angrily on Bond. "You saw that was a number one my caddie found."

Bond shook his head doubtfully. "I didn't really look closely, I'm afraid. However," Bond's voice became brisk, businesslike, "it's really the job of the player to make certain he's using the right ball, isn't it? I can't see that anyone else can be blamed if you tee the wrong ball up and play three shots with it. Anyway," he started walking off the green, "many thanks for the match. We must have it again one day."

Goldfinger, lit with glory by the setting sun, but with a long black shadow tied to his heels, followed Bond slowly, his eyes fixed thoughtfully on Bond's back.

The Finest Course of All

BY PETER DOBEREINER

Wherever the byline of Peter Dobereiner (1926–1996) appeared, the dispatch below was sure to overflow with droll charm. A staple on the pages of the *Observer, the Guardian, Golf Digest,* and *Golf World*—and author of *The Glorious World of Golf,* one of the game's most beautiful tribute volumes—he parted the curtain, in this 1985 column, on the stage of Pine Valley. It's a piece that allows the rest of us groundlings to experience, at least vicariously, how the course generally acknowledged to be the greatest ever coaxed from a landscape in the Milky Way has its own particular way with those lucky—or, double-checking the scorecard, unlucky—enough to actually get on to play it.

The late Bernard Darwin, the father of golf journalism and, indeed, the pioneer along with Neville Cardus of literacy on the sports pages, was a considerable player as well as a fine essayist. When he sailed to America to cover the inaugural Walker Cup match the captain fell ill and the man from *The Times* was co-opted to play and take over the duties of leading the side.

It was from Darwin that British golfers first learnt about Pine Valley. The course already had a fearsome local reputation by the time Darwin was taken there on a private visit in the twenties.

He played the first seven holes in level fours and then came comprehensively to grief at the eighth. He picked up his ball and, sad to relate, retired to the clubhouse after delivering judgement: 'It is all very well to punish a bad stroke, but the right of eternal punishment should be reserved for a higher tribunal than a green committee.'

So far as the outside world was concerned that peppery diatribe set the tone for all subsequent writing about Pine Valley. The course had its label and there was no shortage of lurid anecdote to fuel that myth.

The members relished these horror stories and took pride in Pine Valley's growing notoriety as the most penal, the most difficult and the most malicious course in the world. They offered bets that visitors could not break 100 at the first attempt, or beat the par 18-up with the benefit of five strokes a hole.

So my brain was thoroughly washed by doom and despondency before I set out for the backwoods of New Jersey to tilt my feeble lance at the gorgon of golf. A friend sped me on the way with the words: 'It is all very well for golfers of Walker Cup calibre but for the likes of you and I it is simply unplayable.'

As to that, and to all the rest of the weeping and wailing and spitting of blood about Pine Valley, I am now ready to respond with a cheery cry of 'Rubbish!' True, it demands a standard of accuracy which is beyond most golfers, myself near the top of the list. Equally true it exacts a scale of punishment which is positively Old Testament in its severity, six strokes being a common sanction for missing a fairway or one of the greens which rise like islands in a sea of unraked sand.

As for the bunkers, there is one turf-walled brute at the front of the short tenth whose name is prudishly rendered in official publications as the Devil's Advocate or the Devil's Pit or, getting closer to the truth of the matter, the Devil's ah, Aperture, or just DAH. It is about 8 feet in diameter and the same depth, with steps set into the sand to assist the exhausted and disgruntled golfer to get back to the surface at the end of his shift.

One player, accomplished enough to have scored 35 on the first nine holes, found this bunker off the tee and took 23 for the hole. Devilish intervention caused one four ball to run up an aggregate of 88 strokes at the 10th and another player, having ruined his card and his disposition by taking seven strokes to extricate his ball from the pit, sat on its rim with his feet dangling into the abyss and howled like a baby.

My favourite Pine Valley story is of the four ball which lost one of its members in the woods. Three of them sliced into the trees and the fourth hooked his ball wildly. After playing back into the open country the three slicers crossed the fairway to help their companion's search. They found his ball but he was nowhere to be seen.

The police delivered him back to the clubhouse late at night, somewhat the worse for drink. He had lost his bearings and wandered for miles through the forest and had celebrated his eventual contact with civilisation in the time honoured tradition of *après* golf.

All these tales—and everyone who has enjoyed the privilege of playing Pine Valley has a personal disaster to relate—bear out the horrific reputation of the course. But they tell only the lesser half of the story. Because of the perils which beset the golfer on every side, the charge of exhilaration he receives when he successfully carries his drive over 170 yards of sandy waste is proportionately increased.

The hitting of a green, a routine enough experience at your home club, becomes a thrill. As for holing across those undulating greens with surfaces as slick as polished marble, watching the ball swing as much as 20 feet on its roller-coaster route, the afterglow of achievement lasts for weeks.

So, while playing Pine Valley can be a penance, and nearly always is somewhere during the round, the agonies are the price which must be paid for the ecstasies. Provided you leave your ego back in the locker room, Pine Valley is a delight. The scenery alone is intoxicating and enhanced by the wildlife of what is in effect a 650-acre nature reserve.

When my friends asks what I scored, he will doubtless say: 'I told you that you could never get around it.' In terms of numbers that is a just comment but numbers, far from being the be all and end all of golf, are the least part of the game.

After Pine Valley, by a long way the finest course I have experienced, other courses will seem humdrum so I may very likely retire, to take up pursuits more suited to my creaking bones. It would be a pity to end on a high score but fitting to go out on the highest note of them all.

Workers, Arise! Shout Fore

BY ALISTAIR COOKE

Best known on the western shores of the Atlantic as the original host of *Masterpiece Theater,* Alistair Cooke spent decades observing Americans and American life for the *Guardian* and the BBC. An intrepid golfer, Cooke has, from time to time, enlisted his urbanity and courtliness into making sense of the overall golfing experience; the United States Golf Association once anointed him spokesman for a series of TV spots to instruct the masses on the game's courtesies. Speaking of the masses, in the Cold War thaw of the early '70s, the Soviets hoped to bring its masses a world-class golf course on the outskirts of Moscow. Cooke faithfully reported this Communist plot to his own masses— the TV audience on both sides of the pond—via the multipart BBC/PBS series *The Americans,* and the companion volume that went with it.

There is something I ought to talk about and something I must talk about. What I ought to talk about is the end of the annual General Assembly of the United Nations, a leaden piece of Christmas cake I have obediently chewed on for the past thirty-odd years. What I must tell you about is an encounter I recently had with the Russians that is altogether cockeyed and hilarious, but it is not without deep significance of a ritual kind. Let us skip the cake and come to the icing.

A few weeks ago I was staying in San Francisco, and I had a call one morning asking me to lunch with the Russian Consul General and his deputy. The invitation came from an unlikely host, a friend, a lawyer, an affable and fastidious gent, a Republican, and a first-rate golfer to whom the great game is not only a major exercise in military strategy and tactics but also a minor re-hearsal of the Ten Commandments. He is, indeed, the chairman of the champi-onship committee—and will without doubt soon become the president—of the United States Golf Association. His pairing with the Russian Consul Gen-eral seemed improbable in the extreme. Where, I asked, shall we meet? "At the golf club, of course," was his mad reply. But why, why? "It is very important," he said, "I should surmise that the Consul General is coming under orders, and the whole point of the lunch is to talk golf." This was like being invited by a rabbi to lunch with the Pope to discuss stud poker. I accepted instantly.

The co-host was a young American, a boyish type, who is associated with his famous father in the most successful golf-architecture firm on earth. Golf architecture is the art and science of designing and building golf courses, and it involves much knowledge of landscape, soils, grasses, water drainage, en-gineering, meteorology, and sometimes—I feel—black magic. Let us call the young man Mr. Jones, for that happily is his name.

It seems he had recently got back from Moscow, where he and his fa-ther had responded to what must have sounded like a joke more unlikely than the reason for our lunch: a call from the Mayor of Moscow to consider build-ing the first Russian golf course. The impulse, apparently, had come from a So-viet diplomat who had been exposed to the decadent West and had become one maniacal golfer. This in itself should give us pause. I should have guessed that any Russian who had yielded to such a capitalist diversionary activity as golf would have been, on his first homecoming, bundled off to Siberia, where he'd have been condemned to play golf with a red ball and a snow sled. But he was a close friend of the Mayor of Moscow. When he returned from a foreign, Western, post, he came into the airport carrying a golf bag. The customs men—as also, I imagine, the military and the narcotics squad—examined the weaponry, but reluctantly gave him the benefit of his diplomatic passport. Somehow the man sold the Mayor of Moscow on the idea of a city—public, of course—golf course. I don't suppose things rested there. The matter went up to the Kremlin. And, from all I could gather, Mr. Brezhnev gave the nod.

Well, we sat down to lunch, and the Consul General—a stocky man in the regulation Sears Roebuck suit—turned out to have a puckish humor. When we asked him if the Russians would take to golf, he said: "I think, be-cause you see, the Russian people like quick games." Somebody said, "Like chess." He came back on the hop: "Yes, we like a quick win." He plainly and admittedly knew nothing. But he asked everything. And to help him with the rudiments—of building rather than playing—young Mr. Jones put on a lantern

lecture, with color slides showing rice paddies in Bangkok being trans-
formed—slide by slide—into a bulldozed mess, then into terraced ground,
then into ground being planted with gravel and soil and seed, and eventually
emerging as a pastoral golf hole. Through a series of other slides we went to
Hawaii and Florida and Scandinavia and, in the end, to the five sites around
Moscow from which they will choose the one on which to build the course.

After that, the Consul General was given a lesson in weaponry.
("Golf," said Winston Churchill, "is a game whose aim is to hit a very small ball
into an even smaller hole, with weapons singularly ill-designed for the purpose.") We went off in electric carts, like a little motorized battalion, to the
eleventh tee on the noble San Francisco Golf Club course, a swaying landscape
of lush green meadows flanked with towering cypresses and pine and occasional stands of eucalyptus.

The eleventh hole is a par three: that is to say, you are required to hit
the green with your first shot and then sink the ball with two putts.

Our lawyer host, Mr. Frank (Sandy) Tatum, straightened his waistcoat
(all *ex officio* members of the United States Golf Association board are very sensitive to the ancient amenities and insist on playing in ties and waistcoats, like
the respectable Scots in the old prints). Offhand, I would bet that this Tatum,
on that hole, would hit the green ninety-nine times in every hundred. He hit
about six inches behind the ball, which rose in an unsteady arc and landed
about 150 yards away, well short of a cavernous bunker. "Dear me," he said
with splendid restraint.

"So," said the deputy consul (a pretty fresh type, I thought), "the first
pancake is never any good." Ignoring this gem of Russian folk wisdom, Mr.
Tatum set up another ball, and this time was comfortably on the green. Now,
with many open-handed gestures and facetious bows, the Consul General was
motioned to "have a go." He took off his jacket, looked down at the ball,
gripped the club with all ten fingers (the so-called baseball grip, which about
one professional in a thousand uses). His two hands were far apart. He missed
the ball at the first swipe, but at the second it fell just a little short of Tatum's
first effort. There was general applause. "A natural talent," purred the gallant
Mr. Tatum. "Please!" said the Consul General.

Then the deputy had a go, and he slithered the ball about thirty yards
along the ground. "That deputy," one of our group whispered, "he sure knows
what he's doing." Well, then we all departed for the clubhouse, had our pictures
taken, and the Consul General was presented, by young Mr. Jones, with a copy
of an article I had once written on the origins of golf. Mysterious, this.

"Why?" I asked young Jones. He looked for a second over his shoulder. "Don't you see," he hissed, "it supports the main argument?" And what would that be? "What we kicked around at lunch."

I realized then why I had been seated at lunch next to the Consul General. He had dropped several uncomfortable hints that he knew golf was a rich man's hobby, and I sensed that Moscow has asked him to check on this repulsive legend. I hastened to disabuse him with—young Jones later assured me—deeply moving eloquence. "No, no," I said, "that used to be so long ago, even then only in England and America, never in Scotland." I painted a picture, all the more poignant for being true, of poor little boys going off with their sticks and paying a few pennies to play some of the most hallowed courses on earth. "In Scotland," I said, "the people learn to play golf as simply as they learn to drink tea. And St. Andrews, which is the Vatican—pardon me, the Kremlin—of golf is a public course. On Sundays they close it so that little old ladies and dogs and babies can frolic—can walk around—for it is a public park *absolutely for the people.*" "No?" said the Consul General. "Yes," I said.

"What," he asked, "will our people do, will they succeed at this sport?" No question, I said, "ten years from now"—we were well along with the vodka martinis—"I swear to you the British or American Open champion"— ("Open? What means this open?")—"the golf champion of Britain or America will be a Russian. After all, not so many years ago you sent a Russian basketball team, and Americans shook with laughter. Until you wiped the floor with both the Americans and the Canadians."

"Wiped?"

"Beat, trounced, massacred, defeated!"

"It is so," said the Consul, looking gloomily into his vodka.

"Very well, then," I went on, "maybe the big switcheroo will come sooner then ten years. Maybe four, five years from now, there will be a match between the best player in the world, Jack Nicklaus, and Nicholas the Third."

"There was never any Nicholas the Third," said the knowing deputy.

"But there will be," I cried, "and he will win!"

"Iss possible?"

"Is certain."

I went back to town feeling I had done creditably on my first assignment as ambassador without portfolio. There were, of course, certain little nuisances: of having to learn to play the game (from whom?), to find courses to learn it on, pros willing to spend a couple of years teaching the first Russian golfer how, for God's sake, to hit a golf ball straight. I thought of Nicklaus, at the age of eight, going on the practice tee every day for a year to have his head gripped for an hour on end by the hand of an assistant pro so he could learn to keep his head still. Perhaps I should have stretched the apprenticeship period to ten or twenty years.

Still, if they get around to building the Jones course, I like to imagine Mr. Brezhnev or his successor, or *his* successor, standing on the first tee and approaching a ribbon with a mighty pair of shears. He will carry in his hand a note or two from our San Francisco Summit, and he will proclaim to a vast assembly of the peoples of all the Russias: "So! I have the extremely great honor to say to the citizens of our Soviet Socialist Republics—let us begin to play Goalf! The pipple's sport!"

Left-Handed Golf Courses:
Our Greatest Need

BY RUBE GOLDBERG

The deservedly famous left hand of artist Rube Goldberg (1883–1970) was best known for its skills at engineering amazingly complex and hilariously funny devices for performing the simplest and most mundane jobs, including several dreamed up to help in putting. A Pulitzer Prize–winning editorial cartoonist, he took his golf game pretty seriously, though you might not know it from the left-handed observations that follow, cooked up in 1924 for his friend Grantland Rice's magazine *The American Golfer.*

Soon after the piece was published, Rice insisted Goldberg take his distinctive southpaw stance a step farther. After a particularly frustrating 18, the writer-cartoonist approached Rice in a particularly existential mood. "Is there any way you can play golf *except* right- or left-handed?" Goldberg asked. Rice pondered the question for a moment, then suggested that if Rube ruminate over the conundrum, he'd gladly publish the results of the cogitation.

I have been trying to play golf for the last seven years and have been reading about the game for twice as long. I get no comfort out of the continuous flow of golf reform literature that bellows and splashes against the shores of duffer island. Those who are suggesting new improvements are tackling the game from the wrong end.

When I read that the new rules prohibit the use of corrugated club ends it has as much effect on me as if I had just heard that the Gaekwar of

Baroda had issued a decree calling for purple tassels on all elephant saddles on Mondays and Fridays. The only good my backspin mashie ever did me was to use it as an onion grater when we were fortunate enough to have caviar sandwiches on picnics.

Some people think the new metal shafts are a great improvement over the old wooden ones. I have tried both and I would do just as well with rhubarb or asparagus. Every time they bring out a new ball called "The Purple Flash" or "The Comet's Tail" or "The Galloping Dandruff" I laugh so loud I wake up my caddie. I made the best drive of my whole golfing career with a meat ball I had picked up by mistake from a passing lunch wagon.

Another thing that seems to take up a lot of time and energy among those who are sincerely but unwisely seeking new antidotes for the duffer's poisonous mistakes is wearing apparel. I have actually gone out on the links carrying eighteen sweaters—one for every hole. Each one of the sweaters, according to the ad, was built to give the player a particular advantage in playing certain shots. Some were fashioned to keep the neck rigid, others were made to keep the elbows dry when playing chip shots out of the ocean, and still others were designed with special cartridge belts for carrying spare pencils with which to write down extra large scores. The sweaters were all different, but my shots all remained the same.

I even went and purchased a pair of those terrible-looking English knickers that are baggy enough to hold a radio set, and stop somewhere between the knee and the ankle. They don't look like short pants and they don't look like long pants. They are a first cousin to balloon tires but don't give you near the mileage. I played one round in the pair that I bought and my caddie said to me just before he left, "Gee, your old man must be a pretty big guy, if you can wear his pants cut down and they're still to big for you." I gave the pants to my wife's sister who was having a garden party at her place in the country. She used them for Chinese lanterns.

As I said before, the reformers are trying to reform the game from the wrong end. The thing that needs changing is not the golf ball or the golf club or the golf trousers. It is the golf course. I am surprised that nobody has ever thought of suggesting the left-handed golf course. The left-handed golf course is bound to come if the game is to survive. It is an absolute necessity—for me at least.

I forgot to mention that I am left-handed—and there must be thousands of other unfortunates in this country like myself. I have been advised to switch to right-handed. But why should I? I have been eating soup for forty years with my left hand and I am not boasting when I say that my shirt front is as clean as the average man's. In the ordinary course of things it is no handicap to be left-handed. No woman ever refused to bow to me when I tipped my hat with my left hand—that is, no woman who knew me. I never made a waiter sore by handing him a tip with my left hand.

When I take a practice swing at home people look in through the window and say, "Good morning, Mister Sarazen." But when I go out on the golf course and take the same identical swing, the ball doesn't seem to go anywhere. So I know it must be the fault of the course. Logic is logic.

Here are a few of the handicaps I suffer when I play on the regulation course:

When the average player shoots he stands facing the other people on the tee. Being left-handed I must stand with my back to the crowd. Besides wondering whether or not they are giving me the raspberry, I must try to be a gentleman and say each time I step up to the ball, "Excuse my back." And you know that any talk during a shot throws a man off his stance—even if it be his own voice.

In standard golf courses most of the out-of-bounds limits are on the left side of the fairway. A sliced shot always puts me out-of-bounds. So I naturally stand well around to the right on every tee to play safe, so my drive will slice back into the fairway. Then for some reason or other I don't slice at all. My shot goes straight and I hit the president of the club, who is playing three fairways to the right. This puts me in continual bad standing, besides giving all the club members the extra trouble of finding a new president.

Another thing. When I make a beautiful shot right on the green next to the pin I invariably find that I have played for the wrong green. My left-handed vision has given me a cock-eyed idea of the course.

My greatest handicap is in the traps, where I must admit I spend a good part of my weekends. It takes an experienced miner to go down into a hole with nothing but the blue sky as his only area of vision and still keep his sense of direction. After the seventh shot, my left-handed leanings force me around in an angle of ninety degrees without realizing that I have turned at all. Then elated with the wonderful "out" I have finally negotiated, I rise to the surface only to find that I have shot right back through the foursome behind me and lost about sixty yards. I once had a series of these mishaps and spent an hour and a half on one hole continually losing ground. There was an insane asylum across the road from the course and it took my friends quite a while to convince an attendant who happened to see me that I was not an escaped inmate.

There are many other disadvantages that we left-handers must suffer, including the fact that they're building suburban homes closer and closer to the golf courses. The left-hander, when he dubs a shot, always lands in somebody's back yard and this isn't very pleasant when they're cooking cod fish.

I think I have made my case clear. What golf really needs is a course where left-handers can be segregated like smallpox patients. It would be simple to lay out one of these courses. A golf architect can take a plan of any well-known course and build it backwards. He may run into a few snags in the locker room. It will be quite a feat of engineering to get the attendant to mix cocktails standing on his head, and the water to run uphill in the shower baths. But trifling difficulties have never stopped the march of progress. Did snags and prejudices stop Lysander J. Lentil when he started to construct the first portable sink, now socially known as the finger-bowl?

The Humors of Golf

BY THE RIGHT HON. A. BALFOUR, M.P.

One of the real mysteries of golf is how Arthur James Balfour (1848–1930) found time to play it, let alone write about it. Perhaps it was genetically ordained. A Scotsman by birth, he spent three important years a short niblick away from the Old Course as rector of St. Andrews University. All in all, the first Earl of Balfour was a remarkable man on several counts. When he wasn't sneaking off for a quick nine, he was busy earning respect as a historian, a philosopher, and a statesman. Elected to the House of Commons in his 20s, he rose to run the government, serving Britain as prime minister from 1902–1905. Still active as foreign minister in World War II, he issued the 1917 declaration, bearing his name, that announced Britain's support of the creation of a Jewish homeland in Palestine. When hostilities ended, he represented his country at the Treaty of Versailles. He contributed this engaging essay to the extraordinarily popular 1890 Badminton Library volume on the game. Prose stylings may have changed in the past 100-plus years, but his observations on the nature of the game remain as solid as a well-struck drive.

G radually round all the greater games there collects a body of sentiment and tradition unknown to or despised by a profane public, but dear to their votaries, and forming a common bond of union among those who practise their rites. This tradition relates partly to memorable contests and the deeds of bygone heroes, partly to the changes which time brings about in the most ancient sports not less than in the most memorable institutions. But it does not disdain to concern itself with less important matters. Even games are not to be regarded as wholly serious: they have their lighter side, and he must be unhappily constituted who cannot relieve the graver labours in which his favourite pursuit involves him by watching the humours and comparing notes on the proceedings of others who are similarly occupied.

Now golf gives unrivalled opportunities for investigations of this description. There is more to observe in it than in other games, and there are more opportunities for observing. This is so because the conditions under which golf is played differ fundamentally from those of almost any other form of out-door exercises, and every difference lends itself naturally to the promotion of an infinite variety of characteristic humours.

Consider, for instance, the fact that while the performers at other games are restricted within comparatively narrow limits of age, golf is out of relation with no one of the seven ages of man. Round the links may be seen in endless procession not only players of every degree of skill and of every social condition, but also of every degree of maturity and immaturity. There is no reason, in the nature of things, why golf should not be begun as soon as you can walk, and continued as long as you can walk; while, as a matter of fact, it frequently is so begun, and always is so continued. What an excellent variety does not this give to the game, as a subject of observation, and how humorously is that variety heightened and flavoured by the fact that age and dexterity are so frequently bestowed in inverse proportion! You may see at one teeing ground a boy of ten driving his ball with a swing which no professional would despise, and at the next a gentleman of sixty, recently infected with the pleasing madness, patiently 'topping' his ball through the green under the long-suffering superintendence of a professional adviser.

No greater proof, indeed, can be imagined of the fascinations of the game than the fact that so many of us are willing to learn it—and, what is more, to learn it in public—at a period of life when even competitive examinations have ceased to trouble? Lord Chancellor Campbell, we are told, took dancing lessons at the mature age of thirty-four; in order, as he said, to 'qualify him for joining the most polite assemblies.' But he took them in privacy, under an assumed name, and with every precaution that might ensure his maintaining his incognito. Would even Lord Chancellor Campbell have taken dancing lessons if the scene of his tuition had been a public golf link? If the *chassés* and *coupés* of which he speaks had to be attempted before a miscellaneous and highly critical public? If his first ineffectual efforts at 'figuring on the light fantastic toe' (I still quote the noble and learned lord) had been displayed to a mixed assemblage of professional and amateur dancers? I trow not. Rather, a thousand times rather, would he have remained deficient in any graces lighter than those required for special pleading, and renounced for ever the hope of shining in 'the most polite assemblies'! Yet, after all, no ordeal less than this has been gone through by those of us who have first become golfers in mature life. We have seen ourselves, often at an age when other people are leaving off the games they learned in their youth, laboriously endeavouring to acquire a game which certainly not less than any other punishes with eternal mediocrity those who too long defer devoting themselves to its service. We have been humiliated in the eyes of our opponent, in the eyes of our caddie, in the eyes of our opponent's caddie, and in our own eyes by the perpetration of blunders which would seem almost incredible in narration. We have endeavoured time after time to go through the same apparently simple and elementary set of evolutions. Time after time we have failed. We have, if playing in a foursome, apologised to our partner until we were sick of making excuses and he was sick of listening to them. Yet who has ever been repelled by this ordeal from continuing his efforts until age or sickness incapacitate him? Who, having once begun, has been found to turn back? It might indeed be supposed that, if before beginning all that had to be gone through were fully realised, our greens would be emptier than they are. But a splendid confidence, born of impenetrable ignorance, veils his future from the eyes of the beginner. It is narrated of one intending golfer that he wrote home to a friend, saying that all his arrangements for playing were nearly completed: he had purchased the necessary implements; he had been elected at the club, and he had *hired a bunker for his own exclusive use!* Ingenious commentators aver that for *bunker* in this passage should be read *locker*. But, however this may be, what delicious ignorance is there not displayed in these observations! What blissful unconsciousness of miseries yet to come! The writer little knew that in the case of this particular kind of real estate no process of hiring is by golfing law required; that exclusive possession, though it carries few privileges, brings with it no envy; that he might cultivate it with his niblick and the sweat of his brow till the crack of doom, and no man would be found to suggest that what Providence intended for the people should not be monopolised by the individual!

Strange legends are current as to the fate which has overtaken beginners wrestling with the horrors of a really bad bunker. I have been told of a game in which, when one of the players finally emerged from one of those yawning sandpits, a controversy arose between the caddies as to whether he had played *forty-five* or *sixty-five* before getting out; and so hotly did the contest rage, and so convinced were the combatants, not merely of the righteousness but of the important of their cause, that in the end it was only found possible to settle the point by the ordeal of battle! On another occasion it is said that a player of resolute character disappeared from view down one of these abysses, and only made his presence known to the rest of the world by the clouds of sand driven up from time to time by the niblick. On returning to upper air he was politely asked by his opponent (who must have been at least as remarkable for patience as the other was for perseverance) how many he had played. 'I went into that place,' was the reply, 'at a quarter-past twelve. It is now a quarter to one. You are at liberty to form your own estimate!'

Very marvellous are the expedients sometimes adopted in order to enable the mature learner to acquire some stammering knowledge of a language which might have been acquired so easily and so perfectly during youth. In one case an enthusiastic beginner pinned a copy of the most important golfing maxims in a conspicuous place in his dressing-room, and in the intervals of his ablutions devoted his mind to their perusal during those early moments of the day when it is thought that new ideas most easily and permanently imprint themselves on the awakening soul.

Another wrote his saving formula, 'Slow back, keep your eye on the ball,' &c. on his shirt-sleeve; and before each stroke rend it solemnly in muttered tones to himself. A third, still more original, waited till he had got himself into the exact position recommended by the learned in driving off from the tee; and then, in order to embody in substantial form this evanescent moment of inspiration, sent for the carpenter, and, so to speak, had himself *built in* to a kind of wooden framework, into which he could always again be fitted when the occasion required it. It is said that his caddie was expected to carry this 'mould of form' round the course, so that whenever its inventor had to drive he might be certain, if he missed his shot, at least of missing it 'according to rule!'

Since golf, when it has been once begun, exercises this fatal fascination upon its votaries, it is perhaps fortunate that of all games it appears to the uninitiated to be the most meaningless. A *mêlée* at football may appear to involve a perfectly unnecessary expenditure of energy and a foolish risk of life and limb. But even the most ignorant can see what it is all about. Rackets and tennis, again, at once strike the beholder as being games which require great quickness of eye and great dexterity of hand. But there appears to be something singularly inane and foolish about a game of golf. Two middle-aged gentlemen strolling across a links followed by two boys staggering under the burden of a dozen queer-shaped implements, each player hitting along his own ball for no apparent object, in no obvious rivalry, and exercising in the process no obvious skill, do not make up a specially impressive picture to those who see it for the first time; and many are the curious theories advanced by the ignorant to explain the motives and actions of the players.

Two Englishmen, it is said, visited St. Andrews in the course of a Scotch tour. Looking out of the window of the train at the point where the railway runs along the links, they took their first survey of the game. The weather had been very wet, and at the bottom of some bunkers water was lying. 'These are the places,' said A to B, with ready ingenuity, 'where the Scotch play curling in winter.' 'No,' said B to A, 'these are the holes they use for golf, and the object of the player is to get out of one into another as quickly as he can manage it.' Armed with this superior knowledge, A proceeds down to the links, and finds an old gentleman struggling with destiny at the bottom of a bad bunker. At last the player succeeds in getting out his ball, but only with the result of sending it into the next bunker a few yards farther on. This is not an agreeable incident under any circumstances at golf; but conceive, if you can, the irritation of the player when he finds himself being loudly, and, as he no doubt thought, ironically congratulated by a spectator on the results of his stroke, and the well-merited success with which it had been rewarded! I do not know whether this story be apocryphal or not, but in any case the ignorance which it displays is not likely to be long continued in the southern portion of the island. There will soon be more greens in England than in Scotland, and more players of English extraction than of Scotch. 'Do you have much play here?' said someone to the keeper of a racket court in the neighbourhood of an English golf links. 'We used to, sir,' said the man; 'but ever since this d—d Scotch croquet has come into fashion, no one comes into the court.'

It is hard that a game which seems to those who do not play it to be so meaningless should be to those who do play it not only the most absorbing of existing games, but occasionally in the highest degree irritating to the nerves and to the temper. The fact itself will, I apprehend, hardly be denied, and the reason I suppose to be this, that as in most games action is rapid and more or less unpremeditated, failure seems less humiliating in itself, and there is less time to brood over it. In most games—*e.g.* cricket, tennis, football—effort succeeds effort in such quick succession that the memory of particular blunders is immediately effaced or deadened. There is leisure neither for self-examination nor for repentance. Even good resolutions scarce have time to form themselves, and as soon as one difficulty is surmounted, mind and body have to brace themselves to meet the next. In the case of golf it is far otherwise. The player approaches his ball with every circumstance of mature deliberation. He meditates, or may meditate, for as long as he pleases on the precise object he wishes to accomplish and the precise method by which it may best be accomplished. No difficulties are made for him by his opponent; he has no obstacles to overcome but those which are material and inanimate. Is there not, then, some natural cause for irritation when, after every precaution has been taken to insure a drive of 150 or 180 yards, the unfortunate player sees his ball roll gently into the bottom of a bunker some twenty yards in front of the teeing ground and settle itself with every appearance of deliberate forethought at the bottom of the most inaccessible heel-mark therein? Such an event brings with it not merely disaster, but humiliation; and, as a last aggravation, the luckless performer has ample leisure to meditate over his mishap, to analyse its causes, to calculate the precise effects which it will have on the general fortunes of the day, and to divine the secret satisfaction with which his opponent has observed the difficulties in which he has so gratuitously involved himself. No wonder that persons of irritable nerves are occasionally goaded to fury. No wonder that the fury occasionally exhibits itself in violent and eccentric forms. Not, however, that the opponent is usually the object or victim of their wrath. He is too obviously guiltless of contributing to a 'foozle' to permit even an angry man to drag him into his quarrel with the laws of dynamics. It is true that he may have the most extraordinary and unmerited luck. According to my experience, opponents who are winning usually have. But still he can hardly be blamed because the man he is playing with 'tops' his ball or is 'short' with his putts. Let him only assume an aspect of colourless indifference or hypocritical sympathy, and the storm will in all probability not break over *him*.

Expletives more or less vigorous directed against himself, the ball, the club, the wind, the bunker, and the game, are therefore the most usual safety-valve for the fury of the disappointed golfer. But bad language is fortunately much gone out of use; and in any case the resources of profanity are not inexhaustible. Deeds, not words, are required in extreme cases to meet the exigencies of the situation; and, as justice, prudence, and politeness all conspire to shield his opponent from physical violence, it is on the clubs that under these circumstances vengeance most commonly descends. Most players content themselves with simply breaking the offending weapon against the ground. But some persons there are whose thirst for revenge cannot be satisfied by any such rapid or simple process. I have been told of one gentleman who threw the offending club upon the ground, and then with his niblick proceeded to punish it with piecemeal destruction, breaking its shaft into small pieces very much as criminals used to be broken upon the wheel. Even this procedure seemed inadequate to one infuriated golfer of whom I have heard. A shaft, be it broken into ever so many fragments, can be replaced and the implement be as good as new. Nothing less than destroying both head and shaft can insure its final disappearance from the world of golf. The club must not merely be broken, but must be destroyed, and from its hated remnants no new race must be permitted to arise for the torment and discomfiture of succeeding generations of golfers. This perfect consummation can, it is said, be attained by holding the club upright, the head resting on the ground, then placing one foot upon it and kicking it with the other, just at the point where head and shaft are bound together. By this simple expedient (which I respectfully commend to the attention of all short-tempered golfers) a 'root and branch' policy may be effectually carried out by destroying at one stroke both the essential parts of the club.

If there are any who hold the opinion that measures such as this can never be justified by any series of golfing disasters, however aggravating, I would reply in the language of a gentleman who, when remonstrated with for using his clubs in one of the methods above described, responded with unanswerable logic, 'Is it not better to smash your dashed clubs than to lose your dashed temper?'

While, on the whole, playing through the green is the part of the game most trying to the temper, putting is that most trying to the nerves. There is always hope that a bad drive may be redeemed by a fine approach shot, or that a 'foozle' with the brassy may be balanced by some brilliant performance with the iron. But when the stage of putting-out has been reached no further illusions are possible—no place for repentance remains: to succeed in such a case is to win the hole; to fail, is to lose it. Moreover, it constantly happens that the decisive stroke has to be made precisely at a distance from the hole such that, while success is neither certain nor glorious, failure is not only disastrous but ignominious. A putt of a club's length which is to determine not merely the hole but the match will try the calmness even of an experienced performer, and many there are who have played golf all their lives whose pulse beats quicker when they have to play the stroke. No slave ever scanned the expression of a tyrannical master with half the miserable anxiety with which the performer surveys the ground over which the hole is to be approached. He looks at the hole from the ball, and he looks at the ball from the hole. No blade of grass, no scarcely perceptible inclination of the surface, escapes his critical inspection. He puts off the decisive moment as long, and perhaps longer, than he decently can. If he be a man who dreads responsibility, he asks the advice of his caddie, of his partner, and of his partner's caddie, so that the particular method in which he proposes to approach the hole represents not so much his own individual policy as the policy of a Cabinet. At last the stroke is made, and immediately all tongues are loosened. The slowly advancing ball is addressed in tones of menace or entreaty by the surrounding players. It is requested to go on or stop; to turn this way or that, as the respective interests of each party require. Nor is there anything more entertaining than seeing half a dozen faces bending over this little bit of moving gutta-percha which so remorselessly obeys the laws of dynamics, and pouring out on it threatenings and supplications not to be surpassed in apparent fervour by the devotions of any fetish worshippers in existence.

The peculiar feeling of nervousness which accompanies 'putting' is of course the explanation of the familiar experience that, when nothing depends upon it, it is quite easy to 'hole' your ball from a distance which makes success too often impossible when the fortunes of the game are at stake. 'How is it, dad?' said a little girl who was accompanying her father round the course— 'how is it that when they tell you that you have *two* to win, you always do it in *one,* and that when they say you have *one* to win you always do it in *two?*' In that observation lies compressed the whole philosophy of putting.

It might be thought that among the 'differentia' of golf the conscientious annalist would have to enumerate the facilities for fraud which the conditions under which the game is played would seem to afford. The whole difficulty of a stroke depending as it so often does entirely upon the 'lie' of the ball, which may be altered by an almost imperceptible change in its position, it might appear that there was large scope for the ingenious player to improve his chances of victory by methods not recognised in the rules of the game. As a matter of fact, however, this is not so. In the first place this is no doubt because golfers are an exceptionally honest race of men. In the next place, if there are any persons of dubious morals among them, they probably reflect that, as they are accompanied by caddies, it would be hardly possible to play any tricks except by the connivance of that severe but friendly critic. It is not probable that the connivance would be obtained, and it is quite certain that in the long run secrecy would not be observed by the confidant. Honesty under these circumstances is so obviously the best policy, that the least scrupulous do not venture to offend.

Strange legends, indeed, I have heard of matches played and won by very singular contrivances. A contest is told of one couple who went (without caddies) to play a match that was finally to determine their respective merits. But after a long and rather wild drive, player A lost his ball in the middle of some long bents. A prolonged search ensued, in which both players joined. Suddenly player B espied his opponent's ball, and, wisely reflecting that no simpler or more certain method of winning the hole could be found than that of compelling his opponent to give it up, quietly picked up the ball and secreted it in his pocket. In the meanwhile player A began to be anxious lest that very evil should befall him through natural causes which player B had been endeavouring artificially to produce. His ball was nowhere to be seen, the limit of time was nearly reached, so he bethought him that *his* best course would probably be to take another ball out of his pocket, to drop it in some convenient spot, and to proceed with his play. The plan was no sooner determined on than it was executed, and with a shout of satisfaction he called his opponent's attention to the fact that he had found his ball. 'No, no,' said player B, 'than cannot be it; this is your ball' (producing it from his pocket); 'I picked it up myself awhile ago!'

Another anecdote is told of two players not less well matched than the gentlemen whose performances I have just narrated. They determined to play a match by moonlight. The antagonists were in every respect worthy of each other, and as the match proceeded fortune did not appear to incline to either side. At last they came to a long hole, say 400 yards or so, and to each it occurred at the same time that a critical moment had been reached, and that it was necessary to adopt heroic measures. They drove off two long balls which, to the eyes of the ordinary spectators, appeared to vanish into the night far beyond all human powers of vision to follow. But each of the combatants declared that he saw perfectly where his ball had gone, and they walked off with unfaltering steps in the direction of the hole. When they had gone about 180 yards, each began to be rather surprised that the other showed no signs of indicating that he had reached the place where he expected to find his ball. But no! Both went on with unhesitating stride. Two hundred yards, 250 yards, 300 yards distance from the teeing-ground were successively reached and passed; at last, when they got to the putting-green, some hundred yards or so beyond the longest recorded drive, both balls were found lying within a club's length of the hole, the fact being that each player had arranged to be able to drop a ball through a hole in his trousers pocket when he should reach some point conveniently situated beyond that to which the other should have been able to drive. The plan was undeniably a good one, its only defect being that it must necessarily break down if adopted by both players at the same time.

But what account of the points in which golf differs fundamentally from other games, what study of its peculiar humours would be complete which did not give a place of honour to the institution of *caddies*? Wherever golf exists there must the caddie be found; but not in all places is he a credit to the great cause which he subserves. There are greens in England—none, I rejoice to think, in Scotland—where, either because golf has been too recently imported or because it suits not the genius of the population, many of the cad-

dies are not only totally ignorant of the game, which is bad, but are wholly un-
interested in it, which is far worse. They regard it as a form of lunacy, harmless
to the principals who pay, and not otherwise than beneficial to the assistants
who plenteously receive, but in itself wearisome and unprofitable. Such caddies
go far to spoil the sport. For my own part I can gladly endure severe or even
contemptuous criticism from the ministering attendant. I can bear to have it
pointed out to me that all my misfortunes are the direct and inevitable result
my own folly; I can listen with equanimity when failure is prophesied of some
stroke I am attempting, and can note unmoved the self-satisfied smile with
which the fulfilment of the prophecy is accentuated; but ignorant and stupid
indifference is intolerable. A caddie is not and ought not to be regarded as a
machine for carrying clubs at the rate of a shilling a round. He occupies or
ought to occupy the position of competent adviser or interested spectator. He
should be as anxious for the success of his side as if he were one of the players,
and should watch each move in the game with benevolent if critical interest,
always ready with the appropriate club, and, if need be, with the appropriate
comment.

It need not be said that a golfer, too prone to seek for sympathy from
his caddie, not unfrequently puts himself in the position of hearing the truth
against him instead. 'I went out yesterday,' said a friend of mine to his caddie, 'in
forty-five.' 'You'll never do that again,' was the unsatisfactory if truthful rejoin-
der. 'I beat Mr. So-and-so at half a stroke yesterday,' said another. 'If I were you,'
was the reply, 'I would take care never to play him again.' Even encouragement
is occasionally given in a form probably not wholly agreeable to the recipient.
I have heard of a youth at Westward Ho who was carrying for a distinguished
general, more eminent no doubt upon the field of battle than on the golfing
green. The play of the veteran was more than usually indifferent. He topped his
ball with unvarying success from bunker to bunker. At last the boy lost all patience and exclaimed, 'Come! come! old gentleman, this will never do.'

As I have had occasion to mention Scotch caddies and English caddies, let me repeat a story I have heard about a French caddie at Pau, which
would seem to indicate that the sympathetic criticism of the caddie abroad is
no whit behind that of his insular brother, hampered though he may be by the
difficulties of a foreign tongue. An English player who knew no French made a
fine approach shot with his iron and succeeded in laying his ball dead. He
turned round to his French attendant for applause. The latter saw what was expected of him and did his best to rise to the occasion. He described the shot in
the only English words which he had heard habitually associated with any remarkably successful stroke in the game. Looking full in his employer's face, and

with his most winning and sympathetic smile, he uttered the words, 'Beastly fluke!'

No doubt the French youth conceived himself to be conveying the most agreeable of compliments to his employer, but I would not have it supposed that if players in Scotland are resolved on hearing from their caddies nothing but what is pleasant they cannot be accommodated if they set to work in the right spirit. It is told of a caddie at one time very well known at St. Andrews under the name of 'Long Willie,' that he was in the habit of carrying for a player so ill-endowed by nature for the game, that though his driving was of the shortest, he never could see where his ball went to. He seldom played matches, probably because he seldom could find anybody who cared to play with him. But he used to get hold of Long Willie and make him tee a lot of balls for him, and would strike them off, under Long Willie's directions, one after the other. Long Willie used generally to lead him up close to the Martyrs' Memorial. The present club-house was not then built, and the gentlemen used to drive off one little 'shottie' after another to some such accompaniment as this from Long Willie: 'Eh, Mr. So-and-so, but that's a maist awfu' drive.' 'Guid save us, saw a body iron the like o' that.' Long Willie used to send a boy on ahead, who used to gather the balls and carry them on down towards the burn—some two hundred yards or more, so when the balls were all driven Long Willie used to toddle away down with his short-sighted master further than mortal man had ever driven before, and there they would come on the balls, where the boy had put them. Then they would go back and begin again. And after a few turns of this Long Willie would say, 'Eh, well, Maister So-and-so, I think we've may be done enough for the day. It's nae a guid thing to over-gowf yersel', ye ken.' And so Long Willie would get his half-crown, and the short-sighted gentleman would go home and say that Long Willie was a most invaluable caddie, that he could drive ever so much further when he had Long Willie to carry for him.

After all, however, the humours of golf can be but very imperfectly exhibited in description or illustrated by anecdote; nor has it been my intention in these few pages to add one to the many excellent collections of golfing stories which the piety of golfers in successive generations has given to the world. It is only on the links that these humours can be studied; it is only by those who are familiar with the game that they can be appreciated. To such there is infinite entertainment to be derived from watching the different methods of play, numerous as the multitude of players. 'Some golfers,' explained a novice to his friend, 'when they hit the ball, swing their caddie (*sic*) only a little way, others swing their caddie right round their head.' This gentleman's knowledge of technical terms was doubtless imperfect, but he had the root of the matter in him. No two men use their clubs alike; no two men deal in the same way or in the same temper with the varying changes or chances of the game. And this is one, though doubtless only one, among the many causes which make golf the most uniformly amusing amusement which the wit of man has yet devised.

A tolerable day, a tolerable green, a tolerable opponent, supply, or ought to supply, all that any reasonably constituted human being should require in the way of entertainment. With a fine sea view, and a clear course in front of him, the golfer should find no difficulty in dismissing all worries from his mind, and regarding golf, even it may be very indifferent golf, as the true and adequate end of man's existence. Care may sit behind the horseman, she never presumes to walk with the caddie. No inconvenient reminiscences of the ordinary workaday world, no intervals of weariness or monotony interrupt the pleasures of the game. And of what other recreation can this be said? Does a man trust to conversation to occupy his leisure moments? He is at the mercy of fools and bores. Does he put his trust in shooting, hunting, or cricket? Even if he be so fortunately circumstanced as to obtain them in perfection, it will hardly be denied that such moments of pleasure as they can afford are separated by not infrequent intervals of tedium. The ten-mile walk through the rain after missing a stag; a long ride home after a blank day; fielding out while your opponents score 400, cannot be described by the most enthusiastic deer-stalker, fox-hunter, or cricketer, as otherwise than wearisome episodes in delightful pursuits. Lawn-tennis, again, is not so much a game as an exercise, while in real tennis or in rackets something approaching to equality of skill between the players would seem to be almost necessary for enjoyment. These more violent exercises, again, cannot be played with profit for more than one or two hours in the day. And while this may be too long for a man very hard worked in other ways, it is too short for a man who wishes to spend a complete holiday as much as possible in the open air.

Moreover, all these games have the demerit of being adapted principally to the season of youth. Long before middle life is reached, rowing, rackets, fielding at cricket, are a weariness to those who once excelled at them. At thirty-five, when strength and endurance may be at their maximum, the particular elasticity required for these exercises is seriously diminished. The man who has gloried in them as the most precious of his acquirements begins, so far as they are concerned, to grow old; and growing old is not commonly supposed to be so agreeable an operation in itself as to make it advisable to indulge in it more often in a single lifetime than is absolutely necessary. The golfer, on the other hand, is never old until he is decrepit. So long as Providence allows him the use of two legs active enough to carry him round the green, and of two arms supple enough to take a 'half swing,' there is no reason why his enjoyment in the game need be seriously diminished. Decay no doubt there is; long driving has gone for ever; and something less of firmness and accuracy may be noted even in the short game. But the decay has come by such slow gradations, it has delayed so long and spared so much, that it is robbed of half its bitterness.

I do not know that I can do much better than close this desultory chapter with a brief autobiography, taken down from his own lips, of perhaps the most distinguished professional of the century—a man known by name to all golfers, even to those who have never visited St. Andrews—old Tom Morris.

This transcript of a conversation held on New Year's Day, 1886, is not only interesting in itself, but contains much sound golfing philosophy. I give it to the reader precisely in the shape in which it has been given to me:

'A gude new year t'ye, Maister Alexander, an' mony o' them! An' it's come weel in, the year has; for it's just a braw day for a mautch. Lod, sir, it aye seems to me the years, as they rise, skelp fester the tane after t'ither; they'll sune be makin' auld men o've a'. Hoo auld am I, d'ye ask, sir? Weel I was born June 16, 1821; and ye can calc'late that for yoursel'. Aye! as ye say, sir, born and bred in St. Awndrews, an' a gowffer a' ma days. The vera first time, I think, I hae mind o' mysel' I was toddlin' aboot at the short holes, wi' a putter uneath ma bit oxter.

'I was made 'prentice to Allan as a ba'-macker at eighteen, and wrocht wi' him eliven years. We played, Allan and me thegither, some geyan big mautches—ane in parteecler wi' the twa Dunns, Willie and Jamie, graund players baith, nane better—over fower greens. It was a' through a braw fecht atweens—green an green—but we snoddit 'em bonnie ere the end o't. I canna ca' to mind Allan an me was iver sae sair teckled as that time; though a wheen richt gude pair o' them did their best to pit oor twa noses oot o' joint. But it was na to be dune wi' Allan an' me. An awfu' player, puir Allan! the cunningest bit body o' a player, I dae think, that iver haun'led cleek an' putter. An' a kindly body tae, as it weel fits me to say, sir, an' wi' a walth o' slee pawky fun aboot him.

'I left Allan to keep the Green at Prestwick, and was there fourteen years. Three years efter Allan deed I cam to keep the Green here; an' here I hae been sin syne. Na! sir, I niver weary o' the gemm; an' I'm as ready noo to play any gentleman as I was in ma best days. I think I can play aboot as weel yet as I did in ma prime. No, may be, drive *jist* sae lang a ba'; but there's no muckle odds e'en in that yet. Jist the day I was sixty-four, I gaed roon' in a single wi'

Mr. H. in 81. No that ill for the "Auld Horse" as they ca' me—it'll tak' the best of the young ones, I reckon, to be mony shots better than *that*.

'An it had na been for gowff, I'm no sure that at this day, sir, I wad hae been a leevin' man. I've had ma troubles an' ma trials, like the lave; an', whiles, I thocht they wad hae clean wauved me, sae that to "lay me doun an' dee"—as the song says—lookit aboot a' that was left in life for puir Tam. It was like as if ma vera sowle was a' thegither gane oot o' me. But there's naething like a ticht gude-gowing mautch to soop yer brain clear o' that kin' o' thing; and wi' the help o' ma God an' o' gowff, I've aye gotten warsled through somehow or ither. The tae thing ta'en wi' the tither, I hae na had an ill time o't. I dinna mind that iver I had an unpleasant ward frae ony o' the many gentlemen I've played wi'. I've aye tried —as ma business was, sir—to mak masel' pleesant to them; an' they've aye been awfu' pleesant to me.

'An' noo, sir, to end a long and, maybe, a silly crack—bein' maistly about masel'—ye'll jist come wi' me, an ye'll hae a glass o' gude brandy, and I'll have ma pint o'black strap, an' we'll drink a gude New Year to ane anither, an' the like to a' gude gowffers.'

The Wooden Putter

BY BERNARD DARWIN

Though no one needs a Charles Darwin to suggest we golfers are a species completely unto our own, one of the more prudent means toward understanding the origin of our species entails shimmying out a limb of the Darwin family tree. Bernard Darwin (1876–1961), Charles's grandson, gave up the law to practice golf and, as longtime correspondent for *The Times* of London and *Country Life* magazine, evolved into the progenitor of the job description "golf writer." A superb essayist, his prose survives as some of the fittest, and most elegant, in the language: *The Golf Courses of the British Isles* and *Golf Between Two Wars* remain cornerstones of any golf library aspiring toward sophistication.

Like all deft writers, Darwin understood his subject intimately. As a player, he captained the university golf team his final year at Cambridge. Some 20 years later, he wound up captaining Britain's first Walker Cup team, as well. The circumstance behind that ascension makes a pretty good golf tale in itself. *The Times* had shipped Darwin over to the National Golf Links, on Long Island, to cover the 1922 inaugural between national teams comprised of the best amateurs from Great Britain and the United States. When the British captain got sick before the opening matches, Darwin, the only potential Brit available on short notice, was drafted. As player, he handily won his singles match, 3 and 1. He fared less well as captain; the home team won the competition, 8–4.

Perhaps, in the improbability of his singles victory, Darwin found some of the inspiration that would lead him, two years later, to take one of his few approach shots into the art of fiction.

I t was not for want of clubs that Mr Polwinkle's handicap obstinately refused to fall below sixteen. His rack full of them extended round three
sides of the smoking room. In addition, there was an enormous box re-
sembling a sarcophagus on the floor, and in one corner was a large loose
heap of clubs. To get one out of the heap without sending the others crashing
to the ground was as delicate and difficult as a game of spillikins, and the
housemaid had bestowed on it many an early morning malediction.

The rack along one side of the wall was clearly of a peculiarly sacred
character. The clips holding the clubs were of plush, and behind each clip there
was pasted on the wall an inscription in Mr Polwinkle's meticulously neat
handwriting. There was a driver stated to have belonged to the great James
Braid; a mashie of J. H. Taylor's; a spoon of Herd's.

Nor were illustrious amateurs unrepresented. Indeed, these were the
greatest treasures in Mr Polwinkle's collection, because they had been harder
to come by. The midiron had quite a long pedigree, passing through a number
of obscure and intermediate stages, and ending in a blaze of glory with the
awful name of Mr John Ball, who was alleged once to have played a shot with
it at the request of an admirer. A putting cleek with a rather long, old-fashioned head and a battered grip bore the scrupulous inscription: ATTRIBUTED
TO THE LATE MR F. G. TAIT.

Mr Polwinkle always sighed when he came to that cleek. Its authentic-
ity was, he had to admit, doubtful. There were so many Freddie Tait putters.
Half the clubhouses in England seemed to possess one; they could hardly all be
genuine. His Hilton he no longer even pretended to believe in.

'I bought that,' he would say, 'when I was a very young collector, and
I'm afraid I was imposed upon.' But, at any rate, there was no doubt about his
latest acquisition, before which he now paused lovingly. Here was the whole
story, written down by a man, who knew another man, who knew the people
with whom Mr Wethered had been staying. Mr Wethered had overslept himself, packed up his clubs in a hurry, and left his iron behind; so he had borrowed this one, and had graciously remarked that it was a very nice one.

It must not be supposed that Mr Polwinkle was ever so daring as to
play with these sacred clubs. He contented himself with gazing and, on rare
occasions, with a reverent waggle.

Mr Polwinkle, as I have said, was not a good player. He was aware of
not playing consistently up to his sixteen handicap. If he did not always insist
on his rights of giving two strokes to his friend Buffery, he might, he was conscious, have suffered the indignity of being beaten level by an eighteen handicap player; and with all this nonsense about scratch scores and a raising of

the standard, he saw before him the horrid certainty of soon being eighteen himself.

This evening he was feeling particularly depressed. It had been a bad day. Buffery had won by five and four without using either of his strokes, and had hinted pretty strongly that he did not propose to accept them any more. Confound the tactless creature!

Mr Polwinkle tried to soothe himself by looking at his treasures. Ah! If only he could just for one day be endued with the slash and power of those who had played with them. If only something of their virtue could have passed into their clubs, what a splendid heritage! Such a miracle might even be possible if he had but faith enough. Coué-suggestion—better and better and better—how wonderful it would be!

Suddenly he felt a glow of new hope and inspiration. Greatly daring, he took from the rack the driver WITH WHICH as the inscription lyrically proclaimed JAMES BRAID WON THE CHAMPIONSHIP AT PRESTWICK IN 1908, WITH THE UNEXAMPLED SCORE OF 291; EIGHT STROKES BETTER THAN THE SECOND SCORE, AND PLAYING SUCH GOLF AS HAD NEVER BEEN SEEN BEFORE ON THAT CLASSIC COURSE.

He took one glance to see that his feet were in the right place—long practice enabled him to judge to an inch the position in which the furniture was safe—and then he swung.

Gracious goodness! What had happened? Back went the club, instinct with speed and power, and he felt a violent and unaccustomed wrenching round of his hips. Down it came more swiftly than ever, his knees seemed to crumple under him with the vehemence of the blow, and swish went the clubhead, right out and round in a glorious finish. A shower of glass fell all over him and he was left in darkness.

Never had he experienced anything before in the least like that tremendous sensation; the electric light had always been perfectly safe. With trembling fingers he struck a match and groped his way, crunching glass as he walked, to the two candles on the chimney piece. Once more he swung the club up; then paused at the top of the swing, as he had done so many hundreds of times before, and gazed at himself in the glass. Could it really be?

He rushed to the bookshelf, tore down *Advanced Golf,* turned to the appropriate page, and again allowed the club to swing and wrench him in its grip. There could be no doubt about it. Allowing for differences of form and feature he was Braid to the very life—the poise, the turn of the body, the very knuckles—all were the same.

The miracle had happened with one club. Would it happen with all? Out came the Taylor mashie from the rack. As he picked it up his head seemed to shake formidably, his wrists felt suddenly as if they were made of whipcord, his boots seemed to swell and clutch the ground; another second—crash!—down came the club and out came a divot of carpet, hurtling across the room, while Mr Polwinkle's eyes were fixed in a burning and furious gaze on the gaping rent that was left.

Then it really was all right. If he could swing the club like the great masters, he could surely hit the ball like them, and the next time he played Buffery, by Jove, it would not be only two strokes he could give him.

He was in the middle of being Mr Wethered when the door opened and Buffery walked in. Mr Polwinkle had got his feet so wide apart in his admirable impersonation that he could not move; for a perceptible moment he could only straddle and stare.

'They told me you were in, old chap,' began Buffery, 'so I just walked in. What on earth are you at? I always said that light would get it in the neck some day!' Buffery's heartiness, though well meant, was sometimes hard to bear. 'However,' he went on, while Mr Polwinkle was still speechless, 'what I came about was this. You remember you said you'd come down to Sandwich with me some day. Well, I suddenly find I can get off for three days. Will you come?'

Mr Polwinkle hesitated a moment. He did not feel very kindly disposed toward Buffery. He should like to practice his new styles a little before crushing him; but still, Sandwich! And he had never seen it.

'All right,' he said; 'I'll come!'

'Topping!' cried Buffery. 'We'll have some great matches, and I'm going to beat you level—you see if I don't!'

Mr Polwinkle gathered himself together for an effort.

'I will give you,' he said slowly and distinctly, 'a stroke a hole, and I'll play you for'—and he hesitated on the brink of something still wilder—'five pounds!'

Buffery guffawed with laughter. He had never heard Mr Polwinkle make so good a joke before.

The next evening saw them safely arrived and installed at the Bell.

The journey, though slow, had been for Mr Polwinkle full of romance. When he changed at Minster he snuffed the air and thought that already he could smell the sea. His mind was a jumble of old championships and of the wondrous shots he was going to play on the morrow. At dinner he managed to make Buffery understand that he really did mean to give him a stroke a hole. And Buffery, when at last convinced that it was not a joke, merely observed that a fiver would be a pleasant little help toward his expenses.

After dinner he felt too restless and excited to sit still, and leaving Buffery to play bridge, wandered stealthily into the hall to see if his precious clubs were safe. He felt a momentary shiver of horror when he found someone examining his bag. Had news of the match been spread abroad? Was this a backer of Buffery's tampering with his clubs?

No; he appeared a harmless, friendly creature, and apologized very nicely. He was merely, he said, amusing himself by looking at the different sets of clubs.

'You've got some jolly good ones,' he went on, making Mr Polwinkle blush with pleasure. 'And look here, your mashie and mine might be twins— they're as like as two peas!' And he produced his own from a neighboring bag. They certainly were exactly alike; both bore the signature of their great maker; in weight and balance they were identical.

'Taylor used to play with mine himself!' said Mr Polwinkle in a voice of pride and awe. 'And this is Herd's spoon, and here's a putter of—'

'I expect he'd have played just as well with mine,' cut in the stranger— Jones was the unobtrusive name on his bag—with regrettable flippancy. 'Anyhow, they're both good clubs. Wish I could play like Taylor with mine. Well, I'm going to turn in early—good night!'

Mr Polwinkle, a little sad that Jones did not want to hear all about his collection, fastened up his bag, and thought he would go to bed, too. He lay awake for some time, for the cocks crow as persistently by night in the town of Sandwich as the larks sing by day upon the links; moreover, he was a little excited. Still, he slept at last, and dreamed of mashie shots with so much backspin on them that they pitched on Prince's and came back into the hole on St George's.

'Well,' said Buffery, as they stood next morning on the first tee at St George's, 'it's your honor—you're the giver of strokes,' he added in a rather bitter tone.

Mr Polwinkle took out the Braid driver with as nonchalant an air as he could muster. He could not help feeling horribly frightened, but no doubt the club would help him through. He gave one waggle with that menacing little shake of the club that Walton Health knows so well, and then the ball sped away an incredible distance. It was far over the 'kitchen,' that grassy hollow that has caught and stopped so many hundreds of balls; but it had a decided hook on it, and ran on and on till it finished in the rough on the left.

One of the caddies gave a prolonged whistle of surprise and admiration. Who was this new, unknown, and infinitely mild-looking champion who made the club hum through the air like a hornet? Buffery, too, was palpably taken aback.

'I say, old chap,' he remarked, 'you seem to have been putting a lot on to your drive. Was that what you had up your sleeve?'

However, he managed to hit a very decent shot himself into the kitchen, and then, narrowly escaping that trappy little bunker on the right with his second, lay in a good strategic position in front of the big cross bunker.

Meanwhile, Mr Polwinkle was following up his own vast tee shot in an agitated state of mind. Of course, he reflected, Braid *can* hook. It was, he had read, the one human weakness to which the great man was occasionally prone, but it seemed hard that this should be the occasion. The ball lay very heavy in the rough, and worse than all he had only his own niblick, with which he was singularly ineffective. He had once had the chance of acquiring a genuine Ray, but niblicks were clumsy, ugly things and did not interest him. Why had he been such a fool?

His first effort was a lamentable top, his second only just got the ball out of the rough, with a gaping wound in its vitals. Still, there was a hope if Herd's spoon would behave itself as it should, and he addressed himself to the shot with a desperate composure.

Heavens, what was the matter with him? Was he never going to hit the ball? He felt himself growing dizzy with all those waggles, a fierce little glance at the hole between each of them. There could be no possible doubt that this spoon was a genuine Herd. Just as he felt that he must scream if it went on much longer, up went the club, and away went the ball—the most divine spoon shot ever seen—cut up into the wind to perfection; the ball pitched over the bunker, gave a dying kick or two, and lay within a yard of the hole.

Even the ranks of Tuscany could scarce forbear to cheer. 'Good shot!' growled Buffery grudgingly.

That was four—he would be down in five. The enemy with his stroke had three for the hole, but the big cross bunker yawned between him and the green. Drat the man, he had not topped it. He had pitched well over, and his approach putt lay so dead that Mr Polwinkle, though in no generous mood, had to give it to him. One down.

At the second hole at Sandwich, as all the world knows, there is a long and joyous carry from the tee. A really fine shot will soar over the bunker and the hilltop beyond, and the ball will lie in a little green valley, to be pitched home on to the green; but the short driver must make a wide tack to the right and will have a more difficult second.

Buffery, inspired by his previous win, despite his opponent's mighty drive, decided to 'go for it.' And plump went his ball into the bunker.

The Braid driver was on its best behavior this time—a magnificent shot, straight as an arrow and far over the hill.

'H'm!' said Buffery, looking discontentedly at the face of his driver. 'Is that any new patent kind of ball you are playing with?'

'No,' returned Mr Polwinkle frigidly. 'You can weigh it after the round if you like.' And they walked on in stony silence.

Buffery had to hack his ball out backward, and his third was away to the right of the green.

'Just a little flick with the mashie, sir,' said Mr Polwinkle's caddie, putting the club in his hand.

He took the mashie, but somehow he did not feel comfortable. He shifted and wriggled, and finally his eye was high in the heavens long before the ball was struck. When he looked down to earth again he found the ball had only moved about three yards forward—a total and ignominious fluff. He tried again; another fluff moved it forward but a few painful inches; again, and a third precisely similar shot deposited it in the bunker in front of his nose. Then he went berserk with his niblick, irretrievably ruined a second new ball, and gave up the hole.

'Let me look at that mashie!' he said to his caddie as he walked on toward the next tee. And, after microscopically examining its head, 'I see what it is!' he exclaimed, in frantic accents. 'It's that fellow—what's his damned name, who was looking at my clubs last night—he's mixed them up—he's got my mashie and I've got his! Do you know Mr Jones by sight?' And he turned to his caddie.

'Yes, sir. I knows him. And that's a funny thing if you've got his mashie. I was just thinking to myself that them shots of yours was just like what he plays. "Joneses," his friends call them. He'll play like a blooming pro, for a bit, and then fluff two or three—'

'Where is he now? Is he in front of us?' Mr Polwinkle interrupted. Yes, Jones had started some time ago.

'Then run as hard as you can and tell him I'm playing an important match and insist on having my mashie back. Quick now, run!'—as the caddie was going to say something. 'I'll carry the clubs!' And the caddie disappeared reluctantly in the sandhills.

'Bad luck, old man!' said Buffery, his complacency restored by that wonderfully soothing medicine of two holes up. 'But I'll tell you where to go.

Now this is the Sahara. The hole's over there,' pointing to the left, 'but it's too long a carry for you and me—we must go round by the right.'

'Which line would Braid take?' asked Mr Polwinkle 'Straight at the flag, would he? Then I shall go straight for the flag!'

'Please yourself!' answered Buffery with a shrug, and played away to the right—a mild little shot and rather sliced, but still clear of the sand. Mr Polwinkle followed with another superb tee shot. Far over all that tumultuous mass of rolling sandhills the ball flew, and was last seen swooping down on to the green. Buffery's second was weak and caught in the hollow; his third was half topped and ran well past; his fourth put him within a yard or so of the hole.

The best he could do would be a five, and all the while there stood Mr Polwinkle, calm, silent, and majestic, six yards from the flag in one. He had only to get down in two putts to win the hole; but he had not yet had a putt, and which putter was he to use—the Tait or the Harry Vardon? He decided on the Tait. A moment later he wished he had not, for his putt was the feeblest imaginable, and the ball finished a good five feet short. Still he persevered, and again was pitifully short.

'By Jove, that's a let-off, old chap!' said the tactless one, and popped his own ball into the hole.

'I'll give you that one!' he added magnanimously, and picked up Mr Polwinkle's ball, which was reposing some three inches from the hole.

'I was always afraid it was a forgery!' murmured Mr Polwinkle, mechanically accepting the ball. 'Freddie Tait was never short with his putts—the books all say that!'

Buffery looked at him wonderingly, opened his mouth as if to make some jocular comment, then thought better of it and led the way to the tee.

Much the same thing happened at the fourth. Two magnificent shots by Braid and Herd respectively, right up to the edge of the little plateau, where it stands defiantly with the black railings in the background; a series of four scrambles and scuffles by Buffery, which just escaped perdition. Two for the hole again, and this time the Vardon putter was tried. The first putt was beautiful. How sweetly and smoothly and with what a free wrist it was taken back! The ball, perfectly struck, seemed in, then it just slipped past and lay two feet away.

'Ah!' he said to himself with a long sigh of satisfaction, 'at any rate this is genuine!'

Alas! It was but too true, for when it came to the short putt, Mr Polwinkle's wrist seemed suddenly to become locked, there was a quick little jerk of the club and—yes, somehow or other the ball had missed the hole. Buffery was down in his two putts again, and it was another half, this time in five to six.

'I ought to have been all square by now if I could have putted as well as an old lady with a broomstick!' said poor Mr Polwinkle.

'Well, I like that!' answered the other truculently. 'I ought to have been four up if I could have played a decent second either time!' And this time there was a lasting silence.

Mr Polwinkle felt depressed and miserable. Still his heart rose a little when he contemplated the bunker that had to be carried from the tee at the fifth, and beyond it the formidable Maiden with its black terraces. And, sure enough, Buffery got into the bunker in three—not into the black terraces, because, sad to say, men do not now play over the Maiden's crown, but only over the lower spurs—touching, as it were, but the skirts of her sandy garment. Still, he was in the bunker, and Mr Polwinkle had only a pitch to reach the green. Here it was that he wanted a good caddie to put an iron in his hand—to put anything there but the mashie that had played him false. But Mr Polwinkle was flustered.

'After all,' he thought, 'a mashie is a mashie, even if it is not a genuine Taylor, and if I keep my eye on the ball—'

Clean off the socket this time the ball flew away toward cover point, and buried itself in a clump of bents. Why did he not 'deem it unplayable'? I do not know. But since Mr Horace Hutchinson once ruined a medel round and probably lost the St George's Vase at the Maiden by forgetting that he could tee and lose two, Mr Polwinkle may be forgiven. When his ball ultimately emerged from the bents he had played five; they holed out in nine apiece, for Buffery had also had his adventures and the stroke settled in. Three down.

Worse was to come, for at the sixth Buffery had the impudence to get a three—a perfect tee shot and two putts; no one could give a stroke to that. At the seventh Mr Polwinkle, club in hand, walked forward with elaborate care to survey the ground, walked backward, his eye still fixed on the green—and heeled his ball smartly backward like a rugby forward. For a moment he was bewildered. Then he looked at his club. His Wethered iron! Of course. It was the tragedy of the Open Championship at St Andrews over again!

At Hades his Vardon putter again misbehaved at short range, and Mr Polwinkle looked at it reproachfully.

'I always thought it belonged to a bad period!' he groaned, remembering some of those tragic years in which the greatest of all golfers could do everything but hole a yard putt. He would use the Vardon no more. But, then, what on earth was he to putt with? He tried the pseudo-Tait again at the ninth, and by dint of taking only three putts got a half; but still he was six down.

There was one ray of comfort. There was his caddie waiting for him, having no doubt run the villain Jones to earth, and under this arm protruded the handle of a club.

'Well,' he shouted, 'have you got it?'

'No, sir,' the caddie answered—and embarrassment and amusement seemed to struggle together in his voice. 'Mr Jones says he's playing an important match, too, and as you didn't send back his mashie he's going on with yours. Said they were just the same, he did, and he wouldn't know any difference between yours and his own.'

'Then what's that club you've got there?' demanded Mr Polwinkle.

'The gentleman lent you this to make up, so he said,' the caddie replied, producing a wooden putter. 'I was particularly to tell you it belonged to someone who used it in a great match, and blessed if I haven't forgotten who it was.'

Mr Polwinkle took the putter in his hand and could not disguise from himself that it had no apparent merits of any description. The shaft was warped, not bent in an upward curve as a well-bred wooden putter should be, and decidedly springy; no name whatever was discernible on the head. Still, he badly needed a putter, and if it had been used by an eminent hand—

'Think, man, think!' he exclaimed vehemently. 'You must remember!' But the caddie racked his brain in vain. And then—

'Really,' said Buffery, 'we can't wait all day while your caddie tries to remember ancient history. This is the match we're thinking about, and I'm six up!' And he drove off—a bad hook into the thick and benty rough on the left.

And now, thank goodness, I have reached the end of Mr Polwinkle's misfortunes. The tide is about to turn. At the second shot Mr Wethered's iron, I regret to have to say, made another error. It just pulled the ball into that horrid trappy bunker that waits voraciously at the left-hand corner of the plateau green—and that after Buffery had played three and was not on the green.

Mr Polwinkle's temper had been badly shaken once or twice, and now it gave out entirely.

'Give me any dashed club you like!' he snarled, seized the first that came handy, and plunged into the bunker.

'Good sort of club to get out of a bunker with!' he said to himself, finding that he had a midiron in his hand, and then—out came the ball, as if it was the easiest thing in the world, and sat down within four yards of the hole.

How had it happened? Why, it was Mr Ball's iron—and did not the hero of Hoylake habitually pitch out of bunkers with a straight-faced iron? Of course he did—and played his ordinary pitches with it as well. What a thing it was to know history! Here at once was a magic niblick and a substitute for the mashie rolled into one. And just then his caddie smacked himself loudly and suddenly on the thigh.

'I've remembered it, sir. It was Tommy something—young Tommy, I think.'

'Young Tommy Morris?' gasped Mr Polwinkle breathlessly.

'Ah!' said the caddie. 'Morris—that was it!'

'Give me the wooden putter!' said Mr Polwinkle—and the ball rattled against the back of the tin. That was a four against Buffery's six. Down to five with eight to play.

It is a well-known fact that when golf is faultless there is next to nothing to write about it. The golfing reporter may say that So-and-So pushed his drive and pulled his second; but the real fact is that the great So-and-So was on the course with his tee shot, on the green with his second, and down in two putts—and kept on doing it. That is all the reporter need have said, but he says more because he has his living to earn. So have I; but, nevertheless, I shall not describe Mr Polwinkle's home-coming at full length. More brilliantly faultless golf never was seen. Braid drove magnificently, Mr Ball did all the pitching to perfection and even Mr Wethered behaved impeccably. As for the wooden putter, most of the putts went in, and even those that did not gave Buffery a cold shiver down his spine. What could poor eighteen-handicap Buffery do against it? He must need wilt under such an onslaught. If he did a respectable five, Mr Polwinkle did a 'birdie' three. If he did a long hole in six, as he did at the Suez Canal, that wooden putter holed one for a four.

Here, for those who know the course, are the figures of Mr Polwinkle's first eight holes coming home: four, three, three, four, four, four, two, four. That was enough. Buffery was a crushed man; hole after hole slipped away, and when he had reached the seventeenth green in eight, there was nothing for it but to give up the match. Six up at the turn and beaten by two and one!

As Mr Polwinkle walked triumphantly into the clubhouse he met Jones, and almost fell on his neck.

'My dear fellow,' he cried, 'I can't thank you enough for that putter. I holed everything. Never saw anything like it! I suppose,' he went on with a sudden desperate boldness, 'there's no chance of your selling it me, is there?'

'Oh no, I won't sell it!' began Jones.

'I knew it was too much to ask!' said Mr Polwinkle dejectedly.

'But I'll give it you with pleasure!'

'Oh, but I couldn't let you do that! Give me it for nothing—a putter that belonged to young Tommy—the greatest putter that ever—'

'Well, you see,' said Jones, 'I only told the caddie to tell you that because I thought it might put you on your putting. And, by George, it seems to have done it, too. Wonderful what a little confidence will do. You're perfectly welcome to the putter—I bought it in a toy shop for eighteen pence!'

Mr Polwinkle fell swooning to the floor.

The Bliss of Golf

BY JOHN UPDIKE

In both his essays and his fiction, John Updike—creator of Bech, Rabbit Angstrom, and so many other memorable characters—has written thrillingly about the royal and ancient game. He's written enough, in fact, to fill a book: the thoroughly wonderful collection *Golf Dreams*. As an enthusiastic player himself, his perspective naturally runs the course from blissful—evident in the title of this selection—to deeply pained. I like to think there's some comfort to be found in golf's essential democracy. It treats America's most prominent man of letters no better or worse than the rest of us hackers.

I never touched a club until I was twenty-five. Then, on a shady lawn in Wellesley, a kind of aunt-in-law showed me how to hold her driver and told me, after one swoop at a phantom ball, that I had a wonderful natural swing. Since that fatal encouragement, in many weathers inner and outer, amid many a green and winding landscape, I have asked myself what the peculiar bliss of this demanding game is, a bliss that at times threatens to relegate all the rest of life, including those sexual concerns that Freud claims are paramount and those even more basic needs that Marx insists must be met, to the shadows.

The immensities of space, beside which even polo and baseball are constricted pastimes, must be part of it. To see one's ball gallop two hundred and more yards down the fairway, or see it fly from the face of an 8-iron clear across an entire copse of maples in full autumnal flare, is to join one's soul with the vastness that, contemplated from another angle, intimidates the spirit, and makes one feel small. As it moves through the adventures of a golf match, the human body, like Alice's in Wonderland, experiences an intoxicating relativity—huge in relation to the ball, tiny in relation to the course, exactly matched to that of the other players. From this relativity is struck a silent music that rings to the treetops and runs through a Wagnerian array of changes as each hole evokes its set of shots, dwindling down to the final putt. The clubs in their nice gradations suggest organ pipes.

There is a bliss to the equipment—the festive polyester slacks, the menacing and elevating cleated shoes, the dainty little gauntlet the left hand gets to wear, the leathery adhesion of the grips and the riflelike purity of the shafts, the impeccable lustre of the (pre-Day-Glo orange) ball. The uniform sits light, unlike the monstrous armor of the skier or the football player, and cloaks us in a colorful individuality—not for the golfer the humiliating uniforms, cooked up by press agents and tyrannic owners, inflicted upon baseball players. We feel, dressed for golf, knightly, charging toward distant pennants past dragon-shaped hazards. The green when it receives us is soft, fine, gently undulating, maidenly.

A beautiful simplicity distinguishes the game's objective and the scoring. One stroke, count one. William Faulkner's *The Sound and the Fury* opens with an idiot watching a game of golf, and he grasps the essence well enough: "They took the flag out, and they were hitting. Then they put the flag back and they went to the table, and he hit and the other hit." That's how it goes; golf appeals to the idiot in us, and the child. What child does not grasp the pleasure-principle of miniature golf? Just how childlike golf players become is proven by their frequent inability to count past five. There is a lovable injustice, a comic democracy, in the equality, for purposes of scoring, of a three-hundred-yard smash from an elevated tee and a three-inch tap-in. Or, let's not forget, a total whiff—the most comical stroke of all. A ground-out in baseball or a tennis ball whapped into the net is not especially amusing; but bad shots in golf are endless fun—at least the other fellow's are. The duck hook, the banana slice, the topped dribble, the no-explode explosion shot, the arboreal ricochet, the sky ball, the majestic OB, the pondside scuff-and-splash, the deep-grass squirt, the cart-path shank, the skull, the fat hit, the thin hit, the stubbed putt—what a wealth of mirth is to be had in an afternoon's witnessing of such varied miseries, all produced in a twinkling of an eye by the infallible laws of physics!

And the bliss of the swing. The one that feels effortless and produces a shot of miraculous straightness and soar. "I'll take it," we say modestly, searching about with a demure blush for the spun-away tee. Just a few shots a round keep us coming back; what other sport offers such sudden splendor in exchange for so few calories of expended energy? In those instants of whizz, as-cent, hover, and fall, an ideal self seems mirrored. If we have that one shot in us, we must have thousands more—the problem is to get them out, to *let* them out. To concentrate, to take one's time, to move the weight across, to keep the elbow in, to save the wrist-cock for the hitting area, to keep one's head still, down, and as full of serenity as a Zen monk's: an ambitious program, but a ba-sically spiritual one, which does not require the muscularity and shapeliness of youth. What other sport holds out hope of improvement to a man or a woman over fifty? True, the pros begin to falter at around forty, but it is their putting nerves that go, not their swings. For a duffer like the abovesigned, the room for improvement is so vast that three lifetimes could be spent roaming the fairways carving away at it, convinced that perfection lies just over the next rise. And that hope, perhaps, is the kindest bliss of all that golf bestows upon its devotees.

About the Editor

Jeff Silverman, a former columnist for the *Los Angeles Herald Examiner*, has written for the *New York Times*, the *Los Angeles Times*, and several national magazines. The editor of *The First Chapbook for Foodies*, *The First Chapbook for Golfers*, and *The Greatest Baseball Stories Ever Told*, he now lives with his family in Chadds Ford, Pennsylvania.

Permissions Acknowledgments

Michael Bamberger, "Stark" from *To the Linksland: A Golfing Adventure*. Copyright © 1992 by Michael Bamberger. Reprinted with the permission of Viking Penguin, a division of Penguin Putnam Inc., and March Tenth, Inc.

Glenna Collett, "Dressing the Part for Golf" from *Ladies in the Rough*. Copyright 1929 by Alfred A. Knopf, Inc. Reprinted with the permission of Alfred A. Knopf, a division of Random House, Inc.

Alistair Cooke, "Workers Arise! Shout Fore" from *The Americans*. Copyright © 1979 by Alistair Cooke. Reprinted with the permission of the author and Alfred A. Knopf, a division of Random House, Inc.

Bernard Darwin, "The Wooden Putter" from *The Strand*. Copyright 1924 by Bernard Darwin. Reprinted with the permission of A. P. Watt, Ltd.

Peter Dobereiner, "The Finest Course of All" from *Golf à la Carte: The Best of Peter Dobereiner*. Copyright © 1985 by Peter Dobereiner. Reprinted with the permission of The Lyons Press.

Ian Fleming, excerpt from *Goldfinger*. Copyright © 1959 by Glidrose Productions Ltd. Reprinted with the permission of Penguin Books, Ltd.

Rube Goldberg, "Left-Handed Golf Courses" from *The American Golfer* (1924). Copyright 1924 by Rube Goldberg. Reprinted with the permission of Rube Goldberg, Inc.

Dan Jenkins, "Golf with the Boss" from *Fairways and Greens*. Copyright © 1994 by D&J Ventures, Inc. Reprinted with the permission of Dan Jenkins.

George Plimpton, Chapter 17 from *The Bogey Man*. Copyright © 1968 by George Plimpton. Reprinted with the permission of The Lyons Press.

Rick Reilly, "Day of Glory for a Golden Oldie" from *The Life of Reilly*. Copyright © 2000 by Time, Inc. Reprinted with the permission of Total Sports Publishing.

Grantland Rice, "What Golf Is" from Grantland Rice and Clare Briggs, *The Duffer's Handbook of Golf*. Copyright 1926 by Grantland Rice. Reprinted with the permission of Simon & Schuster, Inc.

Ron Shelton, excerpt from *Tin Cup* screenplay. Reprinted with the permission of Ron Shelton.

Edwin Shrake, "Care to Join Our Little Old Game?" from *Sports Illustrated* (August 15, 1977). Copyright © 1977 by Edwin Shrake. Reprinted with the permission of the author.

Red Smith, "A Hundred and Four Years Old" from *The Red Smith Reader* (New York: Random House, 1982). Originally published in *The New York Herald-Tribune*. Reprinted with the permission of Phyllis W. Smith.

John Updike, "The Bliss of Golf" from *Golf Dreams*. Copyright © 1996 by John Updike. Reprinted with the permission of Alfred A. Knopf, a division of Random House, Inc. and Penguin Books, Ltd.

Pat Ward-Thomas, "The Qualities of Greatness" from *Not Only Golf: An Autobiography* (London: Hodder and Stoughton, 1981). Copyright © 1981 by Pat Ward-Thomas. Reprinted with permission.

Herbert Warren Wind, "Back to Cherry Hills" from *Following Through* (New York: Ticknor & Fields, 1985). Originally published in *The New Yorker* (1978). Copyright © 1985 by Herbert Warren Wind. Reprinted with permission.

P. G. Wodehouse, "The Long Hole" from *Golf Without Tears* (1924). Originally published as *The Clicking of Cuthbert* (London: Herbert Jenkins, 1922). Reprinted with the permission of A. P. Watt Ltd on behalf of The Trustees of the Wodehouse Estate.